Tolerating the Intolerable

DePauw University's war against Janis Price

Jeffrey D. Shively

authorHOUSE™

1663 Liberty Drive, Suite 200
Bloomington, Indiana 47403
(800) 839-8640
www.AuthorHouse.com

First published by AuthorHouse 07/13/05

ISBN: 1-4208-5963-3 (sc)
ISBN: 1-4208-5962-5 (dj)

Printed in the United States of America
Bloomington, Indiana

This book is printed on acid-free paper.

A project as time consuming and difficult as writing a book cannot easily be completed by a solitary individual. It would be remiss of me not to thank the many individuals who made this dream a reality. Mrs. Janis Price, the subject of this book, was absolutely indispensable in making this a success. She provided reams of primary documents from which I built my case, as well as constant encouragement. The Sunday night Bible study with other members of Greencastle Christian Church provided great encouragement. My father, Jerold Shively, has always supported my endeavors, no matter their scope. Dr. John B. Wilson was the reason that I came to DePauw in 1991. He was perhaps the greatest professor that the university has had the sense to hire. Dr. Wilson was taken from us far too early at age 63 in December 1993. Each time I step up to the lectern, I consider the things that he taught me in the brief time I knew him. If I become a fraction of the scholar that he was, I will be very pleased. My friendship with Jim Beatty and Eric Gall date back to our college days at dear old DKE. We've stuck together through trials and tribulations. We've enjoyed the good times as well. They share my concern for our alma mater and have been encouraging me to finish *Tolerating the Intolerable* since the day I put pen to paper. Roy Burnett is one of the finest Christian men that I have ever had the good fortune to know. He was one of the first to suggest that I nurture the gift of writing. Matt Huffman, a longtime co-worker and friend, has been a constant encouragement in this project. He has a keen sense of justice. I must thank the love of my life, Mila Mineyeva for her prayers and words of encouragement. She knows me better than I know myself. Finally, I must thank the Lord for giving me a mind that can research and hands that can translate my findings into prose. Without His help and protection, this work would never have come to fruition.

Contents

Introduction

On a blustery day in December 2001, I was enjoying a short break at home between my day job and my part-time evening job. I had hoped that returning to my alma mater, DePauw University, to add a teaching license to my history degree, would open doors. Instead, I was working two jobs six months after completing the Teacher Education Program. As I was preparing to walk out the door, the phone rang. DePauw University Education Department Chair Dr. Esther Lee was on the other end of the line. She told me that I needed to supply some transcripts of my class work at Indiana State University. I replied that those items had been supplied after I completed each course. She insisted that I needed to provide new copies to insure that my license would be valid. I agreed to locate new copies, but told her that it might take some time, considering my schedule. Shortly thereafter, I left for my night job, a little confused by what I had just experienced.

The one person who I believed could explain the situation to me was DePauw's Certification Officer, Mrs. Janis Price. We attend the same church, so I had known her for quite some time. Two years earlier, I had gone to her for advice about returning to school five years after graduation to pursue a career in education. My plan had been to attend Indiana State University, but she convinced me that DePauw would be a better choice. Mrs. Price explained the course work that I would need and advised me how to proceed. I suspected that she had the answer to my current problem.

I told Mrs. Price about the call from Dr. Lee. Mrs. Price and I had talked the previous month about the problem with my file, and I had resolved it to her satisfaction. Apparently, irregularities arose in the files of two other non-traditional students. It was clear that something was amiss in the basement of DePauw University's Asbury Hall. Why had three students had their Education Department files altered? There had to be more to the story, and I was determined to get to the bottom of it.

Being a very curious individual, I started digging into the mystery. I quickly discovered that my troubles were just the tip of the iceberg. Mrs. Price had been disciplined in July 2001 for "improper conduct" in the classroom. According to the university, Mrs. Price had committed three policy violations. First, she had overstepped her authority by questioning a student's placement in the Indianapolis Public School system for her student teaching. Secondly, Mrs. Price had made disparaging comments about the department in class. Most importantly, she had distributed "hate" literature in a classroom. These allegations, made by a single disgruntled student, would have been quite damning if true.

Upon closer examination, it appeared that Mrs. Price was being singled out for persecution by some DePauw University faculty members and administrators. She had been asked her opinion on student teaching at an Indianapolis Public School system facility by student Angela Morris. Mrs. Price noted that a suburban school might be a better choice for a beginning teacher to learn her trade. This opinion was identical to the concerns voiced by another faculty member. The second charge was equally bogus. Other students confirmed that Mrs. Price had not spoken ill of the Education Department in class as Ms. Morris had alleged. The true character of the case became crystal clear when the nature of the "hate" literature surfaced. In a March 2001 class, Mrs. Price had made four different issues of *Teachers in Focus* magazines, published by Focus on the Family, available for students to take if they desired. Providing these magazines for those who wanted a copy was not an uncommon practice for Mrs. Price, as I had taken an issue or two during my time in the program. The topic of this issue, homosexuality, was the problem. Mrs. Price had allowed Biblical truth about homosexuality to enter her classroom. She had not required the students to read it, nor had she made any assignments from this magazine. Its mere presence was enough to cause outrage. Her pay was cut by one quarter, a class that she had successfully taught for thirteen years was taken away from her, and she was put on probation, a rather Draconian punishment for a non-offense.

Suddenly, the disappearance of my transcripts made sense. As certification officer, Mrs. Price had to approve every education student's class work and test scores before she could recommend that student's application to the Indiana Professional Standards Board for a teaching license. Permitting an unqualified person to be certified would show that she was not doing her job and would legitimize the university's case against her. Having three improperly licensed teachers slip through the cracks would certainly have been grounds for even harsher sanctions. I was being used as an unwitting pawn by someone to cost a Christian woman her job.

Due to her abuse at the hands of DePauw University officials, Janis Price was left with no option but to file a lawsuit against DePauw University. Prior to filing, she pursued the proper internal university channels for nine months following her reprimand. Mrs. Price made eleven appointments with three different administrators during this time, but her concerns were never adequately addressed. Starting in the spring of 2002 and continuing for nearly three years, the case drew a fair amount of coverage in the Christian media. Some secular outlets covered the story as well. David Limbaugh's superb text, *Persecution*, mentioned the case briefly, as did Jim Nelson Black's *Freefall of the American University*. These authors have done an excellent job of bringing Mrs. Price's case out of the shadows and shedding light onto DePauw University's practices. What has been missing is a comprehensive analysis of issues involved as witnessed by a participant in the case. I know several of the key players in the drama. As a Christian and an alumnus of DePauw University, it is my duty to tell the story.

In *Tolerating the Intolerable*, I will show that Janis Price was singled out by some officials at DePauw University for persecution because of her Christian faith. Academic freedom, a cause championed by the radical Left during the 1960s, is not a luxury granted to conservative Christian professors. Additionally, I will demonstrate that her situation was the result of a shift at the university from an upstanding bastion of Methodist education to an institution that caters to the basest elements of society. To that end, I have examined court documents, interviewed witnesses, and studied DePauw University publications. The conclusions that I draw in this book are based primarily upon these sources. As a historian who reveres the *Holy Bible* and the United States

Constitution as the pillars of American civilization, I analyzed the situation at DePauw University through those time honored lenses.

My research uncovered some disturbing trends. Since the 1980s, Christians and conservatives in general have been marginalized at the university. At the same time, rabidly anti-American liberalism has been promoted. Homosexuality has moved from a quiet undertone to a cacophonous, university sponsored roar. Non-Christian groups, ranging from Buddhists to Wiccans, have come to the forefront, receiving official sanction from a university founded by the Methodist Church to rescue the lost and nurture believers. Some administrators have taken it upon themselves to abuse the power granted them by the DePauw University Board of Trustees. A student journalist questioned university hiring practices in an article in the campus newspaper, *The DePauw*. For his trouble, he received a scathing letter of rebuke from an administrator. Feeling that he was being mistreated, the student appealed to the university for help. A committee comprised of two administrators investigated the matter, and concluded that no wrong doing had occurred. This opinion was finalized by President Robert G. Bottoms, who had seen the letter prior to the student receiving it. Equally disturbing are the incidents of uneven treatment of DePauw employees by the university. A staff member who was arrested for drunken driving while returning home from a university function was promoted. The university rabbi who was caught smoking marijuana with students at a university sponsored function received a mild slap on the wrist from the administration. Janis Price's life was thrown into chaos by the unsubstantiated words of one disgruntled student and an overzealous administrator. There is clearly a loss of sensibility on the part of some at DePauw University.

It is not my intention to besmirch the reputation of DePauw University. The actions of a small number of faculty and administrators have already done that. Since my undergraduate days, I have maintained friendships with DePauw alumni from many eras. The tales some of them told about the school in the 1930s and 1940s made me wish that I could have attended the university during those golden years. The institution that they loved so dearly has been perverted into a breeding ground for anti-Americanism, homosexuality, and godlessness. Most alumni want to believe that DePauw is still the way they remember. Every June, hundreds of alumni descend on Greencastle, Indiana to recall the good old days at DePauw. For that weekend, the posters decrying

American imperialism and homophobia are removed. The remains of "Peace Camp" and chalk signs about the "Drag Ball" disappear. A clean, modern university that still respects tradition is presented to mature men wearing faded senior cords. The school song, "A Toast to Old DePauw," rings through the Union Building and East College. Nostalgia softens the hearts of wealthy alumni, who think back to their youth and write large checks so the next generation can share in their memories. The following Monday, everyone goes home remarking how wonderful the alma mater still is. It is my hope that alumni will read this account of the true state of affairs at DePauw University and demand a restoration to the values that made DePauw great. The problems are not insurmountable, but they will require a concerted effort by alumni. With their help, perhaps DePauw's true glory days still lie ahead of it.

Part I

The Problem with Janis Price

As with any good drama, the stage must be set for the case of *Janis Price vs. DePauw University*. The most logical place to begin is with the university itself. Although it was founded by men with the highest Christian ideals, DePauw University has gradually been transformed into a bastion of liberal intolerance. The most damaging changes have occurred under the tenure of Dr. Robert G. Bottoms since his elevation to university president in 1986.

No drama would be complete without a hero. Mrs. Janis K. Price, an instructor and administrator at DePauw University since 1988, is our protagonist. Her background and function within the university's Education Department are vital parts of the story. Equally important is her faith, which has allowed her to survive extraordinary pressures at DePauw.

To claim the title of hero, that person must have one or more foils. Mrs. Price's life was thrown into turmoil by the allegations of one student, Angela Morris. Her unfounded claims fed into already volatile intradepartmental rivalries. Doctors Esther Lee and Eva Weisz must have seen a golden opportunity to remove a popular and competent faculty member. With the help of Vice President of Academic Affairs Neal Abraham, they nearly succeeded.

Christophobia, perhaps the ugliest of all prejudices, was on full display in DePauw's response to Mrs. Price's alleged infractions. The university's over-reaction to a non-issue was quite shocking. The need to resolve this matter in the courts will be quite clear by the end of Part I.

Chapter 1

A Brief History of
DePauw University

Indiana was little more than an untamed frontier in the early 1800s. Settlements were confined to the southern part of the state, not far from the Ohio River. As settlers from Pennsylvania, Virginia, and Kentucky streamed across the border, new towns sprang up farther north. One of these new settlements, Greencastle, was founded in 1823 by Ephraim Dukes as the seat of newly formed Putnam County's government.[1] This west central Indiana town has since grown to be the home of 10,000 residents, a far cry from its humble origins.

Early Indiana was sparsely populated. The only access many inhabitants had to the Gospel was the family *Bible*. The Methodist Church sought to change that. Circuit riders first reached the Indiana Territory in 1801. These itinerant preachers rode from settlement to settlement holding revival meetings. This technique reached scores of lost souls. By the 1830s, Methodism counted 20,000 believers in Indiana, making it the largest denomination in the state.[2]

Methodist Church leadership soon realized that circuit riders simply could not service the growing number of converts. The logical next step was to set up an institution to train new ministers for formal congregations. The Indiana Conference of the Methodist Episcopal Church convened in New Albany on October 17, 1832. One of the topics of discussion was the creation of a conference seminary. A year later, the conference appointed a committee to actively pursue establishing a seminary in Indiana.[3] At the same time, an effort was made to gain access to the state college, now Indiana University. The Presbyterians firmly controlled that institution and refused to share power.[4] In 1834, the Methodists filed a petition with the Indiana legislature to return the election of state college trustees to the legislature, hoping to wrest absolute control from the other denomination. This action enraged the Presbyterians and ended any chance of gaining access to that institution.[5]

The drive to create a Methodist seminary gained momentum in 1835 and 1836. At the Indiana Conference meeting in Lafayette, the Committee on Education presented a proposal for Indiana Asbury University, a Methodist institution. It was decided that $10,000 was a sufficiently large sum to endow the university for the immediate future.[6] A site for Indiana Asbury was then sought. Greencastle, Indianapolis, Lafayette, Madison, Putnamville, Rockville all competed for the honor of hosting the university. Greencastle's presentation, and the offer of $25,000 toward construction, sealed the deal. [7] Indiana Asbury, the earliest incarnation of DePauw University, opened its doors in Greencastle, Indiana in 1837.

Indiana Asbury started life in a rented building. Cyrus Nutt, a twenty two year old graduate of Allegheny College, arrived in Greencastle on May 16, 1837 after an arduous journey from Pittsburgh. He was to be the first faculty member of the new university.[8] Soon he was followed by Matthew Simpson, the school's first president. President Simpson's arrival was met with some skepticism on the part of the locals. He was not yet thirty years old. Although there were seventy students enrolled, the school's new main building was far from complete. Simpson was quite an impassioned orator. It took but one sermon to win the people of Greencastle to his side.[9] As funds were tight in the early years, President Simpson taught many classes during his decade long administration. Natural theology and "Christian Evidences" were a few of the classes that he administered during his tenure. The latter class was considered to be the capstone of the curriculum. For most of the nineteenth century, the honor of teaching this course was bestowed only upon the president of the university.[10]

On September 14, 1840, President Simpson presided over the very first commencement at Indiana Asbury.[11] Before these young men could have been admitted to the university, they had to display aptitude in subjects that most modern graduates would find alien. According to the school's first catalog, applicants needed "a knowledge of Geography, English Grammar, Arithmetic, First lessons in Algebra, Latin Grammar, Historica Sacra, Caesar's Commentaries, Virgil, Greek Grammar, and Greek Testament."[12] During their stay at the university, these early students built upon their understanding of these disciplines to become the nineteenth century ideal of classically educated men. The Christian roots of the school were quite evident during the president's first commencement address, when, at the climax of the speech, Simpson called for "Christianity in culture."[13] There was no doubt where the university, its faculty, and students stood on issues of faith.

Christian faith was not something confined to the classroom. The professors at Indiana Asbury were also Methodist clergymen. As Dr. John Baughman put it:

> In Greencastle, living away from home for the first time, they found themselves in a sectarian university setting where the adult role models were clergymen-professors who themselves had undergone emotional religious conversion.[14]

The 1840s also brought widespread revival. It was not uncommon in those days for dozens of people to be saved at any given camp meeting around the western frontier. This, coupled with the sad fact that at least one Indiana Asbury student year typically passed away during each school year, added a certain evangelistic fervor to the campus.[15]

By the end of the 1840s, President Simpson had been called to serve as a bishop in the Methodist church. His early concern for keeping Indiana Asbury as a proper Christian liberal arts college remained. His successor, Lucien W. Berry, arrived on campus in June 1850.[16] Under his care, the Biblical Department adhered to very strict admission guidelines. Only those students deemed worthy by the Indiana Methodist Annual Conference were allowed into the program.[17]

There was much excitement on campus about this department. President Berry was very active in the efforts to raise funds for a special Biblical library, traveling great distances around Indiana to further the cause.[18] The daily devotional commitment expected of Indiana Asbury students in the ante bellum period would be incomprehensible to modern students at DePauw University. The faith of many students in this period was very strong, but young people often chafed under adult interference.

> The religious observances demanded of students in all the American colleges before the Civil War were extremely exacting, and Indiana Asbury was no different than others in this respect. The trustees were responsible for the rule that the first rising bell "shall ring half an hour before sunrise," the second bell at sunrise, at which time the president or some member of the faculty shall conduct public prayers, at which all students were required to attend. There was also compulsory church attendance on "Sabbath forenoon." On Sunday afternoons there was a lecture by the president or some other member of the faculty at which student attendance was also required. Student opposition to these requirements began early, but, in spite of many years of vigorous effort, compulsory chapel lasted until 1893, and when finally a voluntary chapel service was established, DePauw [Indiana Asbury] was one of the first institutions in the country to adopt this measure."[19]

By 1871, this rigor helped to produce forty seven ministers and three missionaries out of three hundred twenty seven graduates from the college.[20]

Many Christians noticed an increased need for evangelism during the latter third of the nineteenth century. John Ing, a 1868 graduate of Indiana Asbury, was one of those men. While an undergraduate, he had been a founding father of the Psi Phi Chapter of Delta Kappa Epsilon. He continued to find outlets for his leadership abilities after graduating from college. Commodore Matthew C. Perry opened Japan to the West in 1854. Mr. Ing believed that the country was ripe for evangelism, so he opened a mission school in Hirosaki, Japan in the 1870s. Knowing the influence that they held over Japanese society, he targeted his efforts toward the samurai class. In 1877, he sent four young Christian men to his alma mater. Sutemi Chinda, Keizo Kawamura, Izumy Nasu, and Aimaro Sato were the first Japanese students at Indiana Asbury. Before his untimely death, Nasu translated the *Illiad* into Japanese. Sato went on to a successful career as a diplomat, serving as his country's ambassador to Austria-Hungary, the United States, and the League of Nations. Ing was undoubtedly most pleased with Chinda. While at Indiana Asbury, he followed his mentor into the hallowed halls of DKE. Count Chinda eventually served as Japan's ambassador to Germany, Great Britain, and the United States, as well as Privy Counselor and Grand Chamberlain to the Japanese Emperor.[21] That is quite a record for one humble servant of Christ.

The curriculum slide toward secularism began in earnest after the Civil War. In the 1870s, Indiana Asbury offered four courses of study: Classical, Scientific, Normal, and Biblical. A Military Department was started in 1877. The 1880s saw some changes. The Normal School, the predecessor to the modern day education department, was closed in 1890 for failing to maintain the same standards as the rest of the university.[22] The program would be resurrected a few decades later. The School of Theology made its debut in 1885 and graduated thirty five students during the next fourteen years.[23] Indiana Asbury/DePauw University has been solely an undergraduate institution for much of its history. However, an alumnus in the nineteenth century could earn an M.A. *in cursu* by showing three years of personal and intellectual growth after college. This program was halted in 1894. In addition to these Master's degrees, five Ph.D.s were granted from 1886-1893.[24]

The economic fluctuations common during the "Gilded Age" made the fiscal situation at Indiana Asbury uncertain even in the best of times. In 1884, Washington C. DePauw, a wealthy businessman from New Albany, Indiana, offered Indiana Asbury financial security. In exchange, the school would be renamed DePauw University.[25] The original name lives on as the Asbury College of Liberal Arts, one of two colleges contained within DePauw University. Many changes in the campus took place during the 1870s and 1880s. The original college building, the Edifice, burned on February 12, 1879. The shell was rebuilt and re-christened West College. [26] Nine years earlier, the cornerstone to a new building, East College, was laid.[27] It was hoped that this new building would reduce the strain on the aging Edifice. The troubled economy of the 1870s postponed the dedication of the new building until 1877.[28] Once W.C. DePauw's money began filling his university's coffers, new buildings that would serve the institution into the mid-twentieth century cropped up almost overnight. 1885 alone saw the construction of Ladies Hall, Music Hall, McKim Observatory, and Middle College. All of these buildings were constructed of red brick with Indiana limestone accents, a style still prominent on campus today. [29]

Despite the shift toward liberalism, the Christian roots of DePauw University were still quite evident at the turn-of the-century. As late as the 1880s, the university president, chair of the philosophy department and chair of the Bible department were required to be ordained Methodist ministers. Biblical literature, under the name *English Bible*, was required of all students.[30] John P.D. John was university president from 1889-1895. After he retired, he debated agnostic orator Robert Ingersoll five hundred separate occasions on the topic "Did Man make God, or did God make Man?"[31] John was succeeded by Hillary Gobin in 1896. The Gobin Administration was the last to require church attendance. After he retired in 1903, he stayed at DePauw to teach English Bible until 1922.[32]

Compared to the present day situation at DePauw University, the moral problems that confronted the administration in the 1890s seem rather benign. The Methodist Church was still very conservative, forbidding drinking and dancing. Some at the university saw fit to defy these restrictions.

> Mild-mannered President Gobin, for example, found it necessary to suspend several sorority women for attending an off-campus party involving social dancing, a form of recreation strictly forbidden by university regulations, together with such activities as card playing and consumption of alcoholic beverages.[33]

Incidents of drunkenness and general rebellion to university conduct rules increased during the first decades of the twentieth century as more city-born students were admitted. Enrollment passed one thousand in 1909, making the task of policing the student body more difficult. [34] In 1926, the university discarded the rule against social dancing, despite opposition from many in the Methodist Church.[35] Drinking was still officially forbidden. Nationwide Prohibition during the 1920s might have lent credibility to the policy, but students ignored it just the same. Hoping to protect undergraduate virtue, DePauw University policy forbade co-eds from riding in cars after 7:00 pm.[36] These rules seem quaint in the current era of co-ed dormitories, condom dispensers and homosexual activism.

The 1920s brought a pronounced left-ward shift at DePauw University. G. Bromley Oxnam became president in 1928. He had previously served as the pastor of a liberal church in Los Angeles.[37] President Oxnam was a pacifist and a leftist. In 1932, he invited Socialist presidential candidate Norman Thomas to speak at DePauw University, something that didn't sit well with a student body that overwhelmingly preferred Herbert Hoover.[38] President Oxnam resented the fact that the Reserve Officers' Training Corps had been active at DePauw since 1918.[39] He spoke frequently on the need to rid the university of the R.O.T.C. program. Oxnam's leftist tendencies cost the university heavily in the 1930s. The politically motivated firing of a popular professor damaged the university's reputation with the academic community. President Oxnam left DePauw in 1936 to become a bishop in the Methodist Episcopal Church and was replaced by Clyde Wildman in December of that year.[40]

The university continued to grow during the late 1930s and 1940s. The U.S. Navy chose DePauw to host the V-5 and V-12 programs during World War Two. By August 1944, 2,463 men had graduated from the three month officer training program. After the war ended, former servicemen flooded the campus, swelling enrollment from a pre-war high of 1,500 to an average of 2,300 in the late 1940s. [41]

DePauw University absorbed the returning servicemen into the campus. They joined fraternities, made the Dean's List, played on the football team, and generally contributed greatly to DePauw's legacy. In 1951, the Memorial Union Building was opened, dedicated to the one hundred DePauw graduates who perished during World War II. The secularization of DePauw University continued unabated. Philosophy and religion were merged into one department in 1946, although *Bible* remained a separate field until 1955. Although chapel was still offered, it shifted toward personal enrichment and away from evangelism.[42] The university moved to a non-sectarian academic stance during this period without cutting ties to the Methodist Church, a philosophy that holds sway to this day. [43]

DePauw lurched leftward during the 1960s and 1970s. The existence of an R.O.T.C. program at the university was a constant source of irritation for liberal students. This tension came to a head on May 1, 1970 when two radical students burned the R O T C building. Regrettably, the aerospace program was dropped in 1973, forcing students to travel forty miles to attend some Air Force R.O.T.C. classes at Indiana University or Rose Hulman Institute of Technology. Four years later, DePauw hired its first non-ordained president, Richard Rosser. In 1978, President Rosser appointed Robert G. Bottoms Vice President for University Relations, setting in motion the events that lead to Janis Price's persecution twenty three years later.[44]

Robert G. Bottoms, an Episcopalian, holds a B.A. from Birmingham Southern, a B.D. from Emory, and a Doctor of Ministry from Vanderbilt.[45] In 1983, he moved up the ladder to serve as the Executive Vice President of DePauw University.[46] Three years later, Dr. Bottoms ascended to the presidency. During his inaugural address, he proposed a three point plan for his administration. First, he pledged to bring greater diversity to DePauw University. The administration followed through with this. In 1988, the student body was overwhelmingly white, upper and middle class, and Greek affiliated. Over eighty percent of students lived in thirteen fraternities and ten sororities. The Bottoms Administration aggressively recruited minority students from areas outside the Midwest. These students had little interest in the Greek system, critically weakening that pillar of tradition. By 2005, university policies had caused two fraternities and three sororities to close their doors, including Delta Kappa Epsilon, the home of such luminaries as Vice-President Dan Quayle, Senator Albert J. Beveridge, and Ambassador Chinda. However, the losses suffered by the traditionalists were gains for Bottoms' plans. The first minority editor of *The DePauw*, the student newspaper, was appointed in 1994. The same year, United DePauw, a homosexual advocacy organization, was established on the campus. Secondly, Dr. Bottoms promised a greater emphasis on science. He succeeded wildly here. A state of the art biological science building opened during the 1993-1994 school year, moving out of the fifty year old Harrison Hall. In 2003, the newly renovated Percy Julian Science and Math Center opened, offering advanced facilities for students of the physical sciences. The success of the third point, providing moral leadership in a secularized environment, is far more uncertain.[47] The reader should decide the validity of this point only after examining the evidence put forth in the following chapters.

Chapter 2

Janis Price and Education Department Politics

It is always of the utmost importance to understand the characters in a drama. In this case, we must learn who Mrs. Price is before we can fully grasp the reasons behind her actions. Janis Kay Morgan (Price) was born in Stilesville, Indiana, the daughter of a World War II U.S. Navy veteran. She spent her formative years in this west central Indiana hamlet. In 1956, at the age of eight, she accepted Christ as her savior. Her faith was encouraged by her Christian parents, as well as teachers at her school. One teacher went as far as to say that Jesus was absolutely vital to history as we know it. Janis Morgan graduated from the local high school, Cascade High School, in 1966. She had desired to be a teacher since she was a little girl, so that fall she followed U.S. 40 west out of her hometown to attend Indiana State University in Terre Haute. Indiana State University was founded as a teacher college in 1866. Over the past one hundred forty years, it has turned out thousands of highly qualified educators. Janis Morgan completed her student teaching internship at Reitz High School in Evansville, Indiana, and graduated in 1970 with a certificate allowing her to teach English in grades six through twelve.

Her first teaching assignment was at Martinsville High School, located southwest of Indianapolis. She was there only for one academic year, as she married Geoff Price that December. Mr. Price was still completing his active duty time in the U.S. Air Force at Grissom Air Force Base near Peru, Indiana, so the newly married Mrs. Price took a job at Maconaquah High School. Seventy percent of her students were bussed directly from that base. She took time to attend Ball State University extension classes at Grissom to work on her Master's degree. The next year, she made a professional decision to move to nearby Peru Junior High School. Mrs. Price recounted that she was actually encouraged in her faith as many of her fellow teachers, as well as several administrators, were committed Christians. Two years later, Mr. Price finished his military obligations. He got a job as a music teacher with the South Putnam Community School Corporation in 1974, prompting a move to Putnam County, only a few miles from Mrs. Price's childhood home.

The mid-1970s brought drastic changes for the Prices. A son, John, was born in 1974, with daughter Cathy following in 1977. Mrs. Price chose to stay home with the children until the younger reached first grade. She returned to work in 1983 part-time, as a contract substitute teacher. A contract substitute teacher spends a much longer time in a classroom, perhaps as much as a semester, filling in for an ailing, pregnant, or otherwise incapacitated teacher. Mrs. Price was offered a one year position at South Putnam Junior-Senior High School for the 1987-1988 school year. She completed that term and started looking for new employment. She turned to one of the largest employers in Putnam County, DePauw University. That choice would have a profound impact on the next fifteen years of her life.

Mrs. Price Goes to DePauw

Janis Price started her career at DePauw University on a part-time basis. She came to DePauw seeking a position in the English Department, but was offered a job in the Education Department. Starting in August 1988, she served as the director of both field experience and the Audio-Visual Lab. This was an ideal position for someone with school aged children, as the twenty hour per week schedule allowed her great flexibility.[48] At the end of the fall semester 1988, Education Department Chair Dr. Judith Raybern asked her to teach an intensive class for students going through field experience. This class would be the source of controversy thirteen years later. University Provost Leonard DiLillo offered Mrs. Price a full time position on August 25, 1992. From that moment until July 18, 2001, she would serve as certification officer, director of field experience, director of the AV lab, and part-time instructor.[49]

Janis Price's Job Description

The goal of the Education Department is to produce qualified teachers. To that end, someone must oversee students' progress toward that goal and provide proper guidance. As director of field experience, Mrs. Price was DePauw University's ambassador to the school systems. She arranged for students to be placed with experienced teachers who could "show them the ropes" in the public schools. These visits allowed students to see how the theory that they were learning in college applied to public school classrooms. Good placements were vital, because one bad placement could potentially ruin a student's chances of becoming a teacher, as well as strain the relationship between the university and the school.

To facilitate the transition from theory to practice, DePauw offered Education 375. This class will be explained in greater detail in the next chapter. It is important to note that this was the last class that students would take before doing their student teaching. As the instructor of this class, Mrs. Price was responsible for insuring that students were truly ready for a real classroom.

As certification officer, it was Mrs. Price's job to insure that every student's paperwork was in order prior to graduation. They had to complete the proper course work within the department as well as in their chosen field of licensure. Every student was required to pass the Praxis exam. One portion covered general knowledge, not unlike the SAT. The other portion was content area specific. Only after these requirements were met would Mrs. Price recommend a student to the Indiana Professional Standards Board for licensure.

The Early Years

Mrs. Price enjoyed her first years at DePauw University. She was very organized and efficient at her job. Students always had positive things to say about her and she enjoyed the opportunity that she had to impact the lives of young educators. She built strong relationships with Putnam County teachers and school administrators. Her faith was not an issue. She kept a Bible in her office, which was a tiny room nestled in the basement of 1929-vintage Asbury Hall. Her office was decorated with framed Scripture verses. She became a faculty sponsor for Cross of Light, a small Christian student group. Mrs. Price was a founding member of the Full Armor Fellowship, an organization for faculty and staff that met every other week. While DePauw University allowed the group to exist, administrators offered no financial assistance to them in the university budget. Dean of the Chapel Wes Allen suggested changing the name to something less "offensive" in order to get university funding. This suggestion was rejected by Mrs. Price and the planning team for Full Armor Fellowship. The name stayed; funding was never given. It is indeed odd that a Christian organization would have trouble getting funding at a university founded by devout followers of Christ.

Education Department Faculty and Staff- 2000-2001

To better understand the nature of the conflict, it is important to get to know the other actors in this drama. Dr. Judith Rayburn had taught at DePauw since 1974. She served as department chair for seventeen years, resigning for family reasons after the 1996-1997 school year. University Provost Len DiLillo replaced her the following year, taking on the chair duties in addition to his own university responsibilities. A temporary faculty member, Dr. Sam Henry, was hired for one year to fill the vacancy in 1998.[50] Dr. Esther Lee arrived at DePauw University in the summer of 1999, fresh from Southern Arkansas University.[51] She was hired as the chair of the

Education Department, and by 2000, was the highest paid faculty member on campus.[52] Dr. Eva Weisz was in charge of the Secondary Education Program. Dr. Rachel Marshall, a native of Liberia, taught Multi-Cultural Education and Content Literacy during this period. Dr. Paula Birt, a devout Christian, was the technical expert of the department. Every student had to pass her rigorous computer proficiencies in order to become a licensed teacher. Dr. Marcelle McVorran also taught Multi-Cultural Education and eventually succeeded Dr. Lee as department chair. Dr. Jamie Stockton was still completing her Ph.D. during the 2000-2001 school year. She was the most junior of the faculty, and therefore had one of the heaviest course loads. It should have been easy for the faculty to develop strong camaraderie within this small department. This was not the case, and would bode ill for Mrs. Price.

Education Department Courses

The Teacher Licensure Program at DePauw involved coursework spread over all four years of school. These classes were divided into "Blocks," one for each year. In a very real sense, Education majors were double majors, being required to take a significant number of courses in their respective areas of specialization. Block One, usually taken one's freshman year, consisted of a fundamentals class, Ed 170, and a multi-cultural education class, Ed 180. Ed 170 provided a very basic introduction to the program, as well as observation of actual elementary, middle school, and high school classrooms. Ed 180 students were not taught how to deal with the special needs of various minority groups, but were instead required to read literature from these cultures.

Block 2 consisted of Ed 222, "Education Psychology" and Ed 230, "Introduction to Exceptional Children." These were more application oriented classes than those in Block 1. The former shed light on the complex psychological terrain of the classroom. Students spent time working with real students, testing what they had learned in the classroom in a realistic environment. The latter was particularly helpful, as "exceptional children" referred to those on either extreme of the spectrum, the gifted and the handicapped. "Inclusion" is the buzzword of the modern classroom, and these future teachers would face children with exceptionalities like this once they entered the workforce.

Block 3 represented a parting of ways between the Elementary and Secondary Programs. The classes in this block were geared toward the specific needs of teachers headed for high school, middle school, or elementary classrooms. Ed 335, "Methods and Management (Adolescent)" dealt specifically with the problems that teachers would face in a high school classroom. "Content Literacy and Learning," Ed 340, allowed students to compose individual lessons and semester long lesson plans specific for their area of instruction, be it history, English, or math. The capstone of Block 3 was Ed 375, "Field Experience." Students spent the bulk of their class time in a public school classroom, observing and assisting the teacher. This class was the source of Mrs. Price's troubles, and will be discussed at length in a later chapter.

Block 4 consisted of a content specific methods class that allowed students to develop detailed lesson plans under the guidance of a practicing teacher. "Senior Seminar," Ed 430, was taken concurrently with student teaching. The former met infrequently during this semester to discus the trials, tribulations, and triumphs of student teaching. After completing this rigorous regimen, students where then eligible for licensure, a process facilitated by Janis Price.

Conflict

Harmony and tranquility did not reign in the Education Department. Janis Price did her job well, much to the delight of students. However, this did not sit well with two members of the department, Dr. Lee and Dr. Weisz. It did not take long for me to see the situation clearly after my return to DePauw University in January 2000. It was readily apparent to me that these two professors were quite jealous of the rapport that Mrs. Price had with my fellow students. This good rapport was based on the ability that Mrs. Price had to answer students' queries swiftly and accurately. Regrettably, neither Dr. Lee nor Dr. Weisz impressed me with their teaching or advising abilities. As the head of the Secondary Education Program, Dr. Weisz should have taught Ed 335 in the fall of 2000. She broke her foot at the beginning of the school year and took the rest of the semester off on medical leave. The class could have been moved to the main floor of Asbury Hall, which was made handicap accessible when I was an undergrad in the early 1990s, allowing Dr. Weisz to continue her teaching duties. Instead, Dr. Lee took charge of the class. I got very little from the class under her direction. After a few weeks, Jamie Stockton was recruited as the instructor. She did an excellent job, as she had worked as a public school teacher prior to joining the DePauw faculty. It must have been a burden for her, as she already had a full class load to teach, as well as a dissertation to write.

Dr. Weisz also was responsible for arranging for student teaching placements for everyone in the secondary teaching program, then monitoring their progress in the classroom as the semester progressed. Two teachers had requested that I work under them, and I forwarded this request to Dr. Weisz. As the semester wore on, I realized that I would have to resolve the issue myself. Dr. Weisz's role in arranging for my student teaching was granting permission once I had ironed out the scheduling conflicts.[53] It was indeed fortunate that I am native of the area and had known the proper people to contact at the schools, an advantage that a twenty two year old from out of state would not have enjoyed.

I was not the only one to have problems with Dr. Weisz. During Dr. Len DiLillo's tenure as provost, he had accumulated a sizable file on the less than stellar performance of this professor. When Dr. DiLillo retired from the university in 1998, he asked Mrs. Price to make an appointment with him to discuss the situation in the Education Department. The provost was pleased with the quality of her work and apologized for her low pay. He then made her aware of the file that he had been keeping on Dr. Weisz. Students, teachers, and school administrators had all complained to Dr. Len DiLillo about the quality of her work, so he kept copies of the complaints for possible future use. By maintaining such files, the public school employees had a record of the problems that they had been having with Dr. Weisz, providing hard evidence in the event that a situation needed to be resolved legally. He then directed Mrs. Price to maintain a similar file. As the director of field experience with an excellent reputation with the local school systems, she was trusted by administrators and teachers as a worthy professional to hear and deal with their complaints concerning Dr. Weisz. Dr. DiLillo noted that Eva Weisz's greatest problem was laziness. [54] Mrs. Price left the provost's office charged with the difficult task of maintaining her department's reputation in the face of growing unrest at the local schools.

A short time later, when Dr. Lee started visiting the schools, local administrators began complaining about her performance as well. In one incident, she contacted Todd Crosby, the principal at Reelsville Elementary School, wishing to have a meeting for all of the teachers in the school. It was far too short notice to arrange such a meeting, so he declined. She showed up at the school on the Friday that she had requested and demanded that he call all of his teachers together for a meeting. He explained again that that was not possible and gave her a tour of the building. She finally left the school angry. Mr. Crosby reported the situation to DePauw via Mrs. Price. To insure that complaints like this could be substantiated, Mrs. Price started a file on Dr. Lee. Ironically, when Dr. Lee took charge of the Education Department, she stated that one of her goals for her tenure was to develop good relationships with the local schools.[55] It is important to note that no one in the Education Department knew that Mrs. Price was maintaining these files, which eventually became rather thick from school teachers' and administrators' complaints. She did not maintain files on any other professors, as it was unnecessary.[56]

Brooke vs. Eva and Esther

Brooke Hefner (Marsh), a 2002 DePauw University graduate, had extreme difficulties with both Dr. Weisz and Dr. Lee. She was a social studies education student. In the spring of 2001, she turned in her application for student teaching placement for the following academic year. She had already discussed the possibility of teaching in her hometown of Columbus, Indiana.

> I explained to her [Weisz] that it was farther than sixty miles from Greencastle, but I still wondered if it would be possible because it was only about fifteen extra miles. Dr. Weisz said," I live in Indianapolis, therefore I do not see a problem with this. In fact, it may be easier because I can come straight from home." With this settled, I sent out my application to Columbus East High School. While I was waiting for a response, Dr. Lee took it upon herself to

calculate the miles, then told me that I could not student teach in Columbus. Of course, I was very distraught and tried to talk this out with Dr. Lee and Dr. Weisz. As in the past, neither of them, especially Dr. Lee, was willing to listen, let alone consider what I had to say. I did get very upset with the meetings we had about the situation, but again, Dr. Weisz attempted to place the blame upon me. I was looking through my files in the Education Department and found the "Instructor's Qualitative Evaluation of the Teacher Education Student," which was supposed only to be an evaluation of me in the course I was taking from Dr. Weisz, Education 335: Methods and Management. However, Dr. Weisz used it as an evaluation of how I handled meetings about my placement. In the comment section, she wrote, "Brooke at times appears frustrated and even angry- she walked out on two meetings with me- and was not as forthright as she could have been about mileage to Columbus, Indiana." [57]

It is quite clear that Brooke was the victim of duplicity that could have cost her a student teaching placement and delayed her graduation. She dealt with this inconsistency with greater patience than many people would have been able to muster.

Brooke's troubles intensified when it was time for her to receive her license. Dr. Lee, who was now serving as certification officer, rejected her application because she had allegedly not completed the correct courses to be licensed in social studies in Indiana. If this were true, it was due to the lax advising that she had received from Dr. Weisz. When Brooke dared to ask what the Indiana Professional Standards Board, the organization responsible for issuing teaching certificates within the state, had to say on the issue, Lee was incensed. "The State requirements have nothing to do with your licensing," she claimed.[58] The same was true, in Dr. Lee's mind at least, with national standards. The requirements of DePauw University's Education Department trumped all others. Brooke had the good sense to contact the I.P.S.B. directly and was assured by the director of licensing, Shawn Sriver, and the executive director of the I.P.S.B., Marie Theobald, that Indiana state standards supercede anything in individual departments.[59] Dr. Lee appears to have been engaging in a power-play by sabotaging the efforts of a student to become a licensed teacher. Brooke's respect and admiration toward Mrs. Price did not help her with either Dr. Lee or Dr. Weisz.

It is hard for outsiders to understand the volatile mix that had been simmering in the Education Department from 1999. Two adults with advanced degrees were jealous of one of their peers who had a better rapport with students and public school administrators despite not having a Ph.D.. One cannot ignore the anti-Christian bias that both of these professors brought to the office with them. When these two elements mixed, an explosion was imminent. All that was needed was a catalyst. As it would be unseemly for academics to openly attack a peer, they required a student who was willing to say whatever was needed to sully Mrs. Price's good name. That was quite a difficult task, given her overwhelming support and appreciation by the student body within the Education Department. Fortunately for Dr. Lee and Dr. Weisz, they found just what they were looking for in Angela Morris, a fifth year senior English major with an education minor.

Chapter 3

The Class- March 15, 2001

One "offensive" magazine allowed into an infrequently held class is a rather flimsy reason to ruin a valued educator's career. The most reliable accounts of the events of March 15, 2001 come from the instructor, Mrs. Janis Price, and Brooke Hefner, one of four students in the class. I have known both of them for a number of years and have great confidence in the accuracy of their accounts of that fateful day. I took the very same class the previous semester, so I am quite familiar with Mrs. Price's conduct in the classroom. The "offensive" material will be explored as well. Most importantly, the motives of all the parties involved will be revealed.

Mrs. Price taught Education 375 for thirteen years. In all that time, she only had one student who had complained about the class, Angela Morris. What follows is the syllabus for this class for the spring semester, 2001. Passages that aid in the understanding of Mrs. Price's situation are printed in bold type.

Education 375 Syllabus- Spring 2001

Field Experience: AYA/EA - Education 375
Instructor: Mrs. Janis Price
Asbury Hall
658-xxxx
Spring Semester 2001
Office Hours:
Mondays-9:00-3:00
Tuesdays-9:00-12:00 & 1:00-3:00
Wednesdays- 2:00-4:00
Thursdays- 9:00-3:00
Essential Dates for Students to Record
January 30- 3:00-4:00- First Class- AH9
February 2- 12:00-12:30- Second Class Session AH9
March 15- 6:30-8:30 Third Class Session- AH9 [sic. Moved to AH21]
(Mid-term paper is due.)
May 8- 4:00-4:30- Final Class Session- AH9
(Final Paper Due)
Education 375 AYA/EA- Field Experience- Course Overview
Instructor- Mrs. Janis Price

Mission Statement-
"The Mission of DePauw University's Teacher Education Program is to prepare candidates to enter a profession that requires content and professional knowledge, skill competence, and the appropriate dispositions. To this end, our development of professional educators is grounded in a comprehensive liberal education integrated with a professional teacher preparation program that relies heavily on complementary field experiences."

The Ed. 375 course is the final course which you will take in the secondary program that has a strong emphasis on field experience just prior to student teaching. *Be sure to make the most of this course in light of the Mission Statement, and in consideration of the of the fact that it is in Block III.*

Departmental Theme- Teachers for Unlimited Horizons
This course is designed to give you practical experience in a public school classroom for 24 class periods. This opportunity will give you a better "view" of the teaching profession generally, and a closer look at the unlimited potential to teach your particular discipline specifically.

Conceptual Framework-

24

Throughout your college experience at DePauw in the Education Department, you have had multiple opportunities to participate in public school classrooms, whether as an observer or active participant, and whether with an individual, a small group, or an entire classroom. **In this course, you will not be observing as much as actively participating to the extent that the public school supervising teacher believes you are capable. In a practical sense, this is a "pre-student teaching" course.** *The concept you should have is one of teaching as much as possible in preparation for your student teaching semester in Block 4.*

INTASC Principles to be Developed, Reinforced & Assessed-
There are two major pieces of writing that you will produce for this course. One is due at the mid-term class and is a reflective paper in which INTASC principles may be referred to generally or specifically. By contrast, the final paper will speak directly to a minimum of 2 INTASC principles. Information concerning these papers is found further in the syllabus.
While all INTASC Principles are taught in Ed. 375, those which are stressed are the following:

Principle #1- Successful completion of teaching in a public school classroom for 2 class periods per week and for 12 weeks.
Principle #9- Clarity of thought as a reflective practitioner will be expressed through the mid-term paper and the final paper.
Principle #10- Successful relationship building with the supervising teacher (s) over an extended period of time is essential.

Portfolio-
As you are developing your portfolio throughout several semesters and from several courses
and experiences, may I suggest that the materials you will be preparing and the papers that
you will be writing for this course would be excellent opportunities to write well, and then include the final products in your portfolio. This is especially true of the final paper with its emphasis on INTASC.

Performance Based Assessments-
Note that your supervising teacher in the public school to which you will be assigned will be completing an evaluation form and an attendance form. These will be returned to me by the end of the semester and become part of your final grade.

Technology Proficiencies-
Due to the fact that this course is arranged and we do not meet on a regular basis as a traditional class, please use e-mail to communicate with me as you feel is necessary. Additionally, look for creative ways to use technology in your teaching- build on the knowledge that you have gained from the technology workshops in Blocks I and II.

Connection to the Professional Community-
This Field Experience course will afford you with the opportunity to be actively involved in a classroom for 24 class periods. However, it is my suggestion that you build on this opportunity by attending school functions after school hours, have multiple conversations with your supervising teacher about school issues, and generally look for opportunities to make the most of this pre-student teaching course.

Evaluation Information
Ed. 375 AYA/EA

There will be numerous opportunities for your public school supervising teacher and Mrs. Price to evaluate your progress throughout the semester. The following is a list of formal evaluation opportunities and the number of points assigned to each.

1. Attendance and participation in two class sessions prior to the school placement for Field Experience, one class session at mid-term, and one class session at the end of the semester.
First Class Session- 10
Second Class Session- 10
Mid-term Class session- 50
Final Class session- 30

2. Two written reports/papers.
A. Mid-term paper that is 2-4 pages in length. Detailed instructions on the writing of this paper are on a separate page of the syllabus- 100 (20 points are deducted for each day that the paper is late).
B. Semester final paper that is 3-5 pages in length. Specific instructions concerning the writing of this paper are also on a separate page of the syllabus- 100 (25 points are deducted for each day that the paper is late).

3. One observation

An observation will be arranged with you and your supervising teacher. You will need to be actively teaching the entire class for at least a portion of one class period. This observation will be scheduled between mid-term and the end of the semester- 100

4. A final evaluation form and an attendance form will be completed by the supervising teacher with whom you work in the assigned public school.
Evaluation Form-120
Attendance Form-120

Note: Attendance at the assigned school will also be checked by Mrs. Price via the Sign-In Folder which is in the central office of each participating school.
Information is based on research, reading, and previous evaluation procedures used for this course. The basic text used in preparation for teaching of Ed. 375 was the following:
Posner, George J. Field Experience- Methods of Reflective Teaching. New York: Longman Inc., 1996.

Semester Mid-Term Paper
Cover Page:
Your name
Class information (Ed.375, etc.)
Date paper is turned in

Mid-term Paper Text:
2-4 pages in length
It is important that you develop the skill of being a reflective professional educator. As you reflect on the past 6 weeks/12 class periods working with students, choose one of the following quotes, agree or disagree with the quotation, and relate the quote to your experience in the classroom (s) where you are assigned. Support your position with personal classroom experiences, reading, research, facts, statistics, etc.

1. There is more to teaching than chalk.
2. It takes a family and a community (not just a teacher in a school for a few hours each day) to properly raise (educate) a child.
3. It is very hard to grow and learn around impatient people.
4. I hear- I forget; I see- I remember: I do- I understand.
5. The classroom is not a mausoleum, library, or a funeral parlor. It is more like a factory where productive noise is okay.

6. *If you want to do something good for a child/adolescent, give him an environment where he can touch things as much as he wants.*
7. *It is the stillness you have to justify, not the movement.*
8. *What I teach is important, but why I teach is more important.*
9. *One vital key to the teaching/learning process is accountability.*
10. *To avoid criticism, say nothing, do nothing, be nothing.*
11. *As a teacher, I not only teach the lesson, I am the lesson.*

Semester Final Paper

Cover Page:
Your name
Class information (Ed. 375, etc.)
Date the report is turned in
Final Paper Text:
3-5 pages in length
The text will need to be divided into 2 separate parts-

Part I- Review the formula "K+D=P." Assuming that you are Knowledgeable in your content area, what Dispositions have you clearly identified in your field experience as being critical in the teaching/ learning process? Due to your subject matter knowledge and your recognition of
critical teaching dispositions, has your Performance improved/ significantly improved this semester? Give specific examples.
Part II- After carefully reviewing the 10 INTASC Principles, choose a minimum of 2 principles. Describe how this course helped to prepare you as a new teacher in relationship to those
principles you chose.

DePauw University
Education 375
Field Experience- AYA/EA
Evaluation Form
Due: The Week of May 7 (2001)
As a professional educator, please indicate your evaluation of the DePauw student on a scale of 1 to 10. A suggested evaluation key to guide your numeric marks is as follows:

10 points- Outstanding. Student has completed each assigned task in a professional manner and has asked for additional work, showed a special element of creativity, or in some specific way has exceeded work requirements.
8 points- Excellent. Student has completed each assigned task in a professional manner.

6 points- Satisfactory. Student is adequate in teaching. He/she has a command of the subject area and can relate the information well to students.

4 points- Needs substantial improvement. DePauw student has difficulty with students in the classroom and/or with the subject matter.

2 points- Unsatisfactory. Student did not complete assigned work, did not relate well to the students, and/or demonstrated weakness in the subject area.

1. Knowledge of subject matter
(INTASC 1)
2. Small group instruction
(INTASC 5)
3. Whole class instruction
(INTASC 2)
4. Production and/or use of classroom materials/media: bulletin board, quiz, study sheet, video, etc. (INTASC 6)
5. Dispositions- positive attitude, etc.
(INTASC 9)
6. Professional appearance
7. Maturity
(INTASC 9)
8. Rapport with students
(INTASC 6)
9. Performance- ability to teach subject matter
(INTASC 1)
10. Use of a variety of teaching strategies/techniques
(INTASC 3)
11. Pedagogy- ability to communicate what one knows about a subject
(INTASC 2 & 4)
12. Sensitive to needs of diverse learners/students
(INTASC 3)

A summary of your general observations and involvement with the student is most helpful. Please mention any "special" contributions made by this student. Either write your comments on the back of this form, or attach another paper as needed. Thank you for taking the time to help evaluate this student. Doing so will be most helpful to me in determining the student's final grade.[60]

Education 375 was one of the most important classes offered in the Education Department for a variety of reasons. The class only met four times during the semester, so the students had to learn to be self-reliant regarding assignments. The bulk of the class was spent in a public school classroom. The student applied what he or she had learned from Education Department classes during the previous three years to an actual classroom situation. In this way, the theoretical became real. The supervising teacher became more important to the student than the DePauw instructor because he or she would be spending twenty four class periods with this educator over the course of the semester. As such, the observations made by the supervisor carried considerable weight with the DePauw instructor. Education 375 was the last chance that a student had before student teaching to see if he or she was really ready to become a teacher. For all these reasons, a good experience in this class was vital to success in student teaching.

Recollections of Education 375- Fall 2000

When I returned to DePauw in January 2000, I went through the teacher certification program in an unconventional manner. As I already had a degree, I was able to concentrate solely on education classes at the university, taking freshman level classes in spring semester 2000, followed by sophomore and junior level classes during the fall semester. I was in Education 375 the semester before the Angela Morris incident, permitting me to speak as accurately about the nature of the class as anyone could without sitting in the March 15, 2001 class.

We met four times during the semester, just as the spring 2001 class did. I spent my time at Greencastle High School under the tutelage of social studies teacher Ken Mitchell. Mrs. Price visited to evaluate my performance on a lecture regarding 1930s racial stereotyping. Her evaluations clearly and concisely told me the areas that needed improvement, as well as the things that I was doing well. She was always willing to take time to explain her assessments, allowing me to improve my technique for the next class. Similarly, Mr. Mitchell provided me with input on my teaching performance. Both Mrs. Price and Mr. Mitchell were experienced educators, so it was to my benefit to use their suggestions to improve my teaching ability. I knew that their criticisms were meant to be constructive, as were their words of praise. As will be shown later, some students in the Teacher Education Program lacked this mature understanding of honest evaluation.

Angela Morris claimed many things regarding Mrs. Price's classroom behavior. Each will be analyzed and corrected in turn. One claim that I personally know to be false is the suggestion that Mrs. Price "distributed" anti-homosexual literature. After the end of each Education 375 meeting, I recall that she made a variety of education publications available for students to take if they so desired. *Teachers in Focus* was one of the publications that students could take, as well as NEA magazines. She did not hand them out, nor did she make any assignments from them. Based on this experience alone, it is quite improbable that Mrs. Price would change her behavior for the very next session.

The Accuser- Angela Morris

The Education 375 class held on March 15, 2001 is the genesis for the persecution that Mrs. Price suffered at the hands of DePauw University. Three versions of the events of that class will be given. First, Angela Morris's account of that day will be given, followed by the more accurate recollections of Brooke Hefner and Mrs. Price. In a September 20, 2002 letter published in *The DePauw*, Ms. Morris stated the following about the class in question.

> I am the student who was originally 'offended' by the "Teacher's in Focus" article by Janis Price. I am not writing this letter to defend myself or the University, but rather to share a different point of view about the series of events that have been, in my opinion, dissimulated through the biased information in the media thus far.
>
> The Education Field Experience course taught by Mrs. Price was not meeting in a classroom the given day of the incident concerning "Teachers in Focus." Mrs. Price and her four students met in a small room known as the Education Lab. There were no desks and no back table. Rather, the class sat around a small rectangle table with six chairs. Mrs. Price sat at the head.
>
> Mrs. Price distributed two different editions of "Teachers in Focus." She passed them around the table by handing them first to me, on her left, and then I continued the

rotation. She did also comment that there were more editions available in her office.

Although the magazines were distributed at the end of class, I still tried to inquire about the article that immediately caught my eye (concerning gay and lesbian students in the classroom) before my peers could exit the session. After being asked to clarify why she was handing out prejudiced material, Mrs. Price remarked that children go to school to learn the three R's (Arithmetic, Reading, and Wring). The discussion was dismissed and Mrs. Price left the lab.

The controversial "Teacher's in Focus" issue did not land in Academic Affairs the day of the incident. The magazine was passed around among staff members, as well as students, for contemplation, criticism, and conversation. The many responses were weighed into account before further, higher deliberation took place.

Since I participated in the unfolding of this incident from day one, I can say that this is not a Christianity issue, nor one that reflects on academic freedom. Rather, the Janis Price case is an educational matter. By this case, I mean Mrs. Price was in charge of directing future teachers through their final stages of instruction on effective classroom practices. Since the class met less than six times during the semester, it was vital that each meeting was organized to discuss pertinent education issue. For the topic of 'gay and lesbians in the classroom' to be brought up without discussion, through an article that discourages acceptance of these lifestyles, was insulting and potentially detrimental on many levels.

As a practicing teacher in the Indianapolis Public School system, I can say that gays and lesbians in the classroom is one of the most addressed and talked about issues among counselors and teachers. We don't discuss strategies for teaching these children how to be straight because homosexuality is an illness, something to be corrected; instead, we talk about how we can make our classrooms comfortable and conductive for all students. Because children are our future and peace is our mission, we work

> very hard to create a nurturing, accepting environment,
> not a judgmental rejecting one. [61]

Although Ms. Morris' letter has an initial ring of credibility to it, many aspects undermine the piece. It was not a particularly well written piece. One should at least expect decent writing from an English major. The tone of the latter portion is rather arrogant and condescending toward Mrs. Price. This is particularly irritating, considering that the subject of Ms. Morris' criticism has been teaching for longer than this young woman has been alive. In the letter, she admitted to seeing an article that caught her eye. She raised an objection without having sufficient time to read one article, much less the entire magazine.[62] Had she read the magazine, she would have known that this issue of *Teachers in Focus* dealt primarily with homosexual activism in public schools. Ms. Morris stated that "the class met less than six times during the semester.' This is true, but misleading. Had she bothered to consult her class syllabus, she would have been able to state the accurate number of meetings, four. Ms. Morris was also incorrect in her description of room 21 in Asbury Hall, the Education/AV Lab. She stated that there was one large table in the middle, with nothing else in the room. As I used this particular room to work on projects during that same semester, I am quite certain that this description is incorrect. There was a large table in the middle of the room, but the walls of the lab were lined with work tables and computer stations, upon any one of which magazines could have been placed. Ms. Morris also stated that the issue of *Teachers in Focus* was passed around the department amongst students and faculty before the matter was moved to a higher level. According to the deposition of Vice President of Academic Affairs Neal Abraham, the person responsible for the Draconian punishment of Mrs. Price, an incident was reported to him on March 16, the very next day. [63] It is uncertain who saw the magazine prior to it arriving in Academic Affairs, nor is it certain when it arrived in Dr. Abraham's office, but less than twenty four hours had elapsed before a complaint of some kind was raised by her. Perhaps most importantly, Ms. Morris contradicts herself regarding the importance of homosexuality in the classroom. At one point, she downplayed the importance of the issue, chastising Mrs. Price for not spending time on more pertinent issues. In the very next paragraph, she related how often the topic of homosexuality was raised in the school system in which she taught at the time. Without realizing it, Ms. Morris damaged her own case by writing such an erroneous letter.

The Truth- Brooke Hefner (Marsh)

Another student in the class, Brooke Hefner, wrote in to the campus newspaper, *The DePauw*, to correct some of the inaccuracies in Angela Morris's letter. Ms. Hefner took classes in the Education Department from January 1999 to May 2002. [64]I had the good fortune to get to know Brooke when we commuted with another student to observe classrooms in Indianapolis. She is a outstanding young Christian woman who possesses a fine memory. What follows is the unedited text of her letter that appeared in the October 15, 2002 issue of *The DePauw*.

> As I sat in my dorm room one evening of my freshman year reading *Beloved* by Toni Morrison (because it was a mandatory English assignment) I was encountered with acts of incest and witchery. As I sat in an Education class one day of my junior year I was given the opportunity, upon my own choosing, to take copies of *Teachers in Focus*, one of which happened to have an article about homosexuality. What is odd to me about these two classes is that the individual teaching the English class, Dr. Henry, apparently was in the right while the individual, Mrs. Price, teaching the Education class has been classified as intolerable and in the wrong.

> It is interesting to me how a university founded on religious beliefs can tolerate students being forced to read (or forced to fail if they chose not to read) about such things that are found in *Beloved* but in no way tolerates a teacher making available but not forcing students to read a Christian based education magazine. Yes, the magazine had an article about homosexuality, but Angela Morris's interpretation of the article was completely off. The article was not "judgmental and rejecting" of the lifestyle, it simply stated that "Rather than affirming teens as gay, counselors should affirm them as individuals, but encourage them to wait until adulthood to make choices about sexuality." The article was focusing on middle

school aged students, which as many of us know, is an identity seeking time for children, meaning many of them are confused and should not make a decision right then and there that they are homosexual or heterosexual. In other words, take their time and find out what they are really feeling... do not "jump the gun."

Mrs. Price always did a wonderful job of answering students' questions, and Angela Morris's claim that Mrs. Price "dismissed the discussion" without answering her question is ludicrous. First off, Angela's question was about homosexual teachers and what if a student brings up their personal life. Mrs. Price never said anything about "children going to school to learn the three Rs," and she did not leave the room without answering the question. Instead she said, "An English teacher should teach English the best s/he can. The same goes for a Science teacher or a Math teacher. If the teacher is doing the job correctly, there should be no room for her/his personal life inside the classroom." Because Angela was satisfied with the answer is why the class ended and we left the room.

I did not write this letter to call Angela Morris a liar. Yes, her story is a little different than what actually occurred, but not everyone's memory works the same. Rather, I am here to defend an excellent teacher, a warm-hearted person, and a dedicated Christian; all of which I thought that DePauw University was founded on. I guess that what they tell you when you apply and what you experience when you get here are two totally different things. I have graduated, but I hope that those of you still at DePauw will take it upon yourself to be the bigger person, rise above the administration, and bring DePauw back to what it was founded on. God Bless![65]

The contrast between Angela Morris's claims and the reality of the events of March 15, 2001 could not be more stark. Brooke Hefner had actually read the "offensive" issue of *Teachers in Focus* and found nothing wrong with it. She had been offended by passages in *Beloved*, but knew not to make an issue of it. Many students at DePauw and other universities can sympathize with being forced to read literature and participate in discussions on topics that are truly offensive. They remain silent, knowing that saying anything against the professor would result in a lower grade. Ms. Hefner also pointed out that the behavior attributed to Mrs. Price, avoiding answering questions, was out of character for this instructor. She noted during our discussion in May 2004, "She (Mrs. Price) was always there for me to help me through my problems that I was having in the Education Department."[66] It is indeed odd that Angela Morris could not accurately remember the question that she raised with Mrs. Price, but Brooke Hefner did. In her letter, Ms. Morris claimed to have asked a question about homosexual students. In actuality, she queried Mrs. Price on homosexual teachers. Based on Ms. Hefner's recollections, the answer provided to Ms. Morris was apparently satisfactory, because class filed out of the room shortly thereafter.[67] Had the student had further questions, it is quite clear, from what has been established about Mrs. Price's classroom demeanor, that she would have given Angela Morris all the time needed to ease her concerns. Ms. Hefner's recollection of the "distribution" of *Teachers in Focus* contradicts Morris's allegations.

> It was just a normal class. Mrs. Price had some extra magazines, which is the way she presented it. She said, "I've got several copies of these. I'm going to put them on the table, and you can take them or not. You don't have to, there's no assignment out of it." And she laid them on the table for us to take of our own choosing. She had extras and thought that maybe we might enjoy looking at them, just as a different type of magazine that we might not have access to. [68]

Only Ms. Morris and Ms. Hefner chose to take any of the four different magazines at the end of class.[69]

The Truth- Janis Price

Mrs. Price's recollections of the March 15, 2001 class reveal that there was no real problem of which she was made aware. The mid-term paper was due at during this class. This assignment indicated that Angela Morris was an adequate writer. Her efforts in the classroom showed her to be a less than stellar teacher. Her rapport with students was poor. The same was true in her dealings with both Mrs. Price and Mrs. Tona Dobson, Morris's supervising teacher at South Putnam Junior-Senior High School. At the end of the March 15 class, Mrs. Price made several publications available, including *NEA Today, Music Education,* and four different issues of *Teachers in Focus.* She made no assignments from any of these magazines, merely placing them on a table in the classroom for students to take if they wished. Angela Morris picked up the October 2000 issue of *Teachers in Focus.* After glancing at the cover, she asked Mrs. Price in a taunting voice, "Mrs. Price, what do you think of homosexual teachers?" Mrs. Price replied that she felt strongly that "if you are hired to teach English, you should do the best job you can teaching English. And if you're hired to teach math or science, then you need to do the best job you can teaching math or science. " Ms. Morris appeared to be satisfied with the answer and left the room.[70] It is now quite clear that she was still upset about the content of *Teachers in Focus.* If she truly wanted to handle the situation maturely, Angela Morris should have made an appointment to discuss her concerns with Mrs. Price prior to scurrying across campus to the Administration Building.

Teachers in Focus- October 2000

Teachers in Focus was a high quality education oriented magazine printed by Focus on the Family. Each issue dealt with real life problems experienced by teachers in public schools and provided possible solutions from a Christian perspective. In the October 2000 issue, the topic of discussion was homosexual activism in schools. One article, "But what do I say?," provided a Christian response to the dangerous homosexual agenda directed toward schoolchildren. The author, J. Budziszewski, was a professor of government and philosophy at the University of Texas at the time.[71] In another article, former public school teacher Heather Koerner praised "Love Won Out," an organization of ex-homosexuals that help others leave that lifestyle.[72] Dr. Joseph Nicolosi, a psychologist and counselor who extensively researched homosexuality, exploded many pro-gay myths in "Is This Really Good for Kids?"[73] A teacher who wrote under the pseudonym "Pen Master" revealed the manner in which homosexual activists penetrate schools and destroy their opponents in "Notes From the Underground."[74] Finally, "To Those Far Off," a piece written three hundred years earlier by the author of *The Pilgrim's Progress*, John Bunyan, was included as inspiration for those who might be struggling with the sinful effects of homosexuality.[75] As one can easily see, there was nothing remotely offensive or radical in these pages.

When the March 15, 2001 class ended and the last student left Asbury Hall room 21, neither Mrs. Price nor Brooke Hefner had any indication that the last few moments would have such a tremendous impact on their lives. Angela Morris appeared to have been satisfied with Mrs. Price's explanation of the October 2000 issue of *Teachers in Focus*. It seems rather odd for her to keep a magazine that had initially offended her. That magazine quickly made its way into Neal Abraham's hands and Janis Price's nightmare began in earnest.

Chapter 4

Angela Morris' Complaint

Angela Morris made a series of claims against Mrs. Price shortly after the March 15, 2001 class that went far beyond the alleged distribution of Christian material in the classroom. One of these dealt with Mrs. Price putting down the Education Department. According to Vice President of Academic Affairs Neal Abraham, she (Mrs. Price) apologized to a student for the trouble she was having with the department, something that Ms. Morris believed was inappropriate.[76] Sympathizing with a student and trying to help her navigate a rather dysfunctional organization should be considered anything but inappropriate. Despite Angela Morris's claims to the contrary, Brooke Hefner remembered quite clearly that "Mrs. Price handled herself very professionally. She never put down the department. She never forced any views of her own on us."[77]

Angela Morris lodged a second complaint against Mrs. Price. In the words of Neal Abraham:

> She (Morris) described a set of comments in several discussions that they had held about that, with the general impression that Mrs. Price had been quite derogatory about the possibility of a placement in the Indianapolis Public School system.[78]

Dr. Weisz, who had agreed to the placement, was visibly upset that someone had usurped her authority by contradicting her advice regarding this issue,[79] The truth is far less sinister. Ms. Morris and Dr. Weisz had agreed that the urban environment at an Indianapolis Public School campus would be a reasonable setting for a fledging teacher to learn her trade. The young woman must have had some doubts about the placement, as she then consulted Dr. Rachel Marshall, an Indianapolis resident who was quite familiar with the Indianapolis Public School system. Dr. Marshall advised against the placement, not knowing that Dr. Weisz had already approved it. Ms. Morris then went to see Mrs. Price to ask her for a second opinion on the subject. Mrs. Price, noting that Angela Morris was actually seeking a third opinion, concurred with Dr. Marshall's assessment. She reminded the student that inner city schools were difficult places even for experienced teachers to work. When asked whether she had visited the school, Ms. Morris replied that she had not. Mrs. Price then suggested that she visit the school to see for herself if she really wanted to teach there. Ms. Morris assured Mrs. Price that she would stop by the school soon and left the office in a good mood. She did decide to student teach at that school the following semester.[80] It is indeed odd that Ms. Morris did not complain about Dr. Marshall's "unprofessional" conduct, as she had rendered the same verdict as Mrs. Price. It would also seem that she had her mind made up prior to talking to Dr. Marshall and Mrs. Price regarding the placement. What could Angela Morris have gained by asking two different professors questions to which she already had answers?

Neither of Angela Morris' first two claims warranted investigation according to Neal Abraham.[81] They were matters of hearsay, with no documentation to back up her claims. Only the third claim, that Mrs. Price distributed "controversial" material, warranted university action. In May 2001, the situation grew worse. Brooke Hefner went to see Abraham about another Education Department issue. The vice president pulled out the copy of *Teachers in Focus* and asked her what she knew about this magazine. She explained what happened in class and when Dr. Abraham asked if she was offended by the article, she rightly said that she was not. It will become crystal clear in succeeding chapters why DePauw University was willing to pursue Mrs. Price on the issue of permitting Christian educational materials that show homosexuality for what it is into her classroom. The question remains as to why Ms. Morris might have been willing to be an accomplice in the tarring of a fine educator.

The Muscle

Vice President of Academic Affairs Neal Abraham is a key figure in DePauw University's persecution of Janis Price. Without his cooperation, Angela Morris' complaints would have been dismissed as frivolous. Reading Abby Lovett's 1998 "puff piece" on the newly arrived V.P., one would never suspect that this man would behave in an unprofessional manner toward one of his subordinates. Dr. Abraham talked about the need to make sure that DePauw students got their money's worth at the university. He was concerned about the close nature of the campus breeding factions among faculty and students. Dr. Abraham had spent the previous twenty two years as a physicist. He was well traveled, having seen several continents with his family. The new V.P. was a cat lover, sharing his temporary lodgings with two furry friends. In his free time, the good doctor could be found on the tennis court.[82] One would conclude that Dr. Abraham was the type of fellow that everyone would want to have over for dinner. More sinister aspects of this administrator's personality would emerge a few years later.

The Motive

Angela Morris spent the majority of her time in Education 375 under the tutelage of Mrs. Tona Dobson, an English teacher at South Putnam Junior-Senior High School. Mrs. Dobson had experience in the classroom and a complimentary recommendation from the South Putnam Junior-Senior High School vice principal when she agreed to take on a student observer. In a letter dated February 2, 2001, Mrs. Price explained Ms. Morris's responsibilities in Mrs. Dobson's classroom. She was to help with some light managerial work, like stapling and copying, as well as classroom teaching when she was ready. Limited grading and tutoring of individual students was also expected of her. Mrs. Price made certain to explain to Mrs. Dobson that she was to report any problems that the student had, as well as the successes. [83] An honest assessment of the DePauw student would help correct deficiencies before that student did student teaching, was granted a license, and then sent into the working world.

Mrs. Dobson had several issues with Morris' classroom performance. She lacked understanding of high school level grammar and literary terms.[84] More alarming was her idealism.

> My only concern about Miss Morris is her idealism. I am aware that most beginning instructors are and should be optimistic. As an educator, I always strive to provide the best education that I can for each student. However, class size, time constraints, budget restrictions and individual student limitations make teaching a complicated task of give and take. I am concerned that Miss Morris may not adjust to the reality of the public high school classroom. She may have a difficult time making the necessary compromises that teaching demands. I do not know if she will be able to work with colleagues and accept ideas that differ from her own. I have spoken to her a number of times about choices and compromises that teachers have to make. Miss Morris admitted that other people have expressed concern over her idealism.... I anticipate that her greatest struggle will be in adapting to a school system that may not function according to her personal ideal philosophies and those she has learned in college.[85]

This excerpt makes it quite clear why Angela Morris continued to press forward with her crusade against Mrs. Price. She was a typical liberal who was simply unwilling to accept that the rest of the world might not agree with her point of view. Mrs. Price was apparently intolerant of a lifestyle favored by Ms. Morris and the modern Left, so she had to be dealt with harshly.

The other issue that Angela Morris had with Mrs. Price was the grade that she was given for Education 375, a B+. When I was an undergraduate at DePauw in the early 1990s, that was a fine grade to receive from a university that billed itself as the "Harvard of the Midwest." The situation must have changed by 2001, because Angela Morris filed a grade grievance with the university over this grade. Mrs. Price made it very clear why Ms. Morris received a B+.

> The work that you received back from me was A or A-quality, but that was not the case with the evaluation form

that I received from Mrs. Dobson at South Putnam High School. As you know from the course syllabus that you received at the beginning of the semester for Education 375, your supervising teacher was also responsible for a percentage of your final grade in the course.[86]

Upon reviewing Mrs. Dobson's evaluation of Angela Morris' performance, one notices that she received 78 out of 120 points possible, or 65%.[87] This is not a particularly bad grade for this class, as the four students involved averaged 85.75 points in their respective evaluations. Considering that the supervising teacher's appraisal carried roughly a quarter of the weight of the course's grade, it is very easy to see that Ms. Morris was fortunate to get a B+.

Under normal circumstances, a complaint such as this would have been dropped. Ms. Morris already had three complaints against Mrs. Price. It is important to note that Angela Morris took the October 2000 issue of *Teachers In Focus* to Mrs. Dobson and that she found nothing offensive in it, effectively agreeing with Mrs. Price. Since these two Christian women held views opposite those of Ms. Morris, something had to be done.

Whenever a student feels that he or she has been wronged by an instructor, that person can file a grade grievance with DePauw University. Angela Morris did so after spring semester grades were issued in May 2001. A quick review of the syllabus and of Angela Morris's grades from both Mrs. Price and Mrs. Dobson should have ended the issue. Neal Abraham refused to listen to reason, choosing instead to allow Ms. Morris to continue with the grievance. A committee within the Education Department was empowered to look into the matter in early September 2001.[88] Dr. Lee, Dr. Weisz, and Mrs. Stockton could not come to a unanimous decision.[89] This is understandable, as Weisz and Lee already had known biases against Mrs. Price. As a result of the deadlock, the case was referred to a university committee chaired by Dr. Abraham.

Vice President Abraham had it in his power to stop this travesty after he received the e-mail that explained the grading system for Education 375, as well as the hard data on Angela Morris's grades. Instead, he empanelled two faculty members, Bill Morgan and Aaron Dziubinski, and two students, Jane Bankhurst and Jeff Cohran to serve with him on the grievance committee. A date for the hearing was set for October 9, 2001.[90] Mrs. Price brought Dr.

Judith Raybern along as support, while Angela Morris chose to bring Judy Mays, a secretary at the university who would eventually become her mother-in-law.[91] A university picked panel would sit in judgment of an educator with twenty four years of classroom experience to her name.

Grade Grievance Policy

DePauw University has very strict guidelines for filing and hearing grade grievances. During my time as an undergraduate, I do not recall ever hearing of a student successfully filing one, so they are quite rare. The following explains in detail the proper procedure for filing and hearing a grievance.

Preliminary Steps

The student meets with the Associate Dean of Academic Affairs who listens to the student's complaint, reviews policy and procedures, and makes sure that the student has followed the steps outlined in the policy up to this point. If the student decides to pursue the grievance, then the Associate Dean asks for a written statement explaining the nature and grounds of the complaint. When a written statement has been received, the Associate Dean sets a date for the hearing, assembles the committee, and sends a copy of the written statement to the faculty member. The faculty member must receive this statement at least one week before the date set for the hearing.

The faculty member may choose to make a written response to the student's complaint. In this case, the faculty member gives the response to the Associate Dean so that a copy can be delivered to the student at least two days before the date set for the hearing.

Procedure for the Hearing

I. The Vice President for Academic Affairs meets with the University Review Committee approximately one half hour before the hearing begins. The Associate Dean for

Academic Affairs is present to take notes and to audiotape the hearing, but does not take part in deliberations.

The Vice President reviews the task that the committee is being asked to do, the standards it will be expected to apply (as passed by the faculty in March 2000; see the 2000-2001 Student Handbook, pages 94-96), and the possible resolutions that can come about in cases of this nature. The committee reviews the issue of confidentiality.

The Committee reads the student's statement explaining the nature of the grade grievance. The committee is also given copies of the course syllabus, the faculty member's written response (optional), and other materials relevant to the case.

II. A. The Vice President convenes the hearing with all present, including the student and the faculty member. He reviews
* procedure for hearing.
* policy on advisors. (either party may have a faculty, staff, or student advisor. Advisors serve as advocates; they may be present and may advise privately, but may not enter into the proceedings of the hearings)
*policy on witnesses. (Both student and faculty member may call witnesses.)
*materials that have been distributed to members of the committee.
*confidentiality. (of the hearing and of the discussion)
*audio taping of hearing (and policies about storing and using the tape)

B. The student makes a presentation to the committee and may call witnesses. Presentations must be limited to the issues raised in written statements. Questions from the committee will follow. If the student requests, he or she may make the presentation without the faculty member in the room. The faculty member's advisor will remain in the room during the presentation.

C. The faculty member makes his or her presentation to the committee and may call witnesses. Presentations must be limited to the issues raised in written statements.

Questions from the committee follow. If the faculty member requests, he or she may make the presentation without the student present. The student's advisor will remain in the room during the presentation.

D. The committee may direct further questions to the faculty member and/or the student either together or alternately.

E. The student and faculty member are dismissed. Committee members deliberate in private.

F. The committee's decision is sent by mail to the student with a copy of to the faculty member. This is a final decision. Appeals, on procedural grounds only, may be made to the President of the University.

Grade Grievance Policy, Opening Statement
(revised by SLAAC and passed by the faculty, March 6, 2000)

The normal presumption at DePauw is that the faculty member alone is qualified to evaluate and assign grades to the academic work of students in his or her courses. For this reason, questions regarding a faculty member's grades are not normally subject to review. **The grade grievance process is for exceptional cases only.**

At all levels of the grade grievance process, those who hear grade grievances are to be concerned only with whether the faculty member acted in a fair, reasonable manner and whether the faculty member used the same methods of evaluation for all students in the class.[92]

The tone taken by Dr. Abraham toward Mrs. Price during the meeting was belligerent. Dr. Raybern noted, as a long term department chair, that the proceedings were not fair, as the committee chair, Dr. Abraham, had shown an obvious bias against Mrs. Price. According to university policy, the accused faculty member is to receive a copy of the grievance. When I asked to see this document, Mrs. Price explained that she had never received one. The result of the conference was quite predictable. The committee decided to increase Angela Morris's grade from a B+ to an A-.[93]

The process by which the committee, directed by Vice President Abraham, arrived at the decision to raise Ms. Morris's grade was rather tenuous. In his letter informing her of the decision, Dr. Abraham noted the alleged inconsistency between the grading scale used by Mrs. Price and that used by Mrs. Dobson.

> Ms. Dobson judged your performance to be satisfactory in six categories and excellent and outstanding in two, yet the total points awarded for your work amounted to 76 [sic] out of 120, or 65%, which on Ms. Price's scale is the equivalent of a low D. The Committee decided that because of this discrepancy your final grade was computed improperly[94].

Dr. Abraham's line of reasoning does not stand up to scrutiny. On most grading scales at DePauw University, 65% is a D. Neither Mrs. Price nor Mrs. Dobson were out of line in this regard. Also, it is important to note that the area that Angela Morris was rated excellent in was "Professional Appearance."[95] While it is very important to look professional in the classroom, that aspect should be overshadowed by the teacher's ability. No matter how one looks at it, Morris' performance in Mrs. Dobson's classroom did not warrant an A-.

The real issue here is the ability of a disgruntled student to use university policies against an instructor with whom she has had difficulty. At the time of Morris' grievance, Mrs. Price had had three hundred thirty four students in Ed 375, of which only one had complained about her grade.[96] By siding with Angela Morris, Neal Abraham effectively called into question the ability of Mrs. Price to evaluate students. In the name of fairness, the other three hundred thirty three students who had taken this class might also have needed to have their grades changed. That was not going to happen, as this was little more than a power play against a Christian professor. After her victory over Mrs. Price, Angela Morris was overheard talking loudly with Dr. Eva Weisz. They were both delighted at the outcome, saying that it didn't matter what "the bitch," Mrs. Price, said about Ms. Morris's performance. [97] It is reassuring that professional standards are held in high esteem in at least some parts of the Education Department.

The Slippery Slope of Offense

Angela Morris succeeded in damaging the career of a gifted Christian educator by misusing a system meant to protect students from tyrannical or abusive professors. The grievance guidelines demand that the process only be used in exceptional cases. Getting a B+ while doing average work does not rise to this level. Real cases of arbitrary grading might occur at DePauw University. Students are truly and rightfully offended by the statements made by peers and instructors in the classroom. Most go unreported. Conservative students know better than to complain, because they will be the ones labeled as bigots, or intolerant, or homophobic. Brooke Hefner recalled passages that offended her in a Toni Morrison novel. She knew not to mention them to her instructor or an administrator, as she would have been turned away by an administration more concerned with "tolerance" than truth.

There are several instances that I experienced during my undergraduate days at DePauw University that might meet the "Angela Morris Level" of offense. In the fall of 1992, I received a low grade on a U.S. History assignment because I pointed out the merits of the atomic missions against Japan, a position counter to the beliefs of the professor. That same semester, I took Sociology 100, "Contemporary Society." In the course of discussion one day, the subject of free condom distribution by the schools was raised by a female student. After listening to her tirade, I borrowed a page from Rush Limbaugh's playbook by "illustrating absurdity by being absurd." I told her that I would gladly pay for her condoms if she would be willing to foot the bill for some engine work on my 1965 Cadillac. It seemed to be a fair trade, as these were both leisure activities. Needless to say, she was incensed. How dare I compare my hobby with her being "responsible!" To this day, I can't fathom how having sex with someone other than a spouse is responsible. This young woman went on to denigrate my character because I drove this old car daily. I was "worse than a Nazi" because I was destroying the world with my antique Cadillac.

During the spring of 1994, I took "Human Cultures," Anthropology 151. The professor was extremely liberal, noting that he liked doing research in New Guinea because he didn't have to listen to Rush there. As an avid listener of talk radio, I found his comments uninformed and intolerant. The class was assigned a text that included a rather graphic description of a coming of age ritual among the Sambia tribe involving sodomy. "The immature male semen organ is 'solid and dry' and only changes after the ingestion of semen through homosexual contacts."[98] I was offended, but I knew that complaining would do no good. My concerns would have been chalked up to "homophobia," and I might have gotten a lower grade in the class. Thanks to Angela Morris and Neal Abraham, I now realize that, at least according to them, nothing offensive happened in either class, nor was I given lower grades because of my opinions. Being equated with Nazis due to one's choice of transportation was not offensive, nor was reading about nausea-inducing behavior in New Guinea tribesmen. As a result, it would have been pointless to file grievances against my fellow student or these professors. If they had permitted me to read a Christian magazine, evaluated me on the same scale as all previous students, or given me sound career advice, I would have been well within my rights to object.

Conclusion

It is clear to even the most casual of observers the real cause for DePauw University's action against Mrs. Price. Angela Morris was a young woman on a mission to destroy someone whose ideals did not match her own. She was aided an abetted by two members of the Education Department, Esther Lee and Eva Weisz, who were jealous of Janis Price's excellent reputation with students and public school officials. Dr. Lee and Dr. Weisz had failed to ruin this reputation with Ms. Morris' claims of improper conduct regarding the department and her student teaching placement. The grade grievance was a matter of pettiness. Had Ms. Morris received a final grade of a C or lower, she might have been justified in her actions. Moving from a B+ to an A- despite inadequate field performance was an abuse of the system. Even if Mrs. Price had misgraded Angela Morris, the bulk of her record was impeccable. A much larger stick would be needed to hurt Mrs. Price. Neal Abraham would wield that stick.

49

Chapter 5

DePauw's Response

By May 2001, DePauw University had decided that Mrs. Price was a problem needing solved. She had made the mistake of permitting a point of view that the university scorned into her classroom. On May 7, 2001, she met with Dr. Neal Abraham regarding the October 2000 issue of *Teachers in Focus*. The following exchange ensued during the meeting.

> *Abraham*- "How do students know that you are a Christian?
> *Price*- "The same way they know that Nancy McMurty is a Christian and the same way they know that Marcia Ellett is a Christian.
> *Abraham*- "Do you teach Christianity in your classes?"
> *Price*- "No."
> *Abraham*- "This is not a Christian university."
> *Price*- "I understand that this is not Taylor University, or Grace College, or Indiana Wesleyan. However, DePauw is a liberal arts university and as such I thought that diversity and tolerance of many differing beliefs and cultures was valued. Perhaps you can help me understand how it is that I am to be tolerant of others' beliefs, but they don't need to be tolerant of mine."

Abraham- **"We can not tolerate the intolerable."**[99]

The truth finally was revealed at this meeting. Mrs. Price's classroom ability was without fault. Her relationships with public school teachers and administrators were equally admirable. The intolerant words of one disgruntled student, backed by two jealous faculty members, were enough to erase thirteen years of good will. Janis Price's real crime, in the eyes of the university, was being a Christian.

Abraham's Vitriol

Two months passed before Neal Abraham unleashed his punishment on Mrs. Price. To legitimize his position, he claimed that there was a precipitous drop in enrollments in upper level Education programs.[100] While it is true that the most recent semesters had showed a decline in registrations for Education 375, falling to a total of seven for 2000-2001, the numbers rebounded for 2001-2002, reaching twenty four students for both semesters. [101] This raw data does not take into account the difficulties students like Brooke Hefner had with faculty at these levels, causing some to drop out of the program. Such situations were out of Mrs. Price's control. It is important to remember that, while field experience placements on all levels dipped during the 1999-2000 to a low of nine hundred forty five, they rebounded to nine hundred eighty two for the 2000-2001 school year.[102] With an upward trend in overall placements, a staff reduction in the Field Experience Program made little sense. Dr. Abraham pointed out that as an administrative staff member and part time instructor, Mrs. Price was employed on a continuing need basis.[103] This too is accurate, but thirteen years and three hundred thirty three satisfied students suggest that her skills were both needed and appreciated. Finally, and most seriously, he noted three incidents that he had discovered with the help of Education Department Chair Lee. [104] It is not surprising that someone jealous of Mrs. Price's ability and rapport with students would find many flaws in her performance.

The biggest issue that Neal Abraham had was with Mrs. Price's alleged "distribution" of the *Teachers in Focus* magazine. His reasoning was quite flawed on this topic and has been refuted time and again by reliable sources such as Mrs. Price and Brooke Hefner.

> (1) In your recent teaching you provided students with certain magazines that you suggested they might find useful. This material included provocative and critical material which is very intolerant with regard to issues on which DePauw stands firmly in favor of a tolerant environment which should be free of harassment. One might easily conclude that the uncritical distribution of this material represented professional intolerance on your part or the deliberate creation of a hostile environment in violation of DePauw's policy otherwise. Your response was that you had ordered the magazines to make them available to students because some students in prior years had found them useful but that you had not read each magazine in detail before you offered them to the class. I conclude that there are three significant inappropriate aspects of this incident.[105]

Dr. Abraham told the reader more about himself and DePauw University than perhaps he had wished. It is quite clear that this material was "offensive" because it did not give the politically correct spin on homosexuality, favoring Biblical truth instead. An objective reading of the text in question shows how flawed Dr. Abraham's thinking was on this issue. Mel Winninger, a homosexual in the English Department, claimed not to be offended by the content of the October 2000 issue of *Teachers in Focus*.[106]

Dr. Abraham noted that it was unacceptable for Mrs. Price to have not read the entire issue of the magazine before offering it. He admitted under oath that DePauw University has no requirement for professors to read all of the documents that are assigned to a class.[107] In 2004, art history professor Mitch Merback sponsored a "teach-in" regarding "The Passion of the Christ." The first session was held prior to the panel participants seeing the film, with the second "teach-in" following some time later after a trip to the theatre.[108] From my personal experience, it was not unusual for professors to assign a book or an article without having read the item in its entirety. Typically, they chose to use the text based on a review or on the basis of the quality of the author's other works. Since Mrs. Price did not distribute the magazine, it is clear that her actions were well within the norms in many college classrooms. She was being held to a higher standard than her peers with Ph.D.s,

> (a) You provided students, without commentary or critique (except to say that it was "material from a Christian perspective"), resource material that was not provided by an authoritative professional source from the Education community. The implication of uncritical distribution of material by a faculty member or staff member to students in a course or department of material on academic topic is that this is professionally valuable resource material drawn from and prepared with appropriate academic authority. This was not the case and the presentation and manner of presentation were both inappropriate and represent a serious lack of good professional judgment.[109]

In Dr. Abraham's mind, the only way that this material could have been presented to a class was to point out that it was not printed by the NEA or another liberal organization, and that the authors took a view inconsistent with the politically correct views of the DePauw University administration. Perhaps she should have mentioned how terribly "judgmental" and "intolerant" Christians are for good measure. Mrs. Price would have been fine then.

Once again, Neal Abraham failed to do his research. *Teachers in Focus*, while not endorsed by the NEA, contained a great deal of useful information written by authorities in their field. Perhaps being an associate professor at the University of Texas or a licensed psychologist and an expert on homosexuality does not qualify a writer as authoritative in the eyes of Neal Abraham, but these titles mean something to most reasonable people. The vice president was still holding Mrs. Price to a much higher standard than other professors at DePauw. For example, I was required to read parts of Al Gore's *Earth in the Balance* as part of a mandatory Winter Term Core class on the environment in 1992. At no time during the class did the professor suggest that we should consider Senator Gore's work critically, as he held no scientific or academic credentials. Since Dr. Abraham's background is in physics and not in education, it is questionable as to whether he would be qualified to recognize a professionally useful education publication if he were presented with one.

Neal Abraham went on to reinitiate shop-worn claims that Mrs. Price spoke ill of the Education Department and solicited similar comments both from students and faculty. Brooke Hefner's testimony handily refuted this claim. Dr. Abraham was upset that Mrs. Price had maintained files on Dr. Weisz, as she had been instructed to do by his predecessor, Provost Len DiLillo. Dr. Abraham promised to keep these files confidential, but then chose to use them as evidence against Mrs. Price during his deposition two years later.[110] Perhaps most irritating to him was the fact that Mrs. Price dared to try to correct the damage done by the behavior of her colleagues while visiting the public schools.[111] As vice president of academic affairs, Neal Abraham should have investigated the legitimate concerns raised by local educators and administrators. He would have found that some faculty members were in fact raising serious concerns in the public schools about Dr. Lee and Dr. Weisz. Instead, he chose to punish Mrs. Price for doing her job as the liaison between the school districts and DePauw.

Based on his "findings," Vice President Abraham concluded that significant changes were needed in the Education Department. Mrs. Price was to be removed from her teaching duties in Education 375, with the department retaining six full-time faculty members. The Education/Audio Visual Lab was to be maintained by the department secretary. The department chair, Dr. Lee, was given greater power, becoming the authorized signature on matters of licensure and certification. She also became the official liaison to the public schools.[112] Dr. Abraham's restructuring of the Education Department made very little sense in light of many items. Esther Lee did not demonstrate a working knowledge of Indiana licensing procedures when Brooke Hefner had her disagreement with the chair in 2002. Most people know more after being on the job for a year than when they started. If this was the case with Dr. Lee, Neal Abraham's decision was political, not practical. As vice president of academic affairs, it is quite likely that Dr. Abraham had access to data that showed the increased number of students enrolled in Ed 375 for the 2001-2002 school year. By prohibiting Mrs. Price from teaching a class that she had taught for thirteen years, Dr. Abraham left the Education Department short-handed. His concern was clearly not for the welfare of the students.

It is of special interest that while Mrs. Price lost wages and the work titles she had carried for thirteen years, she did not lose the responsibility that these titles carried with them. For example,

Dr. Lee had the title of certification officer, but she merely signed her name to the licensing documents that Mrs. Price prepared. An especially unusual twist of logic was that Mrs. Price was removed from her teaching duties at least partially because she couldn't fairly assess Angela Morris' work. However, she was given the additional responsibility of being the only consistent scorer of students' portfolios in the Education Department, a very time intensive task that requires professional assessment of students' work.

Finally, the vice president ignored the concerns of neighboring school districts by sending Dr. Lee out as DePauw's ambassador. It is logical to presume that the number of complaints did not decrease, so this decision made little sense for the university. It is quite clear that Neal Abraham's concern was with punishing a Christian faculty member who dared not to leave her faith at home.

Crime and Punishment

Janis Price's career at DePauw University was in serious jeopardy. The very same day that Neal Abraham "solved" the problems caused by her alleged conduct, he saw fit to issue the conditions for keeping her job.

> In light of staffing needs and the most recent assessment of your performance, I offer you a three quarter time, 10 month appointment as Education Program Coordinator, at a salary of $31, 225 for 2001-2001.(sic) Your salary will be paid in 12 equal installments over July through June. In this administrative role you will be responsible to the Chair of the Department, Esther Lee, with the duties of Field Placement in Blocks I and II, work with the Unit Assessment and portfolio assessment programs, assisting the chair on matters of teacher certification and licensure including processing of applications, and **other duties as assigned by the chair.**
>
> Benefits, including vacation will be appropriately prorated. For example, you will earn over the course of the year 20 x 10.5 x .75= 12.5 full vacation days (or 16.66 6 hour days) which you may take **based on advanced**

approval of your schedule by the department chair.

Salaried positions are not based on a precise counting of hours, but the expectation should be that you will work through the academic year (from August 13 to May 24) at 6 hours per day plus a modest supplement of additional time to complete the work except on days when the University is closed or on days of scheduled vacation. Adjustments in your work schedule to achieve this average may be made **with the approval of the department chair and with notification to me.** In addition, during the summer you should work an average of two mornings or two afternoons each week, again on a schedule to be determined **with the approval of the department chair.** You and the department chair and I should periodically review your workload to ensure that the assignment of duties remains consistent over the year with the ¾ time, 10-month salaried nature of your position.

You are expected to provide a quarterly activity report and performance self assessment and Dr. Lee and I will provide formal responses to those reports.[113]

The Draconian nature of Mrs. Price's punishment is quite evident in this document. The pay cut was significant on its own. The accompanying reduction of allotted hours to perform her job added a significant burden. Demanding that Mrs. Price pass everything through Dr. Lee was something more appropriate for a freshly hired staff member, not one with an long and exemplary track record. Perhaps the most vindictive aspect of Neal Abraham's action was the requirement that Mrs. Price file a lengthy report each quarter. Under great pressure to keep a job that she loved, and knowing that it was too late in the summer to be hired by another university, Mrs. Price agreed to these onerous measures the very next day.

Quarterly Reports

Janis Price was the only DePauw University employee required to file extremely detailed quarterly reports during the 2001-2002 school year. Neal Abraham had required another employee to file similar reports, but she was only in her second year with the university and had had trouble the previous year. This individual could not take the added pressure and resigned partway through the next year. [114] Being a good employee, Mrs. Price did as she was asked, even though it created a great deal more work for her. Each report averaged forty pages in length. The first of these was due on October 10, 2001. Others followed on January 14, 2002, March 22, 2002, May 24, 2002, with an annual report on April 9 thrown in for good measure. After turning these in to Dr. Lee and Neal Abraham, Mrs. Price would wait roughly two weeks for the response. Typically, these responses were hypercritical and often error-ridden. Mrs. Price was then required to respond to the criticism within a week. [115] The following school year, she continued to file the reports as per the previous year. The new department chair, Dr. Marcelle McVorran, was not vindictive toward Mrs. Price, so her evaluations were not critical at all. Her kindness toward a subordinate did not go unnoticed. Dr. McVorran was reprimanded by Neal Abraham for not following "proper procedures" for evaluating Mrs. Price's work. [116] It did not matter to him that the new department chair had not been given these "proper procedures."

The quarterly reports typically began with a summary of the time worked during each week of the period. The next several pages consisted of the actual time sheets for the quarter. The second part was a detailed listing, usually a paragraph in length, explaining exactly what Mrs. Price accomplished each day. Part Three dealt with field experience placements. The time, date, and location of each student's activity was then listed. This process took a great deal of time. Part Four listed the students whose teaching license application had been prepared for the department chair's signature. The final section listed the students whose portfolios had been evaluated by Mrs. Price. [117] Since she was already trying to fit forty hours of work into a thirty hour week, compiling extra reports for the administration cut into this already limited time, making it harder for her to do an effective job for the students. Consequently, rather than not do her job well, she worked beyond the required thirty hours to maintain her professional integrity.

A Hostile Environment

It is indeed ironic that Neal Abraham was so concerned about Mrs. Price creating a hostile environment in her classroom. His actions in punishing her gave those in the Education Department who already had issues with her the green light to step up the pressure. By granting Dr. Esther Lee even greater authority over Mrs. Price, it is quite clear that the intention was to force her to resign. This would shift the focus away from DePauw's misdeeds and allow outsiders to conclude that Mrs. Price was a malcontent who quit of her own accord.

The new restrictions placed on Mrs. Price by Dr. Lee were rather petty and made it very difficult for her to do her job effectively. E-mail is one of the useful tools in the modern office. Starting in the 2001-2002 school year, all of Mrs. Price's e-mails to Education Department staff had to be approved by Dr. Lee. Although she was stripped of the title and pay of the certification officer, Mrs. Price was still required to do the same amount of work as she had done previously. Dr. Lee merely signed and dated the applications. This should have been of great concern, as Dr. Lee's knowledge of certification was demonstrably weak. Although it was vital for Mrs. Price to attend Indiana Professional Standards Board meetings to keep up with the latest changes in licensure policy, she was forbidden by Dr. Lee to do so. Members of this organization, realizing the nature of this restriction, sent Mrs. Price the needed material in defiance of Dr. Lee's petty edict.[118] She was also a longstanding member of the Indiana Association of Colleges for Teacher Education (IACTE), but Dr. Lee refused to allow her to attend meetings where field experience was discussed. She was also forbidden to attend Education Department meetings, despite the fact that she had done so since 1988. Mrs. Price had taken documents to the registrar's office and used the university seal to stamp them as official documents since 1993. From this point on, Dr. Lee carried the documents to that office and stamped them herself.[119] None of these items were explicitly proscribed by Neal

Abraham in his July 17, 2001 letter. From all appearances, Dr. Lee took this opportunity to abuse her power over a subordinate.

The actions taken by Dr. Lee were petty and inefficient with the potential to bring harm to the Education Department. People outside the department might not have been immediately aware of these internal problems. However, Dr. Lee took actions that further eroded the reputation of her department in the eyes of students and the public schools. Mrs. Price was forbidden to have any student contact in the area of advising without Dr. Lee's permission. When faculty member Dr. Robert Wenta brought a student to ask Janis Price a question, she was criticized by Dr. Lee in a quarterly report for trying to help a fellow faculty member. The chair attempted to undercut field experience placements without Mrs. Price's knowledge. School administrators called her to tell her that well established procedures had been circumvented by Dr. Lee. Mrs. Price had a simple method for setting up field experience. She contacted the school principals and teachers directly. Thanks to Dr. Lee's meddling, she was now required to talk to the assistant superintendent of the Greencastle Community school district, who would then contact the principal, who would then contact the teacher, who would finally get back to the DePauw student who was seeking a placement. This was grossly inefficient and sparked a great deal of outrage within local school districts.[120] These actions do not appear to have had the best interest of DePauw University, public schools, or students in mind.

Missing Files

I graduated from DePauw University in December 1994 with a B.A. in history. Thanks to Janis Price's encouragement, I returned to DePauw in January 2000 to obtain a teaching license. As a returning "fifth year" senior, I was able to take education courses for a third the normal tuition cost. I had completed my undergraduate education in seven semesters, so I did not take many electives that were not needed to complete a history degree. As a result, I had to take Indiana history, psychology, biology, and macroeconomics to be eligible to teach history and economics in Indiana. To speed the progress, I took these classes at Indiana State University. Not only was this much less expensive, but it allowed me to be ready for licensure by summer 2001.

I took one additional course at ISU during the fall of 2000 that would cause Dr. Lee a great deal of concern a year later. Every student must take a methods and management class in his or her content area to be certified to teach in Indiana. I had intended to take this class at DePauw, but the only person who could be found to teach it was Dr. Dennis Trinkle. While he was an outstanding historian and very knowledgeable about the Napoleonic Era, he lacked public school classroom experience. It would have been an arranged class, forcing him to give up a considerable amount of time to teach one student. It was indeed fortunate that Dr. Wilson Warren was teaching a middle school/high school history methods class at ISU. He had taught social studies on the junior high and high school level before coming to Indiana State, so he had a wealth of useful advice that I use in my classroom to this day. Thanks to the practical experience and teaching ability of Dr. Warren, this class was more than equivalent to the much more expensive class that I could have taken at DePauw.[121]

I did not find a teaching job in west central Indiana after finishing my second tour at DePauw, so I took a job coordinating services for handicapped individuals. It was rewarding but very frustrating work. After finishing eight hours in the office, I often spent another seven hours working in a juvenile detention facility. While this was not my schedule every day, it took a significant amount of my time. I was confident that it was just a matter of time until I got my turn at the lectern. I was licensed to teach social studies to students in grades five through twelve. No one could change that, or so I thought.

On October 26, 2001, Dr. Lee approached Mrs. Price about the validity of my middle school endorsement, as well as that of David Carey and Ron Scurry.[122] Dr. Lee wanted to see our transcripts from other schools. Both of these men were older students like me. Mr. Scurry had graduated from University of South Carolina in 1989 and Akron University in 1992. He student taught under the direction of the same man as I had two years later, obtaining his Indiana license in 1998 from DePauw. David Carey was a 1977 DePauw secondary education graduate who had gone on to get an M.S. from North Dakota State University in 1990 and a Ph.D. from Purdue University four years later. He wanted to update his license to current Indiana requirements. Mrs. Price pointed out to Dr. Lee that Dr. Carey did not need to produce his transcripts, as a copy of his valid Educator's Professional License from North Dakota had been sent to the Indiana Professional Standards Board when she recommended him for Indiana licensure.[123] When contacted by Dr. Lee, Ron Scurry was less than cordial to her, undoubtedly insulted by her questioning the validity of his license. Since these men did not live in Greencastle, it was much easier for them to ignore Lee's persistent questioning. I wasn't quite so lucky.

Mrs. Price contacted me in November, 2001 regarding my license. My Indiana State University transcripts were no longer in my file at DePauw, so I needed to obtain replacements. I assured her that I would get these as soon as my hectic work schedule allowed. Mrs. Price took my word, understanding the difficulty of finding time to resolve this petty issue. In December, Dr. Lee called me repeatedly, and I reiterated what I had said originally to Mrs. Price. I had a meeting in Terre Haute on January 22, 2002, so I ordered replacement transcripts, which ISU sent the following month.[124] As far as I was concerned, this bit of unpleasantness was behind me.

My license was secure, but I still had trouble understanding what had happened to my original transcripts. I can recall quite vividly giving Mrs. Price copies of my grades after I finished each semester at ISU and watching her place them in my file. This folder was kept in a cabinet locked securely in Mrs. Price's office. Only three people had keys to that office: Mrs. Price, the building janitor, and the department chair. It is quite evident that somebody removed my transcripts after they were placed in the file. Mrs. Price had no motive, as she was fighting for her job at this time. The janitor didn't know me, so he or she would have had no reason to tamper with my file. Over three years later, my missing transcripts have yet to surface, and the identity of the thief cannot be proven through documentary evidence.

The issue of the validity of my license should have been settled on December 5, 2001. Shawn Sriver, the director of licensing for the Indiana Professional Standards Board clarified the issue in an e-mail to Dr. Lee that day.

> I have pulled the files for David Carey, Jeffrey Shively, and Ronald Scurry. Based in the information we have in the file, I cannot find anything to indicate that these files were inappropriately recommended for licensure. Every indication is that the recommendations made by

> Mrs. Price were the correct recommendations and that
> the correct license was issued accordingly.[125]

This should have closed the case. Dr. Lee insisted on pursuing the matter, claiming that the IPSB gave the department discretion in licensure recommendations. She demanded that Mrs. Price give her my phone number, as well as that of Ron Scurry.[126] She could have asked someone from the university to call me, and I have would gladly explained the validity of the ISU "History Methods and Management" class. Not surprisingly, no one called.[127] When she called me in December, Dr. Lee knew that my license was valid. While she seemed intent on stripping me of my license, this was not legally possible thanks to Rules 46-47.[128]

Although the issue had been resolved in December, 2001, Dr. Lee chose to bring up my "improper" license in her response to Mrs. Price's Quarterly Report of May 24, 2002. This leads one to question why she would continually bring up an alleged problem that had been solved the previous semester.

> Even though Mrs. Price is organized, prompt and efficient, she is not fully accountable to her assigned tasks. For example, she failed to protect students' licensure application files which she processed, recommended, and filed permanently in her office. Two applicants' [Scurry and Shively] transcripts were not found in their files when Dr. Lee, the new licensing advisor, examined certified applicants' records in the Summer 2001. Later she failed to obtain a certified applicant's [Shively] transcript from another university to replace the mysteriously missing one. The Chair [Dr. Lee] was uncertain of the existence of the first place and questioned her decision of recommending the applicant without the required transcript (s). Although she informed the chair that she had received the replaced transcript of another certified applicant, she did not disclose the titles of the transferred courses to the Chair as licensing advisor. The licensing advisor was incorrectly led to believe the file had been completed and the applicant [Shively] was properly certified. Only later the licensing advisor personally examined applicants' [Shively] records and found out those courses did not meet the program requirements. Mrs. Price explained that the applicant [Shively] told her that the courses were related to the required courses by

> DePauw Education Department. So she took his [Shively]
> word without checking the official course description or
> asking him for a course syllabi when recommending the
> applicant for licensure to teach middle/jr. high school.
> The Chair concludes that Mrs. Price's judgment on these
> matters is unreliable.[129]

In not so many words, Dr. Lee was calling me a liar. She lacked the courage to do so to my face, so she used her response to a quarterly report as forum to assassinate my character. The only thing more repugnant to me than being called a liar is to be used as a tool to harm an innocent person. These issues had been solved much earlier to the satisfaction of the Indiana Professional Standards Board. Whether Dr. Lee chose to accept it or not, I was properly licensed in the State of Indiana, and there was nothing that she could do about it. Neal Abraham was correct to be concerned about a lack of professionalism in the Education Department. He was simply looking in the wrong place.

Conclusion for Part I

It is quite clear to me that much of the unpleasantness that has been related thus far could have been avoided if the participants had been willing to consider other avenues. Students overwhelmingly appreciated the work that Mrs. Price did at DePauw University. They felt that they could trust her advice. Both Dr. Lee and Dr. Weisz were obviously jealous of this situation. Had they chosen to do so, they could have rectified the situation by improving their teaching and administrative abilities. In time, there is no reason why students would not have felt as comfortable working with them as they did with Mrs. Price. Angela Morris could have shown the same tolerance of differing opinions that conservative students were required to exercise daily on the DePauw campus. If every right-thinking student filed a complaint against the professors with whom he or she disagreed, classes would probably be cancelled indefinitely. Neal Abraham could have chosen to do a better job of investigating Angela Morris' complaint. Had he done so, the case would have been dropped. Finally, the person who stole my Indiana State University transcripts could have chosen to perpetrate that caper on someone who was not as curious as I am. This individual could have made Mrs. Price look just as bad without anyone asking too many questions. Had she or he done so, the full story of the persecution of Janis Price might never have seen the light of day. Somebody picked the wrong guy to play the patsy.

Part II

The Case Against DePauw

To a casual observer, DePauw University's treatment of Janis Price makes very little sense. She had served the university with distinction for thirteen years. Public school administrators, teachers, and students always spoke highly of her professionalism. Many of her peers also appreciated her contributions to the Education Department. It is also quite clear that Mrs. Price did nothing wrong by providing students with the opportunity to read Christian education publications if they so chose. Why then, did the university, in the person of Vice President of Academic Affairs Neal Abraham, impose such onerous restrictions on her employment after July 2001?

In the following chapters, the reader will be provided with some possible answers. The *Teachers in Focus* issue that was made available during the March 15, 2001 Education 375 class contained articles that gave an honest, Christian assessment of homosexuality in the schools. Homosexuals have become one of DePauw University's most favored special interest groups. Anyone who speaks the truth about that lifestyle is no longer to be tolerated. DePauw University has a long and unfortunate history of abusing students and employees who hold differing opinions. At the same time, the indiscretions of those who are in synch with administration policies are ignored, no matter the legal implications. Janis Price's biggest problem was her faith. Christians are one of the few groups that DePauw University does not favor. As a devout Christian, she was an easy target for abuse.

Chapter 6

DePauw's Unusual Relationship with Homosexuality

On the surface, Mrs. Price's situation would appear to be a case of intra-departmental jealousy gone too far. As with many things at the academy, the explanation for the Draconian measures taken against this Christian woman goes much deeper. The trigger for the chain of events of the spring of 2001 was DePauw University's peculiar view of homosexuality. Until the Bottoms Administration, homosexuality was largely ignored by the university. The period of 1986 to 1994 would best be described as an era of "tolerance." Since 1994, DePauw University has decidedly endorsed homosexuality, up to an including administrative hiring. In June 2005, an openly homosexual sociology professor was appoined Assistant Dean of Academic Affairs.[130] In less than twenty years, gays and lesbians have moved from the fringes of campus society to being the university's favorite minority, enjoying all the benefits that come with an exulted status.

Public opinion in a dynamic group like the DePauw University student body can be hard to quantify. The following study chronicles the first eighteen years of the Robert G. Bottoms Administration, 1986 to 2004. Although imperfect, the campus newspaper, *The*

DePauw, a bi-weekly student publication, was very helpful in providing insight into the collective mind of the university.

The very first mention of homosexuality appeared in *The DePauw* in 1972. The issue remained mostly dormant until the mid-1980s, shortly before Dr. Bottoms took charge. A homosexual student described the problems that arose when he decided to partake in that lifestyle. He was taunted and had to depledge Alpha Tau Omega fraternity. Interestingly, this individual reacted to opposition to his lifestyle with violence. In one incident, he chased his tormenters down a dorm hallway with a knife. There is no indication that he was ever charged with attempted assault.[131] For its part, the university did not ignore the growing noise coming from the campus homosexuals. Tom Arner, a counselor at DePauw, told the newspaper in May 1986 that he and his wife spoke to many homosexual students. "That Carol (Arner) and I talk to so many gays and lesbians does not mean that there is anything wrong with being gay itself. ...The problem lies with the way gays and lesbians are treated by others."[132] This is the first public pronouncement by a university official claiming that there was nothing deviant about the homosexual lifestyle. The problem, in the view of the author and the Mr. Arner, was the "homophobic" mindset of the majority of the student body.

The assault on normalcy was stepped up considerably during the 1987-1988 school year. During the spring semester, the Gay and Lesbian Association, a support group for homosexuals, was formed for students and promoted by DePauw University's Office of Student Affairs.[133] The pro-homosexual propaganda effort was launched in earnest. The winner of the Lewis Sermon Award, Amie Klempnauer, spoke about the problem of silence regarding perceived injustices in modern society, citing "institutional racism; sexism; homophobia; making assumptions about what is normal, desirable, and good; designating certain ideas, behaviors, and lifestyles as good and others as deviant" as examples.[134] Authors writing for *The DePauw* habitually skewed their stories in favor of homosexuality. The very first "Denim Day" was held on April 15, 1988. The idea behind this was to show support for "equal rights," such as gay marriage and preference in the workplace, for homosexuals.[135] The problem was that blue jeans were and still are the foundation of the average college student's wardrobe. Many inadvertently supported the homosexual cause based upon their dress, no doubt a factor in the choice of garb. This very same ploy would re-emerge in the 1990s and remain a fixture to the present day.

Speaking the Truth

The homosexual assault was met by reasoned voices who eloquently defended traditional Christian morality. Joe Walusel and Reese Watt explained the problems of homosexuality.

> Unfortunately, any and all criticism of homosexuals or gay and lesbian rights has lately been regarded as "homophobia." There are many reasons people reject homosexuality. These reasons include religious reasons, medical reasons, individual reasons, and reasons of personal morality. Yet those who argue in favor of homosexual rights insist that this belief merely stems from narrow-mindedness and homophobia. This stereotyping is exactly what the gay and lesbian community is supposedly resisting.[136]

Mr. Walusel's statement could very well have been written recently. It goes to show that the homosexual movement hasn't changed their rhetoric in nearly twenty years. Reese Watt stated the Christian stance on homosexuality in an article from May 1988.

> Jesus and the whole New Testament teaches that sin leads to death. Sin is the worst thing a person could do with his life. Therefore, when Jesus told the prostitute to leave her life of sin, he wasn't condemning her, but admonishing her to leave the terrible life of prostitution. He did not declare that prostitution was not a sin.[137]

The contrast between the pro-homosexual and pro-normalcy articles was striking. One side used the same worn out arguments to promote a godless agenda, while the other calmly defended the truth.

Slings and Arrows

No good deed goes unpunished. These individuals endured a withering attack on their intellect and integrity in the closing month of the school year. A DePauw sociology professor, Nancy Davis, revived the specter of the Third Reich in her attack. Homosexuality was not a threat to society. "Homophobia, on the other hand, is a danger.... We see what homophobia did in Nazi Germany...[it] resulted in the death of hundreds of thousands of gay men and women."[138] The message was clear. Calling homosexuality what it is, a sin, makes a person worse than Hitler. Others were quick to batter the truthful. The Psychology Department weighed in, claiming that homosexuality was not a psychological problem.[139] They didn't mention that radical activists had forced this definition to be changed in the early 1970s to avoid undermining their message. Others used the tired cliché that Christians could not point fingers because the Bible cites many other sins.[140] Perhaps most telling of the pro-homosexual attitude was one writer who said that it was "unfortunate and embarrassing to the DePauw Community" when people spoke out against homosexuality.[141] The argument against those who spoke out for truth was now complete. They were ignorant of science, unaware of their own sins, Nazis, and a general embarrassment to the DePauw campus. It is no wonder that only a handful of articles challenging the sanctity of homosexuality appeared in *The DePauw* over the next decade.[142]

R.emoving O.pposition T.o our C.ause

While decent people remained silent, homosexual activists, buoyed by the ease of silencing their opposition, pushed to get rid of one of the stalwarts of tradition, R.O.T.C. History professor Rod Clifford led the charge. He and his allies claimed that because the military barred homosexuals, R.O.T.C. was in violation of DePauw University's anti-discrimination policies. When the faculty voted to keep the program and merely condemn it, he was outraged.[143] The anti-military bigots got their wish in 1993, when the faculty voted fifty eight to twenty five to disband R.O.T.C. at DePauw.[144]

Henceforth, students who wished to take R.O.T.C. classes could do so only at neighboring universities. This was not good enough for homosexual activists. As late as 2001, they were demanding the total removal of R.O.T.C. from the curriculum.[145]

Policies sometimes have unintended consequences. The drive to Rose Hulman Institute of Technology near Terre Haute, Indiana, can be quite pleasant in good weather. However, driving conditions were treacherous on the night of February 5, 2004. Kellen Mogck, a Christian and popular freshman member of the DePauw football team, was driving home from a R.O.T.C. class at Rose Hulman when he lost control of his vehicle and crashed. The weather was so bad that the med-evac helicopter was grounded.[146] Mr. Mogck was eventually transported via ambulance to Methodist Hospital in Indianapolis, where he died of his injuries there two and a half days later. [147]

Denim Daze

In the spring of 1992, homosexual activists revived "Denim Day" at DePauw. I was a freshman at the time, so I remember it quite well. Fliers promoting this special day were posted everywhere: tacked to bulletin boards, around the entrances to major buildings, even taped to campus sidewalks. A chapel service scheduled for April 8, 1992 entitled "God has AIDS" became the focus of controversy when fliers promoting it were destroyed. Stuart Lord, a chaplain at the university was upset and quite confused as to why anyone would be offended by the topic of the convocation.[148] When "Denim Day" finally arrived in May, most of the people I saw that day had remembered to wear khakis, and those that forgot often rushed home to change clothes. Thanks to a high percentage of Greek living units at DePauw at the time, the turnout for "Denim Day" always seemed to disappoint the activists. They blamed it on the "conformity" that was allegedly rampant at the fraternity houses. They never considered the most reasonable explanation. Most people simply don't want to be thought of as being homosexual. The next April, a group of twenty DePauw students traveled to Washington D.C. to protest the alleged injustices suffered by homosexuals. Marcher Kerry Ann May enlightened readers by telling them: "DePauw students need to realize that if you're a Republican, you don't have

75

to be super-conservative or anti-gay."[149] For others "Equal rights are not special rights" was their tattered battle-cry.[150] As part of the "Denim Day '93" festivities, like minded souls could view a riveting slide show from the "March on Washington."[151] The success of the event was summed up by Diane Ferguson. "People had to make a conscious decision whether or not to wear denim and support gay rights."[152] This was part of the pattern. Claim success, no matter how many people refuse to wear denim.

Baseball Cap Day

The spring of 1994 brought an increased boldness in the homosexual assault on the DePauw campus. Between March 18 and May 3, no less than eight pro-homosexual articles appeared in *The DePauw*. Some celebrated the formation of United DePauw, a university sponsored homosexual activist group.[153] Carol Arner, DePauw's director of counseling and advisor to this group said of United DePauw, "This is an excellent time for such a group to form. The University is now emphasizing multicultural issues, and the gays on campus are as valid a minority as any other."[154] Rob Riemersma, a student who chose his "lifestyle" over his fraternity and was removed from the same, whined about the homophobic evils of the Greek system.[155] Other authors sought to lecture the student body on the need to be more inclusive of the homosexual minority.[156] The university scheduled a screening of "Philadelphia," the film where Tom Hanks played an AIDS infected lawyer. The atmosphere on campus was becoming increasingly tense. Something was needed to release that tension.

In the days leading up to "Denim Day '94," homosexual activists went about their business of posting propaganda as in previous years. The images were more graphic than ever. Two lesbians were shown kissing, a truly vile sight. Three gentlemen, henceforth known as "Nick L.," "Geoff B.," and "David R.," decided that they had had enough of this nonsense. They set to work on the second floor of a fraternity house, planning a counter offensive. They realized that the apparent success of "Denim Day" hinged on utilizing a very common piece of clothing, blue jeans, as its symbol. This commonness also gave the appearance of greater support for homosexuality than was the case. These men settled on the baseball cap as the symbol of the counter-protest. They set about designing fliers to post the night before "Denim Day." Most of them urged students who were tired of having perversion shoved down their throats to show their disgust by wearing a baseball cap and khakis in lieu of blue jeans.[157] An alternative flier, based on a passage from a Lewis Grizzard book, was also produced. It featured a stick figure who was bent over with a second figure close behind him with a circle and slash drawn over the couple.[158] It was a crude, but humorous, admonition against homosexual intercourse.

The night before "Denim Day," one of these gentlemen, "Nick" went out into the cool of the evening to post the fliers. Sometimes he tore down the offensive fliers; other times he simply taped the counter-protest fliers over them. He returned to the fraternity house a short time later. Knowing that his actions were undoubtedly already stirring up trouble with the other side, a fourth man, "Jerry M.," warned "Nick" not to go out again. "Nick" decided to put just a few more fliers up before the night was done. As he was posting them, a homosexual accosted him, demanding to know if he "had a problem with fags." "Nick" tried to walk away from his accuser, but the homosexual, who might well have been intoxicated, pursued him. He grabbed "Nick's" jacket, tearing the zipper off it. Having taken enough from his assailant, "Nick" decked his attacker and escaped to the relative safety of the Sigma Chi fraternity house, whose front door was luckily left unlocked. When it was safe to leave, he made his way across campus to his girlfriend's apartment.

At 5:30 the next morning, "Jerry" was awakened by the door bell ringing at his fraternity house. The campus police were looking for "Nick." "Jerry" explained that he was not at the house, but the officer was not satisfied and searched the premises. The police eventually left and arrested "Nick" elsewhere.

The incident landed "Nick" in Dean of Students Joan Claar's office. "Jerry" went along to provide moral support. The dean had already made up her mind about "Nick's" case. She found the cartoon depiction of a homosexual encounter to be more offensive than a real photograph of a lesbian lip lock. It did not matter that the homosexual had assaulted "Nick" and that he had struck his attacker in self defense. Later that month, "Nick's" homosexual attacker walked across the stage to receive his diploma from Dr. Bottoms. "Nick" would have to wait two years for that honor and graduate a year behind his class. [159]

The Long Range Impact of Baseball Cap Day

The Baseball Cap Day posters were dutifully destroyed before the morning was over, but the message had already been successfully conveyed. In class that day, I saw more caps and khakis being worn by my peers than ever before. The article that appeared in the following Tuesday's *DePauw* downplayed the success of the counter-protest, but no amount of ink could alter what I saw with my own eyes.

It was rather interesting, even amusing, to read the accounts of the 1994 "Baseball Cap Day" counter-protest in 1995, 1996, and 1997 articles in the *DePauw*. In the May 6, 1994 article, the author claimed that "Nick" had been arrested at 3:00 am.[160] This raises the question as to why the police would have awakened "Jerry" from a deep slumber at 5:30am if they already had the suspect in custody. There was little that the author got right, but it became part of the record. In the May 2, 1995 issue of *The DePauw*, a homosexual professor offered his insight on the issue. He claimed that students were "hit with rocks and beaten up last year during Denim Day. Some students tore down signs about the event and wore baseball caps in protest...."[161] This professor conveniently omitted the fact that being punched in self-defense is not even close to being beaten. The legend continued to grow. For "Denim Day '97," Matt Kingston, a member of United DePauw stated that "Certain groups, will for example put up posters saying to wear khakis and baseball hats, (in protest of the day)."[162] Suddenly, one guy with a small stack of fliers became, in the minds of some, a group who stoned homosexuals, tore down their posters, and caused the gay community to quake in fear. I showed "Nick" copies of these articles. He got quite a chuckle out of that notion. A tiny resistance movement had forced the homosexual juggernaut to take notice. Perhaps the past decade at DePauw would have been different if more had followed this courageous trio's lead.

United DePauw is Born

In 1994, the time was right for a large, university supported organization to spread the message of homosexuality to the DePauw campus. In March of that year, United DePauw met for the first time. The idea was to give homosexuals and their supporters a forum from which to proselytize the rest of the campus. Tedra Williams, the editor of *The DePauw*, enlightened readers as to why it was necessary for these students to organize.

> There are many students who have participated in Denim Day by wearing denim to show their support for gay and lesbian rights, but there are also many that show their disapproval by going out of their way not to wear denim on that particular day. Some go so far as tearing down fliers announcing events...[163]

The mission of United DePauw is quite simple: promote homosexual behavior and condemn those who voice opposition. Homosexuals often complained about the "silence" surrounding their lifestyle.

> There is a level of hate and homophobia at DePauw and it is being allowed to exist and grow because the dialogue has disappeared; we have stopped stirring the pot for fear of what might surface.[164]

In 1994, United DePauw set out on a quest to normalize the homosexual lifestyle on the DePauw University campus. Students and faculty continue to be impacted by this decision to this very day.

Drag Ball and the Queer Center: Gays Go Mainstream

The acceptance of United DePauw by the university opened a Pandora's box that would eventually lead to the demotion of Mrs. Janis Price. It should not be surprising to note that her primary accuser, Angela Morris, was a member of this organization. DePauw's chapter of Alpha Gamma Delta sorority closed in 1993. Several years later, the university bought the house and converted it into a dormitory. In 1999, with the blessing of DePauw, the "Queer Center" moved into the first floor of the old sorority house. [165] A year later they were permitted to customize the interior of the building to suit their tastes, despite a university policy against students repainting rooms in university owned housing.[166] Regulations meant little in the face of tolerance.

As a university sponsored organization, United DePauw receives a portion of the activity fee paid by every student at the school. During the 2001-2002 school year, Student Congress awarded $150,000 to organizations at DePauw. The Union Board received $44,000 for the spring semester to provide programming for the entire campus.[167] J.C. is a Christian group with two hundred members.[168] It received $2,800 for that semester. By contrast, United DePauw, which mustered between twenty and fifty people for its meetings, received $14,500, a far greater amount than any other student club.[169] This princely sum was spent on the annual "Drag Ball" and bringing Communist activist Angela Davis to campus.[170] A recent graduate of DePauw noted that United DePauw spent much of its funding on food from Marvin's, a campus restaurant, in an effort to boost meeting attendance.[171]

In addition to the annual "Denim Day," members of United DePauw found many outlets for their campaign. In October 1997, they celebrated Gay History month. Two months later, United DePauw sponsored a gay film festival.[172] In September 1998, a Gay Lesbian Bisexual Transgender panel was started to help support National Coming Out Day, "Misfits Ball," and "Unity Day."[173] For Coming Out Day, the plan was to continue silencing opposition to United DePauw's cause. Lectures entitled "Speaking Out" and "Religion and GLBT People" were used to bully opponents into silence. The attitude of homosexual activists was summed up by John Ohle and Anisah Miley. "Coming out can be as little as wearing a button, not allowing homophobic language and/or supporting United DePauw events on campus."[174] In response to the university's alleged refusal to decry the beating of Matthew Shepard, two student activists sat silently in front of the DePauw University Administration building wearing signs claiming to be the slain homosexual. [175] Theatrics went hand in hand with activism.

Being a homosexual at DePauw is more than wearing buttons and blue jeans and demanding that others praise your behavior. Each year they have "Drag Ball," where one can dress as anything from Marilyn Monroe to James Dean.[176] As Matt Claus explained in "Eyeliner, Feathers, and Boas, Oh My!"

> The general atmosphere was one of unity. From female professors in suits to male students in skirts, there was no wrong answer when it comes to attire.[177]

There have been a variety of activities in recent years for those who did not wish to cross dress. They could participate in the Speakers' Bureau, a jolly band that roamed from building to building spreading the homosexual message. [178] Film lovers enjoyed such classics as "Paris is Burning," "All Over me," "It's my Party," and "Go Fish."[179] United DePauw made an effort to bring noteworthy speakers to DePauw, such as Kate Bornstein. Ms. Bornstein began life as a man but soon tired of the confines of a traditional gender identity and underwent a sex change. As a woman, she finally found the girl of her dreams. In a bittersweet turn of events, Kate's lesbian lover left her to become a man.[180] Others dressed up trees with ribbons to designate them as "gay" and set up freestanding doors on campus through which people could "come out." The musically inclined could partake of such bands as "Bitch and Animal" and "Super 8 Cumshot."[181] In 2003, six activists with sturdy vocal chords screamed to signal the end of the "Day of Silence" while a crowd of twenty gathered to watch their brilliant social statement.[182]

Literarily gifted homosexuals wrote emotional articles about "coming out" or discussed the proper term to call them.[183] They were at their boldest while attacking Christians. Christians were regularly assaulted for their intolerance to 9 homosexuals. Emily Plemons exposed their alleged hypocrisy in *The DePauw* in October 1998.

> How many people are raped or beaten simply for being a Christian? Did your parents disown you when you told them you are a Christian? Will you be denied housing? Be legally fired from your job? Be thought by some to pose a threat to children?[184]

The young author had probably not heard of the trials Christians endure in Muslim nations, nor read Luke 21: 16-17.

> And ye shall be betrayed both by parents, and brethren, and kinsfolks, and friends, and some of you shall be put to death. And ye shall be hated of all men for my name's sake. [185]

Less than three years after this venomous article was published, Mrs. Price was fired from one quarter of her job because of her faith.

Official Sanctioning of Homosexuality

Perhaps the most disturbing trend at DePauw University was the zeal with which the homosexual lifestyle was promoted by the faculty and staff. As noted earlier, the university allowed its counseling services to hold the position that homosexuality was not deviant while condemning those who opposed that lifestyle. By the mid 1990s, DePauw University as an institution had become an advocate for gays and lesbians.

The DePauw faculty took a stand in favor of homosexuality in 1995. At a faculty meeting in the spring of 1995, they resolved to support "Denim Day" with "A Resolution Affirming the Valued Role of Lesbian, Gay, and Bisexual Students in the DePauw Community."

> WHEREAS DePauw's lesbian, gay, and bisexual students often perceive certain elements of the campus environment to be hostile towards them, and find themselves subjected to social ostracism and verbal and physical harassment; and
>
> WHEREAS DePauw University continues to administer ROTC scholarships which exclude openly lesbian, gay and bisexual students, violating the University's own non-discriminatory policies, and reinforcing the perception that such students have a diminished status at DePauw in which their rights are not fully respected; and
>
> WHEREAS Friday May 5 is "Denim Day," when members of the DePauw Community are encouraged to show

support for lesbian, gay and bisexual, staff and faculty by
wearing denim,
THEREFORE, be it resolved that the faculty of DePauw
University takes this opportunity to reaffirm its support
for the University's non-discriminatory policies; *to voice
its condemnation of all discrimination, particularly that
based on sexual orientation*; and to send its best wishes
to the lesbian, gay, and bisexual students at DePauw on
the occasion of Denim Day, with its assurances that in
the view of the faculty, lesbian, gay, and bisexual students
are highly valued and welcomed members of the DePauw
Community.[186]

Interestingly, *The DePauw* did not publish any similarly glowing
endorsement of Christian or conservative interest groups.

The paper's promotion of "Denim Day '95" did not stop with
this endorsement. The editorial space was given over to the topic on
May 2, where the writer repeated the myth of homosexual students
being stoned by "homophobes" during the previous year's festivities.
This person summed up the spirit of the day thusly. "Take a cue
from your professors this Friday and wear denim- you just might
learn a very important lesson outside the classroom."[187] In February
1996, faculty member Tammy Rae Carland created "Apparitions
in the Aperture: The Visible Lesbian." Dr. Rod Clifford published
"Queer Politics" in 1998. The DePauw School of Music paid tribute
to homosexual composers with "Wouldn't that be Queer?," a May 3,
2000 recital.

Perhaps the most troubling endorsement of the homosexual
lifestyle was revealed in an April 21, 2003 faculty roundtable in
which professors were encouraged to address LGBT (Lesbian-
Gay-Bisexual-Transgender) issues in their classrooms. In section
II of the meeting, "Queering the Curriculum," four professors,
representing women's studies, art history, modern languages, and
sociology, discussed ways to integrate the homosexual agenda into
every discipline.[188] In his June 2003 deposition, Neal Abraham
admitted to bringing homosexual speakers to the university to
speak on the topic of their chosen lifestyle using money from the
president's discretionary fund.[189] He also attended United DePauw
meetings.[190] The faculty and administration at DePauw University
have clearly taken a stand in opposition to five thousand years of
moral tradition.

The normalization of homosexuality continued unabated outside the classroom through the late 1990s to the present day. In 1995, Assistant Director of Admissions Amy Ross said that while the university's mailings to prospective students did not refer to United DePauw, "...that's something that should be definitely included." [191] Three years later, DePauw's Counseling Services ran a large ad in *The DePauw* supporting National Coming Out Day festivities at the university.[192] Under the leadership of Jeanette Johnson-Licon, the Office of Multicultural Affairs was re-christened the Department of Multicultural Affairs, Lesbian, Gay, Bisexual, and Transgendered Services in 2001. [193] When a female student at DePauw chose to live the lesbian lifestyle, her parents removed her financial support. In response, the university created the "Lesbian Leadership Award" as a means of keeping this "valued member" of the student body in school. A significant portion of the faculty and staff were now completely in the back pocket of the homosexual movement at DePauw University.

Thanks to prompting by United DePauw and other interest groups, DePauw considered adding so-called hate crimes to the student handbook in 1998.[194] Hate crimes were subsequently codified. In 2000, the guidelines were made even more strict.[195] In April 2002, a real "hate crime" happened at DePauw. After an argument on the way home from a party, a student, Greg Armstrong, slapped another student, Chris Fitzgerald, dumped a red drink on his head, and said "Bye faggot." For this "hate crime," Mr. Armstrong was convicted of a class B misdemeanor, fined $150, and given twenty five hours of community service.[196] The student body could then sleep well, knowing that streets of Greencastle were rid of youngsters who dumped their drinks on heads of others.

It is quite clear from the evidence gathered from sources published by the university that DePauw has successfully transitioned from an institution that ignored homosexuality into one that embraces this deviant lifestyle. This is shameful on moral grounds alone. When this bias toward homosexuality becomes the basis for discrimination against Christians, the situation has become critical.

Chapter 7

Abuse of Power: 1913-2003

The punishment suffered by Janis Price for her alleged offense was undoubtedly Draconian. Regrettably, her situation was not unique. It is just one incident in a pattern of abuse perpetrated by administrators at DePauw University over the past century. This is not to say that every administration was guilty of abusing its power. Many DePauw alumni fondly remember the Humbert and Wildman Administrations. To fully understand the university's stance regarding Janis Price, it is important to investigate several cases of abuse. Five of the seven cases cited occurred during Robert G. Bottoms' tenure as president. The other two are relevant because some elements in each case have direct parallels to Mrs. Price's situation.

Charles Bruner Thomas- 1913

Charles Bruner Thomas was born on November 19, 1891 in Seymour, Indiana. His family moved to Greencastle in 1902.[197] Thomas' mother had attended DePauw in the 1880s, and it was her desire that her children do the same. Young Mr. Thomas entered

DePauw University in 1909. By all accounts he was a popular man about campus. Mr. Thomas lettered in baseball.[198] "Tommy" Thomas was a skilled outfielder.[199] He pledged Delta Kappa Epsilon fraternity, rubbing elbows with Eugene S. Pulliam, grandfather of future Vice President Dan Quayle.[200] In 1913, he appeared to be poised to join the illustrious list of DePauw University graduates. Fate had planned another path for him.

A few weeks before Mr. Thomas was to graduate, he traveled to Purdue University in West Lafayette, Indiana to interview for a graduate scholarship in engineering. When he returned to Greencastle, he received an angry summons to the office of DePauw President George Richmond Grose. The president had received a call from the Purdue registrar to confirm Bruner's coursework. Grose angrily accused Mr. Thomas of lying about being a DePauw graduate. The young man replied that he applied for the scholarship under the assumption that he would graduate in a few weeks. President Grose responded that he had failed to finish a psychology class during the fall 1912 semester and would not be able to graduate with his class. Unable to tolerate Grose's angry, false accusations, Bruner Thomas walked out of the office, never to return. [201] After serving in France with the Allied Expeditionary Force during World War I, Mr. Thomas finished a Bachelor of Science in Engineering degree at Purdue University in 1920.[202]

Bruner Thomas should have walked across the stage with the rest of his class in 1913. He had successfully completed the psychology class that President Grose had falsely accused him of failing. Mr. Thomas had been having trouble with psychology, but Professor R.B. Von Kleinsmid allowed him to take another exam to complete the course. He left DePauw to pursue a career at a different school, but permitted another professor to administer the test. After Thomas passed the exam, this professor told him that he had now received credit for psychology. DePauw's athletic director was informed that he was eligible to participate in second semester sports.[203] Had he failed this class, he would not have been able to play baseball that spring, a privilege granted only to students with passing grades.[204] Mr. Thomas made a very reasonable assumption that he would graduate in 1913 when he applied to Purdue University for graduate school.

A very important factor kept Bruner Thomas from graduating from DePauw University. He made the mistake of making President Grose his enemy. During a university outing, the president had made unwanted advances on Mr. Thomas' sister Lotta. Being a gentleman of the late Victorian mold, he expressed his displeasure with Grose's behavior and warned him not to harass his sister again. President Grose saw an opportunity for revenge when the Purdue registrar called to confirm Thomas' eligibility for graduate school. The psychology exam and all records of his grade disappeared without a trace.[205] President Grose had allowed his desire for revenge to ruin the academic career of one of his students.

Bruner Thomas lived the remainder of his life in Greencastle. To the day he died, he never forgave DePauw University for robbing him of four years of his life. Subsequent presidents tried to rectify Grose's misdeed, but Thomas refused their offers. He was adamant that he should have received his diploma with the rest of his class, and any attempts to award the degree at a later date was disingenuous. After he died in June 1985, there was a movement at DePauw to grant Thomas a posthumous diploma. His guardian at the time of his death, Mary Tesmer, turned down the offer on the grounds that Mr. Thomas would have wanted it that way.[206] Nine decades after reckless acts of a university president, the injustice done to Bruner Thomas in 1913 remains a blemish on the soul of DePauw University.

Ralph Hufferd- 1933

Professor Ralph W. Hufferd, an Army Reserve officer and a skilled chemist, joined the Chemistry Department at DePauw University in 1922. During his eleven years at the university, he developed a reputation as a gifted and engaging teacher. He wrote numerous articles on military science for many publications, including *The DePauw*. In 1933, he seemed to be on a course to retire from the university after a long and distinguished career. This was not to be.[207]

As an army officer, Professor Hufferd realized the importance of a strong military and saw pacifism as a terrible fallacy. This naturally lead to conflict with DePauw's president. He disagreed with President Oxnam's radicalism, and spoke out against it on several occasions. In retaliation, Hufferd was denied tenure and summarily fired in 1933. [208]

Realizing that his dismissal was politically motivated, Professor Hufferd appealed to the American Association of University Professors. An investigative team from the AAUP found President Oxnam to be quite uncooperative. DePauw's policies on faculty appointment, promotion, and dismissal were vague. This prompted the team to delve deeper into the tenure system at the university. The AAUP found that Hufferd's academic freedom had been abridged and condemned his dismissal on the basis of unsubstantiated charges. The organization also criticized President Oxnam's almost unchecked power in matters of tenure. To back up its findings, the AAUP removed DePauw from its approved list and censured the university at its annual meeting in November 1934. The following year the "Statement of Academic Freedom and Tenure" was released by the university in an attempt to mollify the AAUP.[209] This ploy worked, as DePauw was restored to the approved list in 1936. [210] Nearly seventy years later, a different DePauw administration would similarly abuse a faculty member.

The Bottoms Administration is no stranger to controversial personnel policies. Five cases, covering the years 1997 to 2003, represent some of the difficulties that DePauw University has had in maintaining consistent personnel regulations. Three of the incidents involve substance abuse problems of powerful staff members. Sexual harassment, and the surprising response by the victim, was the subject of the fourth case. The final case regards a student who made the mistake of standing up to the university. These examples serve to emphasize the egregious nature of Mrs. Price's reprimand, in light of DePauw's response to the illegal behavior of some of its employees.

"Dee" Gardner- 1997
Glen Kuecker- 2003

Driving while under the influence of alcohol can have terrible repercussions. Thousands of lives come violently to an end each year as a result of irresponsible people getting behind the wheel of a car after having one too many drinks. Most employers frown upon such dangerous behavior from their employees.

On May 2, 1997, "Dee" Gardner, slid behind the wheel of her car after having a few drinks at an evening social function. On her way home from this DePauw sponsored event, she was arrested by a City of Greencastle police officer for driving while under the influence. Ms. Gardner was the dean of academic services at DePauw University at the time of the incident. [211] Remarkably, she did not lose her job. Instead, Dee Gardner was promoted to dean of first year students and academic services.[212] Driving while intoxicated is a crime in the State of Indiana; allowing materials critical of homosexuality into a classroom is not.

Glen Kuecker was hired by DePauw University to teach history. If one believes what is printed in *The DePauw*, his activities had little to do with teaching history. He wrote articles that perpetuated the preposterous myth that Al Gore won Florida during the 2000 election because the black vote was suppressed.[213] Anyone who passed high school civics realized the fallacy in that argument. Dr. Kuecker liked to stir up fear among the undergraduates regarding the Iraq front of the War on Terror by raising the spectre of a draft.[214] This educator was best known for an annual pilgrimage that he and a handful of leftist students would take to Fort Benning in Georgia to join a few thousand other malcontents to protest the School of the Americas.[215] Prior to their departure, they held a "Peace Camp," where they camped in the Academic Quad and engaged in teach-ins.[216] This behavior, while annoying to patriotic Americans, was fairly harmless.

On June 26, 2003, Dr. Kuecker was arrested while driving back to Greencastle from the Indianapolis International Airport when a police officer observed him cross the centerline. He admitted to the officer that he had been drinking during his flight. The breathalyzer indicated that his blood alcohol level was .08. Kuecker pleaded guilty to operating a vehicle while under the influence and was sentenced to sixty days house arrest and twenty five hours of community service. He convinced the court to allow him to postpone serving his sentence until August 17, 2003, after he returned from a vacation in Mexico.[217] The university's rather mild reaction to Dr. Kuecker's reckless behavior was reported in *The DePauw*.

Neal Abraham, Vice President for Academic Affairs, said Kuecker notified the university in writing of his arrest. Abraham said that he made sure Kuecker was aware of the University's alcohol policy, but no other action will be taken because the incident occurred on personal time.[218]

The message was quite clear. Challenge DePauw's sacred cow, homosexuality, and risk loosing your job. If you chose to commit a real crime, like driving drunk, please do it on your own time.

Rabbi "Buz" Bogage- 2000

DePauw University's founders would undoubtedly have been rather curious as to why a Methodist university would need a rabbi. By the 1990s, the school's Jewish population had grown to the point where the Bottoms Administration thought that it needed a spiritual leader on campus. After popular Rabbi Joe Levine passed away suddenly, "Buz" Bogage, a man with a history of radical activism, was hired to replace him.[219]

Besides teaching classes and leading Jewish students in worship, "Rabbi Buz," as Bogage was soon known, also helped out on Winter Term in Service trips. In September 2000, he and music professor Cleveland Johnson were supervising twenty one students at a Bangladesh Winter Term in Service retreat at the Indiana Baptist Camp near Cloverdale, Indiana. At one point during the meeting, the sixty five year old rabbi smoked marijuana in front of some of the students. Professor Johnson was so upset over this irresponsible act that he pulled out of the trip. When word of Bogage's transgression reached the DePauw's administration, he was suspended with pay while Doug Cox, DePauw's security chief, conducted an investigation.[220]

Part of the DePauw community rose up in support of "Rabbi Buz." Predictably, the faculty signed a petition of support for Bogage. English professor Cynthia Cornell stated the faculty's position on the rabbi's situation.

> Faculty are concerned that Buzz will get a fair hearing and that any disciplinary action be proportional to the nature of the infraction and consistent with other similar cases.[221]

Art history professor Mitch Merback attacked the young authors who dared to expose the story of "Rabbi Buz's" drug use to the campus.[222] Students jumped to their battered hero's defense. "Buzz is passionate about including all students and reaching out to anyone in need," explained student Micah Ling.[223] The editorial board of *The DePauw* opined:

> One night's reported mistake does not undo the positive impact Bogage has had on DePauw University over the past 2 years. Bogage's alleged activities did not hurt anyone.[224]

Any illegal activities were outweighed by the "good" that the rabbi did for the campus. All of this concern was unwarranted.

It took eight days to complete the investigation into Rabbi "Buz" Bogage's drug use during the Winter Term in Service retreat. During that time, he was placed on paid leave and was allowed to perform ceremonies important to the high holy portion of Rosh Hashanah.[225] Despite admitting to engaging in an illegal activity with a controlled substance in the presence of students while on a university sanctioned retreat, Bogage was given the proverbial slap on the wrist. Although he remained employed as the university rabbi, Bogage was not allowed to lead the Bangladesh trip. He was also asked to resign from his part time teaching position and was removed as a member of the faculty. Since it was Bogage's first offense, DePauw recommended that no criminal charges be brought against him. Despite this reduction in duties, he did not suffer any form of a pay cut. The whole affair took less than two weeks to resolve.[226] DePauw University considered an issue of a Focus on the Family magazine to be more dangerous to student well-being than a pot smoking "man of the cloth."

Craig Greiwe- 2001-2002

DePauw University's abuse of power also involved the student media. In December 2001, Craig Greiwe wrote an article for *The DePauw* that questioned the university's faculty hiring practice. This young man was rightly concerned with the very real possibility of quality of instruction being sacrificed on the altar of politically correct diversity. Had this concern been expressed about hiring practices at Focus on the Family, the Heritage Foundation, or Promise Keepers, nothing would have been said. By questioning the motives of the Bottoms administration, Mr. Greiwe brought the weight of the university down upon his head.

On January 3, 2002, Craig Greiwe received a seven page letter from Neal Abraham condemning his article. The vice president claimed that Mr. Greiwe had created a "hostile environment for minority professors" by questioning university hiring practices. He was told that he must atone for his "crime."[227] Freedom of speech is one of the rights guaranteed by the First Amendment that apparently do not apply to students at DePauw University.

The controversial article, "Questions surround quest for faculty diversity," appeared in *The DePauw* on December 4, 2001. As of that date, twenty of the previous seventy five faculty new hires were members of minority groups. Some arrived at DePauw thanks to pre-doctorial fellowships. Others had positions created explicitly for them. Neal Abraham said of this process, "This is just one of the extraordinary opportunities where a university has a chance to use its resources to make its own future instead of being passive."[228] Mr. Greiwe explained the particulars of the new process.

> Yet another technique is making an opportunity hire, whereby the University identifies minority professors who might be a good fit for DePauw and then invites them for their own interview and hiring process. Eventually, if they prove a successful match, a position may be created for the professor. This differs from a normal hiring process where a national search is done, and applicants compete against each other for an already established position.[229]

The goal was ethnic, racial, and sexual diversity, possibly at the expense of quality of instruction. As wrong as this policy was, the mid-1990s saw even more insidious hiring schemes. Minority candidates were put into the pool of white candidates for a job, even if they did not make the first cut.[230] This push for diversity came directly from the president's office. Bruce Stinebrickner, a liberal political science professor, alleged that Dr. Bottoms himself directly told or strongly implied to members of the departments that "applicants of color" were to be favored over others. [231] Bill Harmon, professor of religion had no kind words to say about the policy of administrative intervention in faculty hiring. "When I talk to my colleagues at other institutions, they are aghast that the administration would play such an aggressive role in placing faculty into departments."[232] It is interesting to note that when Dr. Esther Lee, a native of Taiwan, was the hired by DePauw, she quickly became highest paid member of the faculty, being compensated at a much higher rate than faculty members who had faithfully served the university for over forty years.[233] If the university was choosing "diversity" over quality, the policy would certainly warrant investigation by those most harmed by this quest, the student body. Instead, a student journalist had his life turned upside down by an administrator bent on protecting his boss's policies.

Craig Greiwe filed a complaint against Dr. Abraham on April 10, 2002, accusing the vice president of harassment and abuse of power. He requested a special judicial panel investigate this administrator. Dean of Students Cindy Babbington headed the investigation with Vice President of Student Affairs James Lincoln assisting. President Bottoms would then have the final say. Not surprisingly, the panel found no evidence to support Greiwe's claim and it was dismissed by the following September.[234]

By the time the ruling was made final, Craig Greiwe was no longer a student at DePauw University. Despite this, he wrote about the case in a letter published by *The DePauw* in the September 17, 2003 issue. He noted that he only had one interview with members of the judicial panel. Vice President of Student Affairs Lincoln did not even support his right to complain about the harsh treatment that he suffered at the hands of Neal Abraham. In Greiwe's mind, it was unfair to have the case handled by two other administrators and have the final decision rendered by the president. The last point was even more egregious, because Abraham had shown Dr. Bottoms the January 3, 2002 letter to Greiwe prior to sending it to the student.[235] Conflicts of interest did not exist if they benefited DePauw.

It is quite evident that an administrator overstepped his authority by reprimanding a student for daring to question the politically correct hiring policies of DePauw University. Twenty seven faculty members signed a petition recognizing this fact.[236] Equally egregious was empanelling fellow administrators to investigate his behavior, with the final decision resting with the president. Not surprisingly, Dr. Bottoms was pleased with the outcome of the Greiwe case. "I thought it was fair," he said to Andrew Tangel of *The DePauw*.[237] Justice is indeed in the eye of the beholder.

Kimberly Taylor- 2001-2003

Most employers insist that their employees have a harassment free workplace. Those who chose to violate such policies are dealt with swiftly and surely. In some instances, punishment is meted out incorrectly on the victim of the harassment. Kim Taylor worked for DePauw University's physical plant, cleaning Roy O. West Library at night. She loved her job. Her grandfather had been a Methodist minister who had spoken fondly of the university. So enthralled with DePauw was she that she asked archive employees for any extra copies of university memorabilia that they might be discarding. In addition to honoring her family's past, she was working toward a brighter future for her own children. Scrubbing toilets at night would allow them to have the education that their mother could only dream of. By all accounts, Ms. Taylor was very happy with her employer.[238]

Everything changed for Ms. Taylor on July 17, 2001. On that day she filed an official complaint with human resources against her floor supervisor, Richard Gaston. An investigation was launched immediately by that department and DePauw Public Safety. Having heard nothing about her case, she called human resources on July 23, 2001, and was told that her harasser had voluntarily resigned. A restraining order forbade him from seeing her or returning to work at DePauw in the future. A mere three days later, Taylor was written up for excessive absences under the so-called "Nine Day Policy." After the write-up, she claimed to have been treated differently than other employees. She was no longer allowed to park her motorcycle in the same lot as she had previously. The university cut off water to her building and eventually assigned it to someone else. Her working environment degenerated rapidly. She explained, "They started following me. I was so scared. I started seeing a therapist."[239] This doctor advised her not to go to work. She tried to call in to work several times, but no one returned her calls. Officially, she was terminated for excessive absences. Even after she left the university, she claimed that she was harassed at her new job by some of DePauw's public safety officers.[240] The victim apparently continued to be persecuted, this time by her former employer.

The policy under which Ms. Taylor was terminated allegedly stated that an employee was entitled to nine days, or seventy two hours of sick time each year prior to needing a doctor's excuse. If an employee exceeded this limit, he or she would meet with a supervisor to discuss the problem. Ms. Taylor did not have the luxury of a meeting with anyone prior to her termination. Also, the university handbook contains an addition that noted that as of July 1, 2001, an employee was to receive twelve days of sick time each year. It is indeed odd that Ms. Taylor was fired for allegedly missing nine days, not twelve. No other employee had been terminated under the "Nine Day" policy prior to Kim Taylor.[241] University employment practices were quite fluid, able to be bent and shaped to meet the institution's needs, or perhaps just its wants.

Kim Taylor filed a complaint with the Equal Employment Opportunity Commission (EEOC) in an attempt to rectify the situation. The EEOC investigators did not uncover enough evidence, in their judgment, to file a case against DePauw. However, it did note that their investigation uncovered only sixty eight hours of work missed by Ms. Taylor. This is far short of the ninety six hours allowed by the edition of the employee handbook in effect on July 17, 2001. Unable to get any relief from the EEOC, Kim Taylor filed a civil lawsuit against DePauw University on July 23, 2002. [242] Regrettably, the case never went to trial. Ms. Taylor's pockets were not as deep as DePauw University's.

Conclusion: Abuse is not new

The treatment received by Janis Price would have been shameful had it been an isolated incident. It is clear that DePauw University has an unfortunate history of abusing those with whom it disagrees and protecting favored persons. Employment policies shift to meet the needs of the moment or the desires of those in control. Criminally reckless behavior has been ignored because the perpetrators were of the proper political or ethnic orientation. Pot smoking rabbis, drunken professors, and sexual harassers are fine. Christian or conservative professors are not. Student journalists who uncover unsavory aspects of DePauw University are not to express their concerns, nor are employees who don't like to be harassed on the job. The message is quite clear. Students and employees have no rights at DePauw University, other than those granted by the Institution.

Chapter 8

Christians in the Coliseum

DePauw University began its life as a bastion of Christian education on the untamed frontier. Thanks to increasingly liberal and godless policies, the university has itself become the frontier. Behavior that would have made the residents of Sodom blush is now celebrated on campus. Christians are ridiculed and silenced at every turn. A non-credit class entitled "Religion in America: Friend or Foe" was offered in the spring of 2005.[243] Not surprisingly, the curriculum was more favorable to the latter position. Interestingly, DePauw has not become anti-religious. Islam, Buddhism, Judaism, and Wicca are all nurtured by the university. DePauw University simply suffers from a severe case of Christophobia.

Judaism

The Rabbi Bogage incident shows how much DePauw University wants to nurture the Jewish community on campus. His spiritual guidance was simply too important to be bound by silly narcotics laws. Adam Cohen, a coach at the university, explained to readers in a September 2001 article in *The DePauw* that there are multiple routes to Heaven. [244] While Robert Plant and Jimmy Page might agree with this philosophy, Jesus Christ, the Savior of mankind, had a slightly different take on Heavenly admission. "...I am the way, the truth, and the life: no man cometh unto the Father, but by me."[245] If Christians wanted to study their faith at DePauw University in an affirming academic environment, they would have been disappointed. Our Old Testament brethren were far more lucky. In December 2001, the faculty approved a Jewish Studies minor at its monthly meeting.[246] It is hard to imagine the writers of *The DePauw* composing stories celebrating the birth or resurrection of the Lord. However, when one percent of the student body gathered with a handful of professors to celebrate Jewish High Holy Days, it was a cause to rejoice.[247] While it is a fine thing to encourage students of this faith to express it freely, Christians should receive the same support.

Islam

Islam, the self-proclaimed "religion of peace," is the fastest growing faith on the planet. Enlightened souls at DePauw University noticed that the campus needed a greater Muslim presence as early as the 1990s. Professor Mac Dixon-Fyle helped sponsor a seminar on Islam in March 1994, a little over a year after the first World Trade Center bombing. He thought that the impressive turnout by the student body proved a "dire need for an Islamite on campus."[248] A tiny group of Muslims founded Bisillah, the Muslim Student Association, on DePauw's campus in 1999.[249] The slaughter of nearly three thousand innocent Americans on September 11, 2001 did little to dampen enthusiasm for Islam at DePauw. Nisreen El-Shamayleh talked to *The DePauw* about fasting for Ramadan. She simply couldn't understand the animosity many Americans felt toward Muslims that fall.

> I don't see reasoning that associates global terrorism to Islam because these terrorists, in my belief, are certainly using Islam as a political tool.[250]

Perhaps a Special Forces operative hunting the Islamic terrorists responsible for reducing four airliners to scrap metal two months earlier could have enlightened her.

Eastern Religions

While Christianity was being shunned by the politically correct crowd for the alleged offense of intolerance, these people have found a new faith in which to believe, Buddhism. This religion had none of the restraints found in Christianity. According to student author Jesse Rochrich, its adherents claimed that Buddhism was both accepting and tolerant.[251] It was so open and tolerant that another student noted in an article how bad she felt for wishing her Buddhist professor a Merry Christmas instead of Happy Holidays. One must wonder how this contradictory state of affairs could exist with such loving people.[252] Some students and faculty were so enamored with these peaceful, tolerant, and accepting Buddhists that a fifth year senior invited a group of five monks to visit DePauw and impart their wisdom to the masses. They demonstrated their religious chants for a group of fifty open-minded students and faculty in the Memorial Union Building in September 2002.[253] These monks were such a hit that they received front page coverage of them doing sand painting.[254] One can imagine what would happen if Billy Graham were invited by a student to speak about his faith at DePauw University. The tolerant, open-minded people would have been up in arms over such a travesty.

Paganism

New Age paganism has taken root at DePauw University. As far back as 1990, the mystical powers of crystals were being seriously discussed.[255] The following year, a psychology class made a black pentagram, complete with candles, on the sidewalk near the library. The alleged purpose was to test the reactions of people to a disruption of their routines.[256] In 2004, an actual coven of witches set up shop at DePauw, calling themselves "Rede." This small assemblage of seven pagans was able to snare $750 per semester in university funds for their group's usage.[257] This same group has been rumored to be praying against the three largest churches in Greencastle, including Greencastle Christian Church, where Janis Price attends. One must wonder what would happen if those same churches openly claimed to be praying for any of these previously mentioned groups. The ACLU would undoubtedly be kicking down their doors and defiling their sanctuaries within minutes.

Christians are Bad People

For all their professions of tolerance and openness, Christophobic liberals at DePauw University despise Christians above all others. There is nothing but vitriol, hatred, and ridicule for those who profess the forgiveness of Christ. *The Bible*, according to the enlightened ones, instructs only in sexism and slavery.[258] Those Christians who explain Godly truth and attack the insanity of relativism are mocked.[259] Kay Weaver, who worked as a part-time instructor at DePauw University in the early 1990s, summed up the situation of Christians on campus quite well.

> My own experience as a former part time instructor at DePauw and as a parent of a DePauw graduate corroborates Paul's experience. If a person- faculty, staff, or student- openly acknowledges being an agnostic, atheist, or uncommitted on a major issue, few, if any eyebrows will rise and no one will bash him or her. Likewise, professors who regularly use God's name in class, an insult to a Christian or Jew, are not reprimanded. But, confess that you are a Christian, one who loves God as revealed in His Son, Jesus Christ, and you are immediately labeled an ignorant, narrow-minded, rigid, immature bigot.[260]

DePauw University, once the training ground for missionaries and ministers, was now bent on suppressing and mocking that very faith. A decade after Mrs. Weaver related her experiences, cartoonist Damon Xanthopoulos gave Christians a black eye for Christmas. In his cartoon "Give more this year," he showed a Christian gleefully exclaiming that his new Bible had even more passages about homosexuality.[261] Mr. Xanthopoulos spent his four years as a critic of anyone who told the truth about homosexuality. Some of his crudest barbs were reserved for Janis Price.

Ignorance

Those who attack Christians at DePauw do so out of fear and ignorance. As far back as 1989, student's lack of understanding of Christianity has been dwarfed only by their ignorance of the United States Constitution. Christine Cercone opined that, "One principle our nation was founded upon was the separation of church and state."[262] As anyone who has actually read the Constitution would note, the document says nothing of the sort. Joe Mason, a young man who found nothing redeeming about conservative or Christians wrote fearfully of Jerry Falwell.[263] Lindsay Hey also had hateful words for the Reverend. She reported activist Marc Adams' wild claims of raids of homosexual meetings at Liberty University. "You know what is happening to GLBTQ students at fundamentalist universities," the author darkly intoned.[264] Christians are too pushy with their ideas, claimed Scott Liepis. "Too often in our society, we are inundated with Christian ideals, of which we are held accountable to."[265] Catholics were subjected to a great deal of undue criticism. According to *The DePauw* columnist Matt Claus, "There is a lot more to Catholicism than simply abstaining from sex and blowing up abortion clinics."[266]

Evangelicals often found themselves excluded from inclusive religious services. Just about every type of faith was represented at an Interfaith Commencement Worship service in May 2002 except those "awful evangelicals."[267] The tragedy of 9/11 has done nothing to diminish the vitriol heaped on Christians. DePauw student Matt Santoro took renowned evangelist Franklin Graham to task for spreading "anti-Islamic propaganda" by daring to point out the well known fact that "the persecution or elimination of non-Muslims has been the cornerstone of Islamic conquest and rule for centuries."[268] A quick read of medieval European history, specifically the Battle of Tours in 732, would have validated Reverend Graham's assertion. Despite turning a blind eye to the crimes committed in the name of Islam, Mr. Santoro made sure to focus on the alleged wrongdoings of Christians. The best that he could do was regurgitate the same shop-worn claims of Christian extremism to prove his point.[269]

The Alabama Supreme Court Ten Commandments controversy also found its way to the pages of *The DePauw*. Chief Justice Roy Moore was impugned for standing his ground in the face of pressure from a Constitutionally uninformed federal judge. This young author simply did not understand that refusing to follow an unconstitutional order showed the highest respect for our Founding Fathers' intent.[270]

J.C.

In the face of vicious assaults on their faith, it might be surprising to some that Christian students not only exist on DePauw's campus, but are organized as well. In 1997, J.C. was organized by a dozen students who wanted a new venue for worship. A year later, they counted over two hundred participants at their weekly meetings.[271] The organization was officially recognized by the university, allowing them to receive student activity funds. For 2001-2002, J.C. was granted an average of $14 per member. United DePauw averaged $725 per member during this same time.[272] Student cartoonist Nick Partlow poked fun at the outlandish appropriations given to the homosexual group by showing a member trying to buy $14,500 worth of blue jeans for Denim Day.[273] As one might expect, he caught quite a lot of grief over this strip. Despite being recognized officially by the university, J.C. found itself excluded from a September 8-11, 2001 Interfaith Retreat entitled "In God's Name(s)."[274]

DePauw's Christophobes were not content to attack Christians in general. J.C. became a lighting rod for criticism. Despite receiving significantly lower allocations compared to the homosexual group, J.C. found itself the focus of an audit by Student Congress in 2002.[275] Student media seldom missed a chance to be critical. The organization was featured on the front page of *The DePauw* in the fall of 1998, shortly after the death of Matthew Shepherd. Author Nicolas Raleigh was upset that Christians were featured so predominantly when the really big news was the murder of a homosexual.[276] Others gleefully mocked J.C., Christians, and the WWJD craze of 1998.[277] Snide comments about the organization were found even within articles that were generally positive about J.C. Any malcontent who found J.C. too shallow or not inclusive enough was tracked down and interviewed. [278]Articles of this nature published against any other group would have resulted in intervention by the ACLU and Americans for Separation of Church and State.

Young Christians refused to back down in the face of continuous assaults by their foes. J.C. member James Pate pointed out the godless character of modern American society. "Because American culture is Christian in name only, Christians have every right to feel excluded."[279] Other authors quite reasonably expressed the desires of Christian students on campus.

> We're not trying to take away anyone's rights or freedoms; neither is hate or violence a part of a Christian's life. But we're also not asking permission to share our faith with a needy world. Calling us names like 'biased' or 'intolerant' just shows ignorance of issues and an intolerance on their part. [280]

Christians on DePauw's campus wished only to have the same rights as their classmates. Some went to great lengths to show their peers that being a Christian and having homosexual friends did not mean that they accepted that lifestyle.[281] Mr. Pate noted a distinct difference between tolerance and acceptance.

> As far as acceptance goes, no one is entitled to accept anything. This is a free country, and people can like whatever they want. If evangelical Christians want to say homosexuality is a sin, then that is their right, period. Similarly, homosexuals should not ask the whole world to like what they are; they should follow their conscience and not care what anyone else thinks.[282]

It is quite evident that tolerance was not really what DePauw was promoting. Acceptance of homosexuality, regardless of the teachings of Scriptures, has been the demand that the university has placed upon DePauw's Christian community.

Despite this hostility, believers were able to bring a few Christian concerts to campus to help spread the Word during the past few years.[283] The climate among the silent majority on campus tracked four to one in favor of religious expression on DePauw campus without university intervention as of 2002.[284]

Sin at DePauw

The real issue that DePauw University and other institutions of higher learning have with Christians is the stance that believers take on sin, particularly sexual issues. American college campuses have been transformed into breeding grounds of all types of wicked behavior. Many forms of sexual debauchery are permitted and sometimes encouraged, from casual drunken sex to homosexuality. Christians, who point out that sin has consequences, are seen as obstacles standing in the way of a good time. Their motives are impugned and intelligence demeaned.

Condoms and SMART People

College is viewed by many as a time to experiment. Sex is one of the most popular manifestations of this on college campuses. In DePauw's case, pre-marital sex is now not only permitted, but sanctioned. In September 1991, the first Human Sexuality Week was held on campus. The previous spring, *The DePauw* ran an eight page special report on sex.[285] Thanks to condoms, young people believed themselves invincible to venereal disease and out of wedlock pregnancies. In the early 1990s, a group calling itself the Committee for Sexual Maturity and Responsible Thought (SMART) proposed installing condom machines in the dormitories.[286] Concerned DePauw parent Nancy Adams spoke up in favor of abstinence, but to no avail.[287] Those who opposed free lust, particularly Christians, found themselves demeaned by their opponents. Abstinence simply would not work, claimed the condom pushers.[288] Columnist Dale Hrebik was gleeful at the prospect of these new vending machines appearing in dorm restrooms, writing "so let's install condom machines (and use them), and we'll all live to screw forever." [289] That is most certainly a smart, mature, and responsible reaction to the easy availability of prophylactics.

Apparently, the self-serve method wasn't as effective a means of distribution as the safe-sex advocates would have liked, because they moved to passing out condoms in the corridors of academic buildings by 1994.[290] As a DePauw undergraduate, I was accosted by a condom peddler in Asbury Hall. Although I was not yet a Christian, I knew that pre-marital sex was wrong. As this rather large woman tried to shove condoms in my face, her actions were met with a curt "no thanks" and an icy glare. I found it quite insulting that this stranger thought so little of me as a man to presume that I could not control my base instincts without her intervention. As reasonable and informed people know, condoms are unreliable at preventing the transmission of disease or preventing pregnancy. Rush Limbaugh was absolutely right when he said, " ...abstinence works every time it is tried."[291] If only the "enlightened" safe-sex advocates would take time to hear the truth.

Abortion

One of the most common side effects of extramarital sex is pregnancy. There are but two options once the situation has reached this point; allow the child to live or slaughter the innocent one. DePauw University came down squarely against life. Few articles that told the horrific cost of abortion have been printed since the late 1980s. Planned Parenthood's every move was met with approval from *The DePauw's* staff.[292] When the president of Planned Parenthood visited campus in 1990, the university gave this "dignitary" the use of Kresge Auditorium, with a seating capacity of 1,500.[293] A year earlier, Nadia Shloss, the president of Indiana Right to Life, had been invited to speak about abortion by DePauw parent Nancy Adams and local residents Don and Kay Weaver. She was granted use of a classroom in East College.[294] The university would undoubtedly point to this as an example of equal access for conflicting points of view.

Inevitably, politics entered the abortion debate. Such was certainly the case at DePauw University. The policies of Ronald Reagan and George H.W. Bush were excoriated by undergraduate authors.[295]

> The Republican party dominated the last decade, turning back the clock on civil rights, women's rights and the environmental destruction that plagues our planet...[296]

It was not enough for the pro-abortion crowd to rant about the policies of pro-life presidential administrations. They made sure to perpetuate the myths about both sides. Seanna Murphy insisted that pro-lifers bomb abortion clinics and that they were hypocrites because they didn't want to raise the children spared from abortion.[297] It is true that a few radicals have carried out assaults on abortion mills, but those cases pale in comparison to over forty five million lives snuffed out in the name of choice since 1973. Columnist Joe Mason stated, most incredibly, that pro-choicers were tolerant of all views.[298] The actions of DePauw Art Gallery director Susan Watt told a different story. In 1999, a small pro-life insert, "What you don't know can hurt you," was carried by *The DePauw*. That was simply too much for Ms. Watt. In her mind, *The DePauw* should not have printed "propaganda."[299] So much for tolerance.

Feminism

DePauw University is not unusual in that it has had a noisy feminist movement on its campus since the 1980s. A student can major in women's studies if she, or he, so chooses. The roots of this stretch back to March 1989 with the first "Women's Week," themed "Sharing Herstory." As would be expected, the specter of the Religious Right was raised in the film "Holy Terror."[300] The assault on Christians did not end after the lights came up after the film. Two years later, Phyllis Trible delivered "Feminist interpretation of the Bible" at DePauw as part of the Mendenhall Lecture series. University chaplain Stuart Lord noted that this message was important for students to hear. "Her research will cause controversy because some students don't want to know the truth about how women were raped and abused in the Bible."[301] A decade later, a different feminist, Judith Plaskow, opined on sex, ethics, and religion. She encouraged the audience to stop insisting that marriage is the only proper place for sex, as "...it only creates alienation in a community. We need to support a range of lifestyles."[302] One can only imagine what communities might be offended by traditional marriage between one man and one woman.

Modern Methodism at DePauw

DePauw University has come a long way since its founding in 1837. Only thirteen percent of students in 2003 claimed to be Methodist.[303] Among those students, a certain percentage simply did not understand Scripture. In 2002, a special service was held at the local Methodist church. Ten homosexual students served as ushers and readers for the service.[304] Perhaps they neglected to read Genesis 18:20-19:29, which recounts the destruction of Sodom and Gomorrah for the sin of homosexuality. The founders of Indiana Asbury College would be ashamed of the current state of affairs with modern Methodism at their university.

The Christian population at DePauw, while smaller than it was a century ago, has finally begun to reassert itself. Requesting to have the same access to student activity funds and university facilities as their peers is certainly within their rights. Although Christians should be heartened by the renewed boldness of the student body at DePauw, there is much work to do. Christian organizations must get a more equal share of university funding. Christian students need to speak out more often in the pages of *The DePauw*. Christian speakers must to be invited to the university and then be treated with respect when they are here. Academic freedom should be extended to all students and faculty. It is truly shameful that Christian professors do not receive the same level of respect as their peers. Janis Price's case has served to emphasize this travesty.

Part III

The Lawsuit

Janis Price spent the nine months following her July 17, 2001 reprimand attempting to obtain a redress of her grievances within proscribed DePauw University channels. She made numerous appointments with Human Resources Department personnel, but no one wanted to address the real issue behind her case. With no where else to turn at DePauw, she contacted Mr. John Price, a well known and widely respected lawyer in Indianapolis. She explained that she had been persecuted by the university for the crime of being a Christian. Barrister Price took on the case and filed a lawsuit on April 17, 2002.

The final section of *Tolerating the Intolerable* takes the reader on a journey through the tangled jungle of Indiana law, chronicling DePauw's repeated attempts to squelch the truth and deny Mrs. Price justice. The case gained nationwide fame thanks to the "700 Club," the American Family Association, Fox News, and a variety of other credible news outlets. Two DePauw alumni, the author and Jim Poor '54, repeatedly made local citizens aware of the true nature of the case, often drawing scorn from the intelligencia and other uninformed people. Although Mrs. Price's case is of great importance in and of itself, it is also a symbol of a much larger problem at American universities. Being outraged by the mistreatment of a fellow Christian is simply not enough today. As patriots, citizens, and Christians, we owe it to future generations to demand a stop to this type of oppression.

Chapter 9

The Five Counts and Judicial Tampering

Janis Price bore her punishment in a Christian manner, going about her work as instructed. Dr. Lee continued to heap scorn upon her head in her answers to Mrs. Price's Quarterly reports. Knowing that she had been reprimanded unjustly for her faith, she pursued the proper course for redress. She scheduled eleven meetings with several administrators over the nine months spanning July 2001 to April 2002.[305] She provided detailed lists of people who could attest to the veracity of her claims.[306] Not a single contact was ever called. Perhaps they were too busy to listen to these repeated requests for help. A lawsuit was the last resort.

John Price, no relation to Janis Price, is a devoted Christian and skilled lawyer. He started his law practice to help clients in circumstances like Mrs. Price's. He is a 1963 Wabash College graduate, making his selection to try the case against DePauw all the more interesting. His primary opponent, John Neighbors, is a 1971 DePauw grad employed by the Indianapolis law firm Baker and Daniels.[307] DePauw and Wabash have been football rivals for well over a century, so the conflict that normally is carried out on the gridiron every November saw new life in the courtroom.

On April 17, 2002, Cause # 67C01 0204 PL 130 was filed in Putnam County Circuit Court. Mrs. Price was suing DePauw University as an entity, as well as Neal Abraham and the Board of Trustees as individuals. The factual background of the case outlined in section IV of the lawsuit has already been well established. Her status as a Christian, her job at DePauw, the "intolerable" event, and her punishment are repeated here for the benefit of the court. The meat of the case is contained in section V.

The Case Against DePauw

John Price rightly asserted in Count I that Mrs. Price was deprived of her Constitutional rights by officers of DePauw University. Some might claim that this is legal, as the university is a private institution. As a result, it is not bound to the same rules as a public university. However, DePauw receives large sums of federal funding each year in the form of student loans and grants. This money is paid to the students, but the source remains the same. It has been my experience that financial aid is generally given directly to the institution, so cash seldom physically passes through the hands of the students. By claiming that *Teachers in Focus* was impermissible in the classroom, DePauw restricted Mrs. Price's First Amendment guarantee of freedom of speech. The plaintiff sought relief under 42 U.S.C.$1983, demanding that her free speech rights, former duties, and proper pay be restored.[308] Based on the quantity of evidence presented earlier, DePauw was guilty on this account.

Count II dealt with the harassment that Mrs. Price suffered at the hands of Neal Abraham and Esther Lee.

> The hostile, discriminatory action taken by the Defendants against Price was severe, humiliating, unreasonably interfered with Price's work performance and duties, was sufficiently severe and pervasive to alter the condition of Price's employment and created an abusive work environment, and in all other ways violated Title VII, 42 U.S.C.$2000 (e)-(a)(1).[309]

John Price also noted that the basis for this harassment was Mrs. Price's Christian faith. There is no doubt that DePauw was guilty of the afore mentioned charges. Janis Price was treated like a poorly performing employee in her first year on the job, despite a spotless record stretching back to 1988. She was punished because of the complaints of one disgruntled student who was aided by an overly zealous administrator. The real issue was inclusion of a Christian magazine in a Christian woman's classroom. She did not smoke dope in front of her students, drive while intoxicated, or sexually harass anyone. Her crime was being a person of faith.

The first two counts could have involved an employee of almost any type of business. Count III was unique to an education setting, the violation of academic freedom.

> 44. Though Price did not promote the contents of "Teachers in Focus," or even discuss same with her class, beyond answering one student's single question; and in spite of the fact that Price did not discuss the issue of homosexuality in the classroom from either a Christian or any other perspective; nevertheless, Price had the right as an Instructor at DePauw to do so, if she had so chosen.
>
> 45. The blatant and reprehensible efforts by the Defendants to stifle Price's First Amendment rights and prohibit her from discussing, or even distributing information concerning an issue which is of general interest in today's society, constitutes prior restraint, censorship and a denial of academic freedom in the DePauw classroom.[310]

Universities are supposed to promote learning, not stifle opinions that differ from the ruling elites. Homosexuality was a widely discussed topic at DePauw for nearly fifteen years prior to Mrs. Price's reprimand, so she wasn't breaking new ground. The censorship of her choice of optional reading not only violated her rights as a citizen of the United States, but it severely undercut the stated mission of DePauw University.

DePauw saw fit to deny the sovereignty of the United States Constitution when dealing with Mrs. Price. One would think that they would have some constant measure by which to manage its affairs. The current edition of the DePauw University Academic Handbook was first published in 1977. This document has been updated several times over the years. It is logical to assume that DePauw placed some importance upon this tome, as new employees received a fresh copy once they sign on at the university. Today, they no longer receive a hard copy, as it is available to them via DePauw's website. In Count IV, John Price noted that the Defendant ignored its own rulebook when dealing with Mrs. Price.

> 47. In taking the actions which Abraham and the other Defendants took, the Defendants failed to follow the DePauw University Academic Handbook.
> 48. Under the Handbook, the section regarding Personnel Policies, includes Section IV- Procedures for Personnel Decisions which requires that all personnel decisions "shall be considered first by the personnel committee of the school or department." This did not occur in this case.
> 49. Further, Section V- Criteria for Decisions on Faculty Status includes a requirement that decisions concerning personnel matters should "express judgments about candidates' merit and services using the principles of equity, which considers each individual faculty member in terms of his or her unique talents, abilities, in accomplishments in relation to the criteria for personnel decisions and quality." This also did not occur in this instance.
> 50. Section VI- Standards for Release, Dismissal or Non-Reappointment of the Personnel Policy of the Handbook, states that faculty members may be released for stated reason or dismissed for adequate cause. By terminating Price as an Instructor, removing her as Chair of the Unit Assessment Systems Review Committee and Licensing Advisor and reducing her pay by twenty-five percent (25%), the Defendants thus effectively released, dismissed and non-reappointed her from her previous titles, positions and duties. The Handbook requires that only for stated reasons or adequate cause may these actions be taken, and then may only be taken by the President after consultation with the dean or department chair of the committee on faculty and the Vice-President for Academic Affairs. These procedures were not followed in this case.[311]

Even a person of moderate intelligence could see that DePauw only followed the rules if and when they fit into a wider agenda. In Mrs.

Price's case, these regulations would not permit her removal based on the flimsy evidence presented, so they were ignored. As such, there was no rule of law at DePauw University.

The university has displayed no respect for its own regulations, much less the United States Constitution. Not surprisingly, its agents showed the same contempt for the Indiana Constitution, as explained in Count V.

> 52. The Defendants, in taking the actions as set forth above have violated Price's rights under the Constitution of the State of Indiana.
> 53. Article I, Section 3 of the Constitution of the State of Indiana prohibits interfering with, or attempting to control, "the free exercise and enjoyment of religious opinions, or interference with the right of conscience."
> 54. Article I, Section 4 of Indiana's Constitution provides that "no preference shall be given, by law, to any creed, religious society or mode of worship...". The Defendants have thus discriminated against Price's religious beliefs.
> 55. Article I, Section 9 of Indiana's Constitution prohibits "restraining the free interchange of thought and opinion, or restricting the right to speak, write or print freely on any subject whatsoever." The Defendants have clearly interfered with and restrained the right of Price to engage in free speech.[312]

In a fair courtroom environment, the charges would have lead to an immediate ruling in favor of the plaintiff, Mrs. Price. The evidence presented in the first two sections of this book prove that DePauw was guilty of violations of the United States and Indiana Constitutions, not to mention the principles of academic freedom. In their zeal to harm her, DePauw's agents even ignored the school's own regulations. A kind and considerate judge would have pulled DePauw's lead attorney aside and suggested settling immediately to avoid damaging the institution's reputation. Unfortunately, arrogance ruled the day, and the case proceeded.

Judge, Diana LaViolette

Here comes the Judge, Diana LaViolette

Judge Diana LaViolette sat on the Putnam County Circuit Court bench for three terms, from her election in 1992 to her retirement in 2005. [313] Prior to that, she had worked in the prosecutor's office in Greencastle. To fill some time between cases, she taught at DePauw University on two different occasions. During the 1986-1987 school year, she taught Political Science 324,"The Politics of Civil Rights and Liberty." Four years later, she taught Political Science 323, "Constitutional Law and Political Structure." Considering these two incidents alone, she should have recused herself from the case. She had done so in a case that involved the Greencastle Community School System. Interestingly, when Mrs. Price's case was moved to neighboring Clay County, she requested to be appointed the "special judge" to preside over it. Some of her courtroom behavior noted by observers was clearly unprofessional. Making flippant remarks such as "Oh well, that's it. You win!" directly to DePauw's counsel during a hearing in early October 2003 was uncalled for at best, and prejudicial at worst. [314] Despite these obvious reasons to doubt the judge's ability to hear the case fairly, Judge LaViolette had made a statement years before that might indicate that she could give Mrs. Price a fair hearing. In an October 1986 interview with *The DePauw*, she claimed that she had gone into law to have the opportunity to "defend poor, down trodden individuals whose rights were violated by some bureaucrat."[315] Mrs. Price was exactly that type of person, someone whose liberties had been trampled under to politically correct jackboots of DePauw University. Over the eighteen months between the initial filing of the complaint to the final ruling, Judge LaViolette had many opportunities to prove those ideals true.

Judicial Tampering

DePauw's lead attorney, John Neighbors, and his two assistants, immediately set about dismantling Mrs. Price's carefully prepared case. Mr. Neighbors used the considerable might of his law firm, Baker and Daniels, to help in his quest to defend the indefensible actions of his alma mater. He had plenty assistance from disinterested federal courts and a local judge who chose not to see the truth.

One of DePauw's first actions was to move the case to federal court. The court promptly dismissed the federal claims. Perhaps these judges were unaware that DePauw University is located within the United States. Perhaps they did not fully consider the evidence that was readily available to them. Whatever their reasoning, they tacitly agreed that Mrs. Price did not have the same rights as other American citizens.

After the case was sent back to Putnam County, stripped of its federal complaints, it languished for nearly a year. In January 2003, it was venued to Clay County. On February 7, the presiding judge recused himself. His reasoning for doing so is still a mystery, as he had no connection to the case. Diana LaViolette was then sworn in as the Special Judge in Clay County to hear Mrs. Price's case.[316]

Judge LaViolette immediately set about her work of gutting the case. On March 10, 2003 she dismissed three of the four original remaining counts, leaving the violation of the academic handbook as the lone survivor.[317] Her lack of objectivity is clear. It is absolutely absurd to think that Mrs. Price was not harassed because of her faith and that her academic freedom was not violated. For once, a judge actually read the Supremacy Clause and used it to remove the count regarding violations of the Indiana Constitution. The federal court had ruled that DePauw violated no federal Constitutional principles. Logically, then, the "inferior" Indiana Constitution could not have been violated either. Ignoring these counts did not change the facts of the case.

Throughout the spring and summer of 2003, Judge LaViolette catered to almost every whim that John Neighbors could conceive. On March 18, she dismissed DePauw's Board of Trustees as co-defendants. A few months later, in June, Mr. Neighbors insisted that Neal Abraham also be stricken as defendant. This too was granted with haste on June 27. John Price appealed to the judge to reconsider her order, but this was denied. DePauw University stood alone as the sole, faceless defendant. One of the reasons for listing the trustees and Dr. Abraham as co-defendants was to place a human face on the case. Remarkably, Diana LaViolette refused Mr. Neighbors' demand for summary judgment in favor of the university in July. She finally heard the call for summary judgment on October 6, but insisted that the case must go to trial. The trial was set for Monday, October 27, 2003.[318] Both sides compiled their witness lists and prepared for a legal battle of epic proportions at the Clay County Court House.

Janis K. Price vs. DePauw could have been a landmark case had it not been for activist judges that cared more about politics than Constitutional principles. The evidence that I have presented in this book did not come from secret sources. These judges, both federal and local, could have accessed it just as easily as I did, but chose not to do so. As a result, they took the most important issues off the table before the case ever made it to trial. Diana LaViolette could have taken a stand for justice in Indiana by recusing herself from the case because of her close ties to DePauw. A ruling in Mrs. Price's favor on all five counts could have struck a significant blow for freedom. It would have codified the idea of academic freedom in Indiana. Conservatives could have pointed to the case in future years when confronted by liberal activists, showing that they have equal access to express their opinions. This would have been devastating to these special interest groups, as homosexuals, feminists, pacifists, and environmentalists who are allowed to silence their opposition on college campuses. The counts regarding freedom of religion would have neutralized another important weapon of the Left. These miscreants would have had a much harder time silencing conservative Christians, as conservatives could now point to another court case that reaffirms their position as laid out in the First Amendment. All was not lost. The issue of having employee handbooks as binding components of contracts would certainly go a long way in securing fair treatment for all employees. If the jury found in Mrs. Price's favor, DePauw and other institutions would be forced to follow a consistent personnel policy, rather than relying on their own prejudices. *Price vs. DePauw* could still have a tremendous impact on the legal system, if only Judge LaViolette would rule with the law.

Chapter 10

The Trial- October 2003

Janis Price finally got her day in court on October 27, 2003. Despite the best efforts of John Neighbors and the rest of the DePauw crowd, a jury would finally get an opportunity to hear the truth. The first order of business was to select the six people who would sit in judgment of DePauw. Out of a dozen potential jurors, the four who were admitted Christians were summarily dismissed. Interestingly, a man with a DePauw connection was left on the panel, claiming that he could rule without prejudice.[319] Before the lunch break, a jury of five men and one woman was empanelled.

Day One

After lunch, Janis Price was the first to take the stand. John Price asked the witness to recount her story, which she did willingly. Mr. Neighbors raised a number of objections, most of which were overruled by Judge LaViolette. The lead DePauw attorney took so many sidebars that the judge was forced to apologize to the jury. After a break, John Neighbors began his cross examination. He asked her petty questions about minute details of meetings had that happened years before which had no bearing on the case, solely as a means to rattle her. Shortly before 5:00 pm, she stepped down for the day. [320]

Day Two

The second day of testimony got underway late, at 9:20 am. Mr. Neighbors continued to badger Mrs. Price, hoping that she would crack. His intent was to show that she had a poor memory, casting doubt on her claims. He finally gave up and allowed John Price to call the next witness, Dr. Judith Raybern.[321] Since she had hired Mrs. Price, she was able to discuss the quality and quantity of her work in the department. [322] After lunch, Brooke Hefner was called to testify. Mr. Neighbors objected when John Price asked whether she was offended by *Teachers in Focus*. A sidebar was called and Brooke was allowed to answer the question.[323] Her testimony was vital, as her recollections matched the events of March 15, 2001. Of course, it also matched what Mrs. Price had stated under oath in previous testimony.

Perhaps the most interesting witness called by John Price was Eric Edberg. For many years, he had served DePauw as a professor of cello. More importantly to the case, he was a homosexual and faculty sponsor of United DePauw. He talked about United DePauw's mission on campus.[324] He stated quite emphatically that he was not offended by Mrs. Price's actions. Under oath he testified that, "Janis is a model example of how I would like to be treated by someone who disagrees with me."[325] He had offered to testify very early in the proceedings, knowing that the university's actions were wrong.

Executive Director of the Indiana Professional Standards Board Marie Theobald testified about Mrs. Price's work ethic as licensing advisor. When some of Esther Lee's antics were mentioned by John Price, Mr. Neighbors objected, a motion sustained by the judge.[326] After a short recess, Dr. Jamie Stockton took the stand. As a long time co-worker and interim department chair, she testified to Mrs. Price's worth as a co-worker.[327] John Price brought up the harassment suffered by Mrs. Price and Dr. Paula Birt, but Mr. Neighbors objected. Interestingly, Dr. Birt had also been harassed in the Education Department by Esther Lee, and left DePauw to direct the children's program in her church. His objection was sustained, but the jury got to hear that others had suffered the same persecution as Mrs. Price.[328] These previous witnesses had been called on Tuesday due to occupational time constraints. John Price called Mrs. Price to the stand again to finish questioning her. Judge Laviolette concluded the day's proceedings around 4:00 pm.[329]

Day Three

Court began at 8:30 am on October 29. Dan Puckett, principal of Central Elementary, testified on behalf of the Putnam County principals with whom Mrs. Price had worked. He went into detail regarding Mrs. Price's professionalism in dealing with local schools. This apparently upset Mr. Neighbors, who called yet another sidebar.[330] Dr. Mary English, chair of the Economics Department, testified about the academic handbook and academic freedom. She stated that she considered the handbook to be part of her contract with DePauw. Naturally, Mr. Neighbors objected. He was over-ruled, and Dr. English was allowed to answer. Not willing to let her answers stand, John Neighbors made an absurd illustration about academic freedom, asking whether saying "Bob Bottoms is incompetent" would be covered under this proviso. John Price objected to this twice, and the judge sustained both objections. DePauw's chief lawyer then bore in on Dr. English's faith. He demanded to know the nature of the relationship between her and Mrs. Price, as both attend Greencastle Christian Church. He had the further audacity to ask if she had prayed for Janis Price specifically or attended church wide prayer services regarding the case. Mr. Price rightly objected to this line of questioning.[331] Perhaps John Neighbors was unfamiliar with the Constitution, but the place, time, and form of Christian worship was no business of his.

Dr. Robert Newton wrote a significant portion of the current incarnation of DePauw's academic handbook in 1977. He was key in proving that the university had indeed violated the provisions therein when punishing Mrs. Price. John Neighbors called another sidebar, and the jury was sent into seclusion. He demanded to know who Dr. Newton had talked to the day before and what they had told him about the trial. Mr. Neighbors insisted that Dr.

Newton's testimony be stricken from the record, as it was somehow corrupted. The motion was rightly denied by the judge.[332]

The validity of the academic handbook was raised by both lawyers during the trial. It would be in the reader's best interest to see what the text actually says, allowing him or her to judge DePauw's actions based on its own rule book. The appendix contains a significant portion of the relevant material in this case.

After lunch, Mr. Neighbors made a motion for a directed verdict, claiming that his opponent had not proven his case. This demand was immediately denied by Judge LaViolette. Angela Morris was the first of DePauw's witnesses to take the stand. She was flown in from Denver, Colorado, at the university's expense, to testify. Ms. Morris was clearly very nervous on the stand. Her answers appeared to be very well rehearsed. Many times, she began her answer before Mr. Neighbors had finished asking his questions. She often contradicted herself. John Price let her continue without objecting, allowing her to show her true colors. Judge LaViolette appeared to be getting very perturbed with the course of events and stopped Ms. Morris's testimony. She called Mr. Price and Mr. Neighbors into the judge's chamber. The two other DePauw lawyers tried to accompany Mr. Neighbors, but Judge LaViolette insisted that they need not be involved. She dismissed them twice before they left the chamber. Enraged, Mr. Neighbors slammed the door behind them. Judge LaViolette was upset with Mr. Price for not stopping Ms. Morris' shaky testimony. At one point during Mr. Neighbor's questioning, Morris began to cry. This was particularly remarkable in that she had not yet been cross examined. [333]

John Price's questions to Ms. Morris elicited typical liberal responses when light the light of truth is shined upon them. She made interesting claims that Mrs. Price "yelled" at her and that this veteran educator was "immature." Complaining about getting a B+ in a course where one did "D" quality work for a significant portion must have been the height of maturity in Ms. Morris' mind. She tried to portray herself as an innocent victim, caught in the middle of a faculty dispute. The evidence told another story. John Price was very gentle with this potentially hostile witness, something which had not been granted to his witnesses by John Neighbors.[334]

Day Four

Neal Abraham led off this day's proceedings. He spent his time repeating the same shop-worn and inaccurate charges against Mrs. Price that have long since been disproved. In his trial notes, spectator Jim Poor noted a difference in the behavior of the two attorneys with Judge LaViolette. Mr. Neighbors spent his down time engaging in friendly chit chat with her, while Mr. Price maintained the proper professional distance. Mr. Neighbors was quite windy in his questioning of Dr. Abraham, who was equally lengthy in his responses. He was very testy when being cross-examined by Mr. Price, giving the appearance of being terribly inconvenienced by having to answer his questions. Neal Abraham gave direct answers only when ordered to do so by the judge. DePauw rested its case and Mr. Price called Janis Price back to the stand for final clarification. Not being satisfied with his opponent getting the last word, Mr. Neighbors re-examined her as well before proceedings ended for the day. [335]

Day Five

Friday morning brought closing arguments by both parties. Mr. Neighbors told the judge that she must throw the case out, based on *Orr vs. Westminster Village North (1995)*, a motion wisely disregarded. John Price clearly and accurately stated the facts of the case in his closing argument, while Mr. Neighbors prattled on about the "integrity" of DePauw University and Neal Abraham. The jury entered deliberation after receiving its instructions from Judge LaViolette. They returned with a judgment in favor of Janis Price.[336] This panel of ordinary citizens had seen through the fog and found the truth. After thirty one arduous months, justice had finally been served on October 31, 2003.

The Judgment

Janis Price was granted $10,401, the amount of money that she had lost during her first year of punishment. Not surprisingly, the university's agents maintained that they had done their best to follow the letter of the law regarding the case. Director of Media Relations Ken Owen stated the following in *The DePauw* on November 4, 2003.

> While we have tremendous respect for the system of justice, we maintain that DePauw scrupulously followed its employment policies and practices outlined in the sections of its academic handbook governing part-time faculty members every step of the way.... We have substantial reason to be confident that we will be successful on appeal, as the courts have supported DePauw in every other issue related to this complaint.[337]

One of the oldest and most sacred cornerstones of our civilization is trial by jury. Instead of acknowledging that his side had been soundly defeated, Mr. Owen went on the offensive. DePauw's surrogates still had not realized that this whole affair could have been avoided if Neal Abraham had simply followed the university's personnel procedures. Mr. Owen was quite factual in one aspect. The local court had agreed to gut Mrs. Price's lawsuit before it ever got to trial. One wonders if the university would have been accorded the same treatment by a judge who was not a former employee. On November 20, 2003, Judge LaViolette granted Mrs. Price $3,164 in court costs. She threw a bone to DePauw. The judge ruled that the university would not have to pay Mrs. Price's attorney fees, a sum much greater than $3,164.[338]

Prior to her victory in the lawsuit, Mrs. Price had been asked to give her Christian testimony at DePauw University's Union Building Ballroom. People of other faiths had earlier been asked to do so as well as part of a series. She addressed over one hundred people on December 4, 2003. Ken Bode, the Pulliam Distinguished Professor of Journalism, taunted her by asking.

> In the early part of your difficulties with the university you made some indications that DePauw is a difficult

place for Christians to be....I just witnessed a speech given on university property that conflicts with that idea.[339]

Professor Bode must not have noticed the crowd of angry homosexual activists that showed up for the meeting. United DePauw member and winner of the Lesbian Leadership Award Meredith Douglas took the opportunity to belittle Mrs. Price.

> "You said it was difficult to eat when you are worried and talked about feeling of being choked....When I read the material [*Teachers in Focus*] you handed out, that's how I felt. I just wondered if you feel any remorse now.[340]

It is unclear exactly about what, in Ms. Douglas' mind, Mrs. Price was to feel remorse. Allowing students to read articles that address serious issues from an accurate, Biblical perspective is nothing to be ashamed of. Another activist, Doug Waters, continued the party line.

> You were suing the university for being silenced yet your material speaks of silencing homosexuals as if they were a problem.[341]

Had Mr. Waters taken the time to read the issue in question, he would have realized that this statement bordered on lunacy. Perhaps the most telling aspect of the article is the photograph accompanying it. The picture focused on Meredith Douglas, with Mrs. Price standing at the lectern in the distance.

United DePauw Breaks Its Silence

United DePauw has always had a flair for the dramatic. They filled the editorial pages of the November 18, 2003 issue of the DePauw with their hysterics. Meredith Douglas launched the opening salvo by distorting the well-document facts of the case. She "knowingly distributed anti-gay literature to her students." Remember, speaking God's Truth about this lifestyle is hateful in the minds of these activists, even if the material is merely made available, not distributed. This brilliant writer concluded her screed by noting that because Mrs. Price actually believed what was printed in the October 2000 issue of *Teachers in Focus*, that "Neither I nor many of my friends would ever consider enrolling in one of Price's classes."[342] That was truly tolerance in action.

Perhaps even more inflammatory was the tirade engaged in by the executive board of United DePauw. Although it is difficult to read because of the many vague accusations, inaccuracies, and generally nonsensical premise, it is important to understand the mentality of those who opposed Mrs. Price.

> United DePauw remained silent on the Janis Price case. We sat quietly while she framed the issue and set herself up as a martyr for Christendom. We said nothing as she claimed the high moral ground and reveled in her pyrrhic victory. We were silent until now. Today we remember the words of Audre Lorde: "Your silence will not protect you.

> This case has thrived upon silence. When Price disseminated Teacher in Focus magazine without discussion or debate, she silenced the students in her class. She was in the position of power and authority as a professor, and she used it. She silenced lesbian, gay, bisexual, and transgendered people, allies, friends, family members and other Christians whose faith in God is not about hate and exclusion. That day, Price made her classroom unsafe for anyone who has ever questioned their sexuality or her brand of Christianity. Then, to add insult to injury, she cast herself as the victim. Our community may have been silent but we weren't fooled; we know something about victimization.

> In our experience, the line between hate literature, hate speech and hate crimes is very thin. We believe that it is no coincidence that Chris Fitzgerald '02 was reportedly assaulted soon after the Price case went public. Some us were there when Greg Armstrong allegedly assaulted Fitzgerald, grabbed his throat and insisted that he could not be both "a Christian and a faggot." With dismay we watched as certain faculty lined up to support Armstrong, instead of holding him accountable for his actions, just as they have supported Price. And, when we asked our fellow students to denounce hate violence of any kind,

some told us that they wouldn't speak out because they didn't want to "support homosexuals."

Finally, let us call out the hurt and hypocrisy. As a community, we have been hurt by Janis Price- all the more because she claims out of one side of her mouth to have "no problem" with gay people, to have gay friends, even as she disseminates literature that suggests that we are AIDS-infected pedophiles. Price expects the handbook to be followed to the letter on employment issues, but shirks her duty to create "a learning environment free of inappropriate treatment because of sexual orientation (Faculty Handbook).

Make no mistake, we are not asking for censorship. Offensive materials can and should be discussed in the classroom. Price, however, disseminated literature on its face value without discussion or academic relevance. This was her personal attack on our community.

Price, if you believe you truly know the mind of God, then give the students of United DePauw the courtesy of looking every last one of us in the eye as you pass judgment against us. We meet Thursdays at 9:30 p.m. in the Queer Center of Senior Hall. Our agenda will be cleared this Thursday, November 20, anticipation of your visit, but this time we will not be silent.[343]

The DePauw has printed many columns over the years that were hateful, but none quite as toxic as this. It would have been unwise to have gone to this meeting even if Mrs. Price had had more than two days notice. Her story would have fallen on deaf ears, as the disrespectful members of United DePauw had already passed judgment on her. It would take too much time to dissect the inaccuracies in this disgusting, erroneous piece of hate speech, but the reader may wish to look at earlier chapters for clarification of the issues raised.

Homosexual activists at DePauw were certainly afraid of Mrs. Price, but not for the reasons that they stated. Her accuser, Angela Morris, had been a member of United DePauw as an undergraduate. It should not come as any surprise that they would attack someone who had upset one of their alumni. Additionally, no one had stood up to DePauw's homosexual activists since Baseball Cap Day in

1994, nearly a decade earlier. In the ensuing decade, they became overly confident. They printed outrageous articles, and their critics were promptly silenced. They brought obscene movies and bands to campus, and few responded. For one, brief moment, truth had pierced the darkness enshrouding their movement. The curtain was pulled back, and what was revealed was little more than hateful and vindictive people fearful of loosing their power at DePauw University.

Chapter 11

The Truth Will Set You Free
Media Coverage of Janis
Price v. DePauw University

Janis Price's lawsuit quickly garnered the attention of the media. For nearly three years, the media has been covering the case. The partisan media, be it *The Indianapolis Star*; the local paper, *The Banner Graphic*; or the campus paper, *The DePauw* have been decidedly against Mrs. Price. Fortunately, the new media and its allies in the Christian media have insured that an accurate picture of the case was presented.

The 700 Club

The first time many people outside of Greencastle became aware of the situation was thanks to a "700 Club" broadcast on July 10, 2002. Senior producer Andrea Garrett traveled to Greencastle to interview Mrs. Price, as well as university officials. Not surprisingly, Neal Abraham refused to speak to the media, but claimed that the faculty has academic freedom. Ken Owen, the director of media relations at DePauw, stated that the university could not speak regarding the lawsuit, as it was still in progress. Mrs. Price was more than willing to talk.[344]

"Janis Price doesn't look like a trouble maker, but her employer, Indiana's DePauw University, seems to think that she is one."[345] With those simple words, the rest of the world learned about DePauw's harassment of Mrs. Price. During the course of the interview, the facts of the case were recounted in detail. Neal Abraham's famous cry, "We can not tolerate the intolerable," was met by Mrs. Price's reasoned response. "And what is intolerable at DePauw and with him is my Christian faith in general and my view on homosexuality in particular."[346]

Other figures weighed in on the case. John Price noted that the case was really about the Constitutionally protected right to free speech, as well as academic freedom. Dr. Jeff McCall, a DePauw graduate and long time communication professor at the university, discussed the effect on the campus.

> Because Janis has been scolded and disciplined for providing materials, the chilling effect suggests then that other people will then become hesitant as well to make decisions in an academic freedom sense as to what kinds of materials they want to provide as well." [347]

Economics professor Dr. Mary English had even more disparaging sentiments on the university's policies. "We have to be tolerant and politically correct of all other areas except Christianity. So its OK to be intolerant of Christians as long as Christians are tolerant of everybody else."[348]

The report ended with the audience being reassured that Janis Price's motives were pure, seeking only for the university to restore her position and to admit its mistakes. DePauw was making no attempt to settle the case at this point. In the conversation after the piece, Pat and Gordon Robertson discussed the national implications of the case. The elder Robertson pointed out that "John Wesley would be turning in his grave," because of DePauw's actions.[349] He also noted that the goal of political correctness from the beginning has been the protection and promotion of homosexuality. [350] The segment was excellent with one minor caveat. The classroom where the incident occurred was not shown. Instead, a much larger room was filmed. Perhaps this was due to the cramped nature of that basement room. It is a small point, but some of those who are on the wrong side of the issue have pointed out that there was no back table in that classroom as Mrs. Price had claimed, supposedly undermining the case against the university. A tiny point to be sure, but Mrs. Price's opponents have shown themselves to be quite petty.

In October 2003, Mrs. Price was again mentioned on the "700 Club." David Limbaugh was on the program discussing his new book, *Persecution.* He mentioned three cases from the book. The example that he gave for anti-Christian persecution on the college level was *Price vs. DePauw.* [351] Just a few days after this broadcast, a verdict was reached in the case. The outcome was reported on the November 3, 2003 broadcast.[352] The "700 Club" was vital to getting out the truth about Mrs. Price's lawsuit against DePauw. Had Andrea Garrett not taken the time to investigate the story, most Americans would have known nothing about DePauw's abuses of its employees.

Dr. Bottoms Speaks

President Robert G. Bottoms make a strategic error on July 29, 2002. He sent a two page letter to every DePauw alumnus explaining the university's position on *Price vs. DePauw.* This insured that those who missed the "700 Club" would know about the case. As a result of the report and the following letter, he received a mountain of e-mails and letters from alumni who were justly angered by the university's behavior towards Christians.

> I am writing to comment on a matter involving DePauw University which has attracted significant media coverage. Some members of the DePauw community have called or written letters of inquiry and concern.
>
> Janis Price, who continues to hold an administrative staff position in the Education Department, has filed a lawsuit against the University and its Trustees. Mrs. Price, who served as a part-time instructor in the department, alleges that her teaching duties were revoked because of her conservative Christian views. She and her attorney

133

aired the complaint in an article posted on a Web site sponsored by Focus on the Family and, more recently, were profiled in a segment on the Christian Broadcasting Network's *700 Club*.

Because this is a personnel matter as well as the subject of a pending lawsuit, there are numerous particulars that I am not at liberty to discuss. However, I can assure you that Mrs. Price's reduction in duties had nothing to do with her religious beliefs.

Simply put, the reason that Janis Price is no longer teaching at DePauw (but remains an administrator) is declining enrollments in the Education Department which led the University to reallocate resources to other academic departments. In recent years, the number of students enrolled in education classes at DePauw has declined by more than one-third; the number of education majors has declined by 50 percent. Those facts led us to make some difficult decisions in the 2001-2002 school year, reducing the number of full-time faculty members in the Education Department from eight to six. Additionally, the University no longer needed Mrs. Price to teach part-time, and the administrative duties assigned to her were slightly reduced. I would add that the University holds to the general principle that its courses are best taught by full-time faculty members who have completed the most advanced possible graduate study and preparation for their teaching. Consequently, over the last five years the University has increased the percentage of its courses taught by full-time faculty members from 84 percent to 94 percent.

Mrs. Price's claim that the University no longer allows her to teach because of her religious views, an allegation on which she bases her lawsuit, is, in fact, without merit. Because of the litigation instituted against us, DePauw's counsel has advised us not to comment further on the case. Please know that the University is confident its employment decisions regarding Mrs. Price were lawful and appropriate, and I believe that the judicial system will find in our favor....

The CBN story raised questions about this environment we are so proud of, one that embraces and welcomes people of all races, faiths and lifestyles. DePauw prohibits harassment/discrimination against individuals for any reason, including religious practices and sexual orientation. Accordingly, the University allows its faculty, students, and employees to fully exercise their freedoms in these respects. The University recognizes and adheres to the concept of academic freedom so long as it does not infringe on these other protected rights.

Our American judicial system allows individuals who sincerely believe that their legal rights have been violated to initiate a lawsuit to remedy such a wrong. It also affords us the opportunity to rebut these claims in a court of law and that is exactly what the University is doing. As President, I wanted to make you aware of the situation and some of the facts of the case. I assure you we will remain committed to religious principles, academic freedom and social good. [353]

It is clear that Dr. Bottoms had hoped to quell any concerns that alumni might have had after seeing the "700 Club." Instead, he stirred a hornet's nest with his inaccurate portrayal of Mrs. Price's lawsuit.

Faculty Institute 2002

Dr. Bottoms was not content just to send an erroneous letter to the alumni and to the parents of current students. On August 16, 2002, he addressed the faculty for forty five minutes during the annual Faculty Institute. Although he promised not to discuss the specifics of the lawsuit, President Bottoms spent nearly one quarter of the time addressing Janis Price's case under the guise of a discussion of the culture war. He talked a lot about the "formation of an inclusive community," in which we "celebrate difference without eradicating it."[354] This portion of his speech had two common threads running through it. First, he spent a great deal of time belaboring "white privilege." Secondly, he seemed almost obsessed with not being thought of as being politically correct, despite the fact that Mrs. Price's persecution was a textbook case of political correctness run amok.

The president began his discussion of the case itself by noting that "some of you do not watch CBN," the mention of which caused a murmur to roll through the crowd. While he claimed to offer no interpretation of the facts, he certainly put a dizzying spin on them. Twice he referred to *Teachers in Focus* as a "religious tract," something that has been established to be demonstrably false. A professional magazine for educators written from a Christian perspective is no more a tract than an NEA publication. He gave a short overview of the "facts" and continued. "And then the plot thickens. First a lawsuit and then the media enters." At this point, the mainstream media had completely ignored the story, so the Christian press was carrying the load. He then denigrated the lawsuit as "just another little skirmish within the confines of DePauw.[355]

Dr. Bottoms seemed most perturbed by the e-mails that he was sent by enraged alumni. The comment, "why don't you wake up and smell the crematories, you pathetic Nazis, " was met by laughter from the faculty. Another e-mail, this time directed at Neal Abraham posited, "Why don't you contact a physical and schedule an X-ray, and see if he can find a spine, you gutless, godless wonder." A third writer suggested that Dr. Bottoms "resign and move to San Francisco," a comment met by more mindless laughter from the faculty. The majority in the room did not seem to understand the level of anger being directed at the university. Perhaps they saw these concerns as the rantings of unenlightened bumpkins. This was quite ironic, as these "bumpkins" were people who graduated from DePauw prior to its slide into the death grip of political correctness. Dr. Bottoms finished this section with a statement on academic freedom: "Free expression is always welcome as long as it doesn't trample the on the rights of other individuals in the community." This is something that was denied Mrs. Price. Perhaps the most ironic statement of the speech followed shortly thereafter. "We need to address what its like to live the life of integrity in a society that is as pluralistic and broken as ours."[356] Someone who lived a life of integrity on that campus had been forced to go to court to defend her reputation. Indeed, this was an issue that the university needed to address.

The Dynamic Duo-Poor and Shively

Jim Poor, a member of DePauw's Class of 1954, and I took up our pens to set the record straight. Jim and I share the same concern for our alma mater. As Christians, we were bound by our faith to stand up to the misstatements made by Dr. Bottoms in his July 29, 2002 letter and correct them.

> On Friday, August 9, I returned to Greencastle from a week in Detroit at the Cadillac Centennial. My mood was shattered by the letter I found in my mailbox from DePauw University President Robert Bottoms. In this letter, he attempted to convince alumni like myself that the religious discrimination lawsuit that Janis Price filed against the University (sic) was baseless. It was a very well crafted, but highly inaccurate piece of penmanship. Unlike most DePauw alumni, I have had a ringside seat to this affair. It would be best if I told my story as a way of correcting the record regarding Mrs. Price.

> I graduated from DePauw University with a degree in History in December 1994. I decided to obtain a teaching license in late 1999. I contacted DePauw's Certification Officer, Mrs. Price, to see what I needed to do. I had planned to attend ISU, but I knew Mrs. Price would steer me correctly. She convinced me that the 5th Year program at DePauw would suit my needs better than ISU, so I enrolled in the program in December 1999. I completed the necessary DePauw Education Department class work in two semesters while taking non-education classes at ISU. I completed my student teaching in April 2001 and was licensed by the State in 5-12 Social Studies in July 2001. As far as I knew, everything was fine. In the fall of 2001, I was informed by Mrs. Price that Dr. Esther Lee, Education Department Chair, was trying to get my license revoked. It seems that there was no record of the class work from ISU in my file. Thus, I was not qualified as a teacher. Mrs. Price and I both remembered putting my grades from ISU in my file. Suddenly, they had vanished. Dr. Lee harassed me at home regarding this issue several times that fall. I was able to replace the ISU paperwork, securing my license. At the same time two

other non-traditional students were experiencing similar problems with Dr. Lee. It all fit together when Mrs. Price was demoted for passing alleged "hate material." I was being used as a pawn by the University to discredit her and give grounds for her removal.

Why does DePauw want to be rid of Janis Price? Her student evaluations are always very high. She has a reputation for giving honest career advice to students. Quite simply, DePauw will tolerate anything except traditional Christian values. The "hate literature" that Mrs. Price offered, <u>Teachers in Focus</u>, was printed by Focus on the Family. To obtain a copy, a student would have to ask specifically for one. Nothing was ever forced upon anyone, making it very hard to be exposed to "offensive" literature. The issue in question presented a Biblical view on homosexuality. This topic has been a sacred cow for DePauw since my undergrad days in the early 1990s. During the summer of 1992, one of my co-workers at the DePauw library, Carol Emrick, was sent home to change her Christian t-shirt. Apparently, a homosexual had complained that the shirt had offended her. Every May, the homosexuals had a "coming out" day. As a show of support, (or of forgetfulness) students would wear blue jeans to class. To herald this day, the gays would hang posters all over campus that included all sorts of neat things, like two women kissing. In 1994, a small band of freedom loving conservatives decided to stage a counter protest, "Baseball Cap Day." Needless to say, there were a lot of ball caps worn around campus on that warm May day. This success was bittersweet, as one of these brave souls was accosted by a homosexual while hanging posters the night before the counter protest. Needless to say, the University sided with the homosexual.

This anti-Christian, pro-homosexual bias continues to this day. Christian faculty are hounded until they resign, no matter how well they do their jobs. At the same time, part of the old Alpha Gamma Delta house has become home to a "gay resource center." A faculty member adorned his van with pro-homosexual and extreme left wing slogans and parked it on campus a few years ago. University Rabbi "Buz" Bogage was caught smoking pot with students. His "punishment" was two weeks of paid leave. The message is clear; DePauw doesn't want anything to do with the Christian values that its founders held dear.

> If this testimony does not convince you that the attack on Mrs. Price's religious freedom is but a small piece in a much larger puzzle, a quick read of *The DePauw* will. The University of Henry Longden, Albert Beveridge, and Hillary Gobin is but a memory. In its place is an arrogant monstrosity that believes that it can crush its enemies with impunity. Parts of Greencastle look like London during the Blitz because of the University's desires. As an alumnus, I can only hope that the legal system finds in favor of Mrs. Price. If it doesn't, the First Amendment means nothing on that campus. That would truly be a sad day, as DePauw blood was shed at Gettysburg, Havana Harbor, Verdun, and the Ardennes to preserve those very liberties.[357]

This article was my first foray into publishing my thoughts on DePauw's misdeeds. Many readers appreciated my efforts.[358] Not surprisingly, I was attacked in print by liberals in *The Banner Graphic* and in *The DePauw*.[359] A very badly edited version of my letter appeared in the September 24, 2002 issue of the campus newspaper. A very poorly informed student, Janelle van Buiten assaulted the character of DePauw's founders, as well as my own.

> If the 'values that its founders held dear' happen to include the type of prejudice and homophobia that Shively displays in his letter, I applaud DePauw for getting as far away from them as possible.[360]

The ignorance of my attackers would have been humorous if it did not reveal the shockingly limited understanding of American history exhibited by many Leftist college students.

Jim Poor followed my lead and let loose with a series of articles that were printed in *The Banner Graphic*.

> As an alumnus of DePauw University, I (like Jeff Shively, and thousands of other alums) received the "comment" letter from President Bob Bottoms trying to convince us that the lawsuit filed by Janis Price against DePauw was "without merit." The very fact that President Bottoms

felt a letter to thousands of alums was necessary says to me that the opposite is true.

Mrs. Price is definitely being persecuted because of her Christian views. I thought it interesting that Bottoms' letter failed to mention DePauw's Vice President Abraham and his comment that "we cannot tolerate the intolerable." The "intolerable" in this case is Mrs. Price's Christian views.

As a graduate of DePauw University, I have always considered DePauw an asset to the Greencastle community, even though I did not necessarily agree with some positions and actions of the university. Since the shameful and unfair treatment and the failure of DePauw to recognize and change their bias against Christians, I no longer consider my university in a positive way. I am ashamed of their wrongful and injurious treatment of Mrs. Price because she expresses her Christian views.

I am also personally offended that President Bottoms thinks I (also with Jeff Shively and surely many others) will swallow this "explanation" of the events surrounding the removal of this good teacher. I am a Christian, and the persecution of my Christian sister, Janis Price, is persecution of all Christians. We must speak out!

As Joshua challenged the Israelites, "Choose this day whom you will serve... as for me and my house, we will serve the Lord." I call on President Bottoms to do the right thing- not the politically correct thing.[361]

Jim continued his quest to inform the public with another letter to the editor.

The Janis Price lawsuit against DePauw University is being written about quite often in *The DePauw.* (campus newspaper) In an article by Andrew Tangle in the August 27 issue, Mr. Tangle writes, "Bottoms wrote in a July 29 letter to alumni and parents that 'Mrs. Price's reduction in duties had nothing to do with her religious beliefs.' But Ken Owen, director of media relations, said the magazine article did play a role, however small, in her revocation of duties and subsequent probation. 'That's just one marble in the bag,' Owen said."

Mr. Tangel also noted that at the Aug. 16 faculty meeting, President Bottoms talked about the role of the faculty in preparing DPU's students for "citizenship." He writes, "Bottoms said that a multicultural institution like DePauw needed to shrug off moral relativism and mold students' character."

Possibly that is what President Bottoms meant when the Office of Multicultural Affairs sponsored the sex-riddled Mexican film "Y Tu Mama Tambien," shown Sept. 22 in Watson Forum. Advertised on the DePauw website as the "unrated version" and "wildly erotic!," the film was reviewed by Mariana Carreno of www.offoffoff.com. Some clips from the review were "...full of unnecessary sex scenes," "exploration of sexual identity and intimacy" and "full of sex, drugs and ingeniously funny scenes (and not yet rated)."

I think that it is disgusting that a supposedly "church-related" university will sponsor a film like this on their campus but will punish Janis Price for making available to her students an article on the Christian view of homosexuality.

Christians can help Mrs. Price in her brave struggle against the unjust persecution of DePauw by helping with her considerable legal expenses.[362]

Jim and I wrote periodically on the topic of *Price vs. DePauw.* Even after the case was put through the sausage grinder, we continued to write, reminding local people of the truth. Two weeks after the trial ended, "Take Heart America" was published.

The events of the past two weeks should make freedom lovers take heart. After two and a half harrowing years, Janis Price's case was finally heard by a jury. The five men and one woman saw through DePauw University's attempt to obscure the truth and found in favor of Mrs. Price. In the entertainment world, CBS attempted to portray a distorted, slanderous miniseries about President Reagan as accurate. American citizens, outraged at such a vengeful assault upon a man who can no longer defend himself, called the network's hand, forcing them to cancel the CBS broadcast of the miniseries. After six decades, the "Enola Gay" is finally on display at Dulles International Airport as a glorious tribute to all the airmen, soldiers, sailors, Marines and auxiliaries who saved civilization during World War II. After many setbacks, it is refreshing to see freedom take a step forward.

What do these seemingly different events have in common? They show what dedicated, honest Americans can do if they choose to unite for a good cause. Mrs. Price received financial, moral, and spiritual support from people all over the nation. Americans who actually remember the Reagan Presidency stood up to an attempt by part of the Establishment Media to slander a man who served his country well for decades. Even his liberal daughter, Patty Davis, agreed that the filmmakers were inaccurate in their portrayal of her father. Many of us remember the infamous mid-1990s plan to display the incomplete airframe of the fabled Boeing B-29 Superfortress, "Enola Gay," as part of a historically inaccurate exhibit about World War II. Veterans expressed their outrage in such great numbers that the Smithsonian cancelled the inflammatory display. A proper restoration of this magnificent artifact began in earnest, resulting in the respectful and accurate presentation one sees today. Working together, regular Americans made a difference in each case.

These incidents are also quite similar in the attitude of the opponents of truth. A distinct tone of arrogance resonates in their arguments. DePauw is appealing the decision. They did their very best to water down Mrs. Price's case, but still managed to lose once a jury heard the evidence. Their inability to accept defeat has forced them to continue dragging the University's once-proud name through the muck. So-called "free-speech" advocates are howling censorship at CBS. How dare ordinary Americans disagree with their revision of recent history! As a consolation, the mini-series will be aired to a much smaller audience on Showtime. Of course, these people were strangely silent when Dr. Laura and Rush Limbaugh were denied equal access for their views on television a few years ago. Predictably, professional "historians" are ranting about the evils of displaying the "Enola Gay" in a positive light, going as far as to compare it to a slave ship. Again, we are to trust their interpretation of history, rather than our own study of the subject. We are to believe that the citizenry is not sophisticated enough to involve itself in important affairs.

Even with these successes, it is important to remember that the battle is not over. Everyday it seems, a new assault upon the truth is launched. The question comes down to this. Are you, as a citizen of this great land, willing to stand up and be counted for truth? Mrs. Price did, and she has paid heavily for it. If you choose to make a stand, beware. Opponents will hurl cruel, inaccurate and mostly inarticulate assaults at your character. Your position might cost you your livelihood. The rewards are more than worth the cost. Knowing that you helped preserve freedom for your descendants gives one great peace of mind.[363]

The Banner Graphic chose not to publish my final article regarding Janis Price. Fortunately, a small Cloverdale, Indiana based newspaper allowed it to run.

The time honored American system of trial by jury can't be trusted. That would seem to be the position that DePauw University is now espousing. Despite claims to the contrary, the University is intent on dragging the Price affair out for as much as three additional years, the time it would take to get thorough Indiana's appeal process. It is past time to swallow their pride, apologize to Mrs. Price, and write a tiny check for less than $15,000.

It is quite unfortunate that the scope of the appeal will be limited to the events of the October trial, because there are many very pertinent issues that need to be addressed. Although she did not plan on asking for damages beyond her lost wages and court costs, Mrs. Price was pre-emptively denied the opportunity to ask for them. The statement in the DePauw press release that ran in the *Banner* on December 3 is true, that the Laviolette court had ruled in their favor on the other 11 counts. (sic) What is not said is that if these other counts were heard by a jury, the likelihood of a ruling favorable to Mrs. Price is high. The evidence collected by her, as well as the testimony of eye-witnesses, is quite damning. I say this with confidence, as I have been closely involved in the case for over two years.

During the jury selection, potential jurors who had heard of certain Christian publications and broadcasts were summarily dismissed. This was done in the name of insuring an objective jury. If objectivity was truly a concern, it would follow that a former DePauw employee would also be asked to recuse herself. According to the 1986-1987 *DePauw University Directory*, Judge Diana LaViolette served as a Part Time Instructor of Political Science during that school year. How could this not be called a conflict of interest? At the very least, it calls into question her motive for dismissing these counts.

The claim that the jury had insufficient time to understand the Academic Handbook is quite absurd. Creating a handbook that is too difficult for an employee to understand is illogical. We are also led to believe that the handbook is irrelevant to the case, as it has nothing to do with employee contracts. It must have been challenging to create a document that is too complex for a potential employee to understand, while being entirely irrelevant to his or her employment. It would also be an unnecessary expense to print and distribute this handbook to new faculty members if it is not part of the contract. The Academic Handbook was completely revised in 1977. It has been amended since that time. That is a lot of effort to expend on an irrelevant document.

I called one of the gentlemen involved in the 1977 revision to Academic Handbook. He seemed rather perturbed when I asked him if his committee had intentionally made a document that was unclear. He was gracious to send me copies of the portions of the handbook relevant to the case. The text was very detailed, but clear. I must question the claim that the text was too difficult for the jury to understand.

A fine article regarding the case appeared in the October 2003 issue of *The Wabash Commentary*. The author, Paul Stolarczuk, quoted DePauw attorney John Neighbors as saying in court," There are no Constitutional rights at DePauw University." The Framers might take a different view. The Supremacy Clause, found in Article 6 of the U.S. Constitution states that it "shall be the supreme law of the land; and the judges in every state shall be bound thereby, any thing in the constitution or laws of any state to the contrary notwithstanding." South Carolina had a similar disregard for the Constitution during the Nullification Crisis of 1832, a stand which sowed the seeds of civil war. If DePauw wishes to ignore the Law of the Land, what then serves as the basis for governance on the campus? DePauw has argued that it's Academic Handbook is not part of the employment contract. Following this argument to it's logical conclusion, a DePauw employee has no legal rights. That leaves us only one option. DePauw wishes to operate under the Rule of Man, not Rule of Law. This concept flies in the face of eight centuries of legal precedent, effectively overturning the ideals of all legal codes since the Magna Charta.

A key player in this case has been quoted as saying that one of the things that attracted this person to study law was the opportunity to "defend poor, down trodden individuals whose rights were violated by some bureaucrat." Although this motivation certainly applies to John Price, the quote belongs to then- Assistant Prosecutor Diana LaViolette, found on page 8 of the October 14, 1986 issue of *The DePauw.* I wonder what became of those ideals.[364]

It is still a mystery as to why *The Banner Graphic* did not run the final column. Perhaps the fact that I showed Judge LaViolette in an objective light forced the editor to overlook the three copies that I sent him.

The Mainstream Media

The mainstream media's coverage of *Price vs. DePauw* merits very little attention other than to say that it was slanted heavily against the plaintiff. Under the ownership of the Pulliam family, *The Indianapolis Star* was an excellent source for bias free news.

Since it was bought out by a conglomerate, the quality of the writing has sunk to the level of the *New York Times*. Five separate articles appeared in the paper regarding the case between August 22, 2002 and November 23, 2003. None of these articles were sympathetic to Mrs. Price.[365] Many of *The Banner Graphic's* articles about the case read a little too much like press releases to be considered balanced. In all fairness, the editor did print articles by Jim Poor and me, so that allowed some truth to shine through. *The DePauw* had its share of negative articles. One young writer published the particular insightful opinion in saying "a Christian document in secular education is a no-no."[366] One wonders if she has ever read the First Amendment. Homosexual activist and DePauw cartoonist Damon Xanthopoulos spent his undergraduate career demeaning traditional values, but his cruelest barbs were reserved for someone who challenge the politically correct orthodoxy on campus. One cartoon depicted Mrs. Price as a baby throwing a tantrum and screaming "DePauw is intolerant of my intolerance!"[367] After the case ended, he fired a parting shot at this distinguished educator by pointing out that most of the counts that had been dropped, making Mrs. Price's victory a hollow one.[368] Both cartoons were extremely demeaning and intolerant. It is indeed reassuring that tomorrow's leaders exhibit such deep reasoned thought processes as these characters do.

There were a few people at DePauw who chose to stand up to the politically correct pressure and tell the truth about Janis Price. Ryan Pugliano, a member of the Class of 2004, was the object of hateful e-mails, articles, and cartoons because of his brave stand. Despite the risks, he was a consistent defender of Mrs. Price.[369] Drew Humphrey and Seth Kinnett also stood for truth. [370] Their comments met with derision from the "tolerant" members of the DePauw community too.

146

The American Family Association Weighs In

The American Family Association was one of the first publications to pick up the Janis Price story. The writers at the *AFA Journal* made sure that the true nature of the case saw the light of day.

> Janis Price worked for years to build a reputation as a strong, highly respected educator and a Christian. Now, she's fighting to restore her career and defend her religious views.

> Christians have long found themselves the focus of persecution. What adds a twist here, though, is the entity Price is suing: her employer, DePauw University, a college founded in 1837 in Greencastle, Indiana, on Methodist principles.

> That was then. The DePauw University at the center of this debate is far removed from that religious foundation.

> In her lawsuit, Price contends the university, and specifically Neal B. Abraham, vice-president for academic affairs, violated her First Amendment rights and created a hostile work environment. The lawsuit stems from Price's cut in pay and responsibilities in 2001 after Abraham and the university placed her on probation and reduced her position from full-time to 75% time status. The move came after officials said Price distributed material in her classroom that promoted intolerance and created a hostile environment for students.

> The material at the heart of the argument: copies of *Teachers in Focus* magazine, from Focus on the Family. The issue which created the brouhaha contained an article about homosexual activism in the schools. Price had for many years made the magazine available to students in her classes, but hadn't required they read it.

A student, Angela Morris, complained last year to university officials about the politically incorrect magazine, but didn't voice concerns to Price beyond asking her, in class, what she thought about homosexuality. Price said in her lawsuit that she answered the question, addressing the entire class, saying, "Science teachers need to do a good job teaching science, English teachers need to teach English, and math teachers need to teach math, etc. One's sexuality is a private matter and has no place in a public school classroom." Price said that was the end of the discussion.

On May 7, 2001, Price was called before Abraham, who then informed her the student had complained. During the meeting, Abraham asked Price about her teaching practices, and questioned her about how students knew she was a Christian.

Price said Abraham pulled out the copy of the magazine article and read parts of it aloud. He asked her several times whether she believed what the article said, and each time she said she did. According to Price's lawsuit, she asked Abraham how she was to tolerate others' beliefs if her own beliefs weren't to be tolerated. "We cannot tolerate the intolerable," Abraham said.

On July 16, Price was called back into Abraham's office. According to her lawsuit, Abraham said her administrative duties (Certification Officer and Director of Field Experience) had been reduced; she would no longer be an instructor at the school; her future responsibilities in public schools would be monitored; her position as director of the AV laboratory had been reassigned to another person; she was placed on probation; and her pay would be cut by $10,401, in line with her position being reduced from full-time to 75% time.

Abraham accused Price at the meeting of "professional intolerance" and the "deliberate creation of a hostile environment."

In the time since, Price charges in her suit, she has suffered financially from the pay cut, lost her career status by the termination of her teaching duties and lost standing at DePauw and in the state of Indiana by her termination as Chair of the Unit Assessment Systems Review Committee.

Now, Price is having to play a waiting game. No trial date has been set yet, and "the university has tried, in every way it possibly can, to slow things down," she said. "They filed a motion to dismiss the case, which has been denied. They're digging their heels in; they do not want this to go to court. And if it does, then they want to stretch it out such that I run out of money before they do."

Price said she and her husband, Geoff, have found comfort in the outpouring of moral support they have received from the community and from several of her former students. A fund has been established to help the Prices financially with this case. [371]

The *AFA Journal* followed the case through the decision, right into the appeals phase. As it moved through the courts, the Journal was there, reporting the facts.

An Indiana college professor's religious discrimination lawsuit has moved closer to being heard before a judge and jury.

Janis Price won a procedural victory in January that will allow her case to be heard by jurors who don't live in the county where DePauw University is located.

"We were able to have the trial moved to another county, but the Putnam County (Indiana) judge will stay with the case," Price said. "That means the jurors will be from Clay County (Indiana), the trial will be held in Clay County, and the judge will be Diana LaViolette from Putnam County. This is exactly what we wanted."

The trial is now anticipated to begin in September, her attorney, John Price (no relation) said.

Mrs. Price was removed as an instructor and lost 25% of her pay because she kept copies of a Focus on the Family magazine, *Teachers in Focus,* in her classroom, and allowed students to take them and read them.

Price was removed from her position after one student complained to school officials about a particular edition of the magazine, which contained an article concerning homosexual activism in schools.

The legal battle threatened to drain the savings of Mrs. Price and her husband, but after an article in the October 2002 *AFA Journal*, she received an outpouring of support from AFA members around the nation.

"I have received notes, cards, letters, pages from children's coloring books, pictures of families, etc.," Mrs. Price said. "All of this is because *[AFA Journal]* called and asked if I would 'mind if [they] included my home address at the end of the article.' Mind? The notes of encouragement have been such a blessing and they just keep coming. I am amazed at how the Lord is using His children to help me in ways that are clearly from Him."[372]

Mrs. Price was interviewed in January 2005 for the AFA's radio program, allowing even more people to learn about the case. This organization was perhaps the most consistently helpful of all the media in educating the public about DePauw's mistreatment of Janis Price.

Limbaugh, Black, et al

Numerous other organizations covered *Price v. DePauw*. Focus on the Family, the publisher of the "intolerable tract" that nearly cost Mrs. Price her job, made sure its members knew about the case. John Hagee covered the case in a televised sermon, and Fox News spent some time on this issue as well. David Limbaugh published a chronicle of Christophobic behavior in late 2003 entitled *Persecution*. He spent well over a page on the case, a significant amount of time to devote to one subject in this three hundred fifty page book.[373] Mr. Limbaugh mentioned the case again in the forward to Norman Geisler and Fran Turch's *I don't have enough faith to be an atheist*.[374] In 2004, Jim Nelson Black investigated the slide of the modern American college into mediocrity in *Freefall of the American University*. He highlighted Neal Abraham's infamous charge, "We cannot tolerate the intolerable!" in Chapter 10.[375] Despite Dr. Bottoms' best efforts, news of his university's misdeeds escaped the censors.

Financial Impact of Persecution

We will never know the full impact that the persecution of Janis Price had on the financial health of DePauw. Andrew Tangel's article in the November 19, 2002 issue of the DePauw hinted at the problems that the university was having with fundraising. Former $250,000 donor K.C. Mosier '66 renounced any further gifts because of the case. Lisa Hollander, the director of DePauw's Annual Fund noted that four alumni specifically had noted that they too wouldn't give the university further funding either.[376] Eloise Davis, the wife of former DePauw trustee, George Davis '36, wrote to express her family's disgust with the mistreatment of Janis Price.[377] Another Davis, a member of the Class of 1958, wrote to express his outrage as well.[378] A classmate and fraternity brother of Jim Poor, Walter Eugene Danneberg, renounced a $100,000 bequest to DePauw in response to the university's violation of Mrs. Price's rights.[379] These frustrated and angry alumni are just the tip of the iceberg. We will never know how many alumni simply wad up the Annual Fund's request forms and throw them in the trash, never telling anyone why they chose not to give.

Chapter 12

DePauw Appeals

The arrogance of some individuals and institutions knows no bounds. Despite the best efforts of John Neighbors to obfuscate the truth, a jury of five men and one woman saw through his smokescreen. DePauw would be forced to pay Janis Price the wages rightfully owed to her and restore to her the well-earned positions. For a full month, it appeared that justice would prevail over Christophobic ignorance. There were soon signs that all was not well. Judge LaViolette refused to make DePauw pay the court costs that Mrs. Price had accrued thanks to the machinations of its agents. [380] Thirty days after it was soundly defeated by a jury of ordinary Americans, DePauw University appealed this honorable decision.

The rule of law meant absolutely nothing to the agents of DePauw University. So consumed with false pride were these people that they could not fathom that anyone would dare oppose them in a court of law. After all, the most egregious claims against the institution had been struck down under rather dubious circumstances. Now, these same miscreants had to find a higher court, complete with activist judges, to "correct" a judgment rendered by mere citizens. They found such a body in the Indiana Court of Appeals.

Justice Denied

On December 14, 2004, the Indiana Court of Appeals ruled that the Clay County jury had been in error when they found judgment against DePauw. The ruling was thus overturned.[381] They did this without hearing one word of testimony from Mrs. Price's witnesses. They didn't get to see the manner in which DePauw treated its opponents in the courtroom. They ignored the reams of damning evidence that have been presented in these pages. They chose to take the liberal, activist route, and ignore the wisdom of a jury and the Constitution. Ken Owen, the media relations guru for DePauw, was ecstatic over this miscarriage of justice.

> The Indiana Court of Appeals affirms what we have maintained from the beginning: That DePauw scrupulously followed its employment policies practices every step of the way in this matter. [382]

Prior to coming to DePauw, Mr. Owen had had a reputation as being a fair minded television reporter for the Indianapolis CBS affiliate. Based on the evidence available in this case, the reversal by the Indiana Court of Appeals makes no sense. Much more was in play than meets the eye.

Conflicts of Interest

The erroneous ruling in favor of DePauw was written by Justice Terry A. Crone. At the time of ruling, he was serving in the Third District of the Indiana Court of Appeals, based out of South Bend. As a graduate of Notre Dame Law School, one would expect him have a distinguished legal career. Crone served as the president of the St. Joseph Bar Association, St. Joseph County Attorney and as judge of the St. Joseph Circuit Court. He has spent a great deal of time helping minority youth in his areas as well. What is most interesting about Justice Crone is the institution from which he received his undergraduate degree.

It is most fortunate for the university that Governor Frank Kernan, a Democrat from South Bend, appointed Crone to the bench in March 2004.[383] He graduated from DePauw University thirty years earlier after majoring in political science.[384] The 1971 DePauw yearbook shows Justice Crone and DePauw's lead counsel, John Neighbors, on facing pages.[385] While this does not necessarily prove collusion, it makes one wonder why Justice Crone did not recuse himself from this case. A jurist in his position should have done that at the very least, to guard against the appearance of impropriety. Justice Crone most certainly should not have written the opinion. That should have been left to his fellow Democratic administration appointed justices, the Fourth District's Patricia A. Riley or Nancy H. Vaidik of the Fifth District.[386]

Joseph Heller Award For Legal Logic

It is a given that the Indiana Court of Appeal's decision was a grave miscarriage of justice. The reasoning behind this ruling is rather muddled, but with some patience, it can be understood. Justice Crone noted that

> Indiana follows the doctrine of employment at will, under which employment may be terminated by either party at will, with or without reason. However, the at-will employment may be converted to a relationship in which the employer may terminate the employee only for good cause. In order to achieve the termination for good cause status, the employee must provide adequate independent consideration.[387]

It is clear that this is an insurmountable challenge. What does an employee need to do to provide "adequate independent consideration?" Is a second job required to force the employer to recognize his or her worth? Perhaps certification from the federal government would suffice. It is quite clear that a spotless thirteen year record is not enough to gain protected status. In reality, the deck is stacked against the employee, as he or she cannot reach this position as it is not clearly defined. Employment is at the whim of the employer, allowing Christians and other politically incorrect people to be dismissed without good cause.

Justice Crone then went on to attack the fact that DePauw failed to follow its own handbook. The evidence is quite clear that it did not follow the rules, so he was forced to fall back on the tortured logic of *Orr vs. Westminster Village North (1995)*. In Terry Crone's mind, DePauw's academic handbook was not binding because it was not specifically mentioned as a part of the contract.[388] This begs a very important question. If the handbook is not part of the contract, why does the university spend money to update this tome on a regular basis? The handbook was updated five times between 1977 and 2001. This required the formation of committees to study the issue and make changes to the document as needed. This seems like a lot of time, money, and energy to expend on something that isn't worth the paper upon which it is printed.

Judge Crone's most callous assault was left for last, regarding the issue that DePauw had violated its policies by engaging in religious discrimination against Janis Price. The justice's logic makes one dizzy trying to follow its ever tightening circles. By signing Neal Abraham's punishment letter of July 17, 2001, she had negated her ability to sue. The breeches of the handbook had occurred before that time, so she signed a new contract with those injustices already in the record. Following Justice Crone's reasoning, Mrs. Price should have refused to sign this "contract." By taking this action, she would have been saying that the religious discrimination had occurred and that it was unacceptable. This would have made her eligible to sue the university. However, she would have also voluntarily have terminated her employment, making her ineligible to sue. She would have found herself in a "Catch-22" situation. Perhaps Mrs. Price should have sued under the pseudonym Captain Yossarian.

The Orr Decision

Justice Crone based a significant portion of his opinion on a 1995 case involving employees of an Indianapolis retirement home. In this case, employees were terminated and attempted to cite their employee handbooks as a part of their employment contracts in their defense. This ruling further codified the idea of employment at will in Indiana. In its essence, *Orr vs. Westminster Village North (1995)* denied that handbooks were legally binding documents unless both parties agreed on that status from the onset of employment. Employees could not claim that their employer had violated the company handbook, as it was merely implied as part of the contract. The court did allow for a form of redress for employee grievances. They could file a suit against their employer to obtain letters explaining their termination. While that might be a nice memento of a former job, it doesn't provide a real recourse to employees who were wronged by their employers.[389]

The real issue here is that Janis Price was not necessarily an at will employee. She had signed a new letter of employment annually since she started working for DePauw in 1988. Each letter was essentially a one year contract of employment. Using *Orr* was a very poor idea, as she was not covered by the at will portion of the case.

> Historically, Indiana has recognized two forms of employment: 1) employment for a definite term; and 2) employment at will.... A contract for term employment is created when the parties agree that employment shall continue for a fixed or ascertainable period. If no definite or ascertainable period of employment is agreed upon, the employment is at will... and is presumptively terminable at any time, without liability, at the election of either party.[390]

As long as Mrs. Price continued to receive one year appointments, it should be clear that she was functioning as a term employee. As such, all of the harassment that she endured at the hands of Dr. Abraham, Dr. Lee, and Dr. Weisz should have been covered by anti-harassment laws. That would most certainly include Dr. Lee's harassment of Mrs. Price over my missing transcripts as well as her consistently error-filled personnel evaluations during the 2001-2002 school year.

Curious Timing

There are many odd coincidences that have arisen out of the Indiana Court of Appeals miscarriage of justice. First, they chose to make their ruling while John Price was on a much needed Christmas vacation. Professional courtesy would have had them issue the ruling while both he and Mr. Neighbors were in their offices. The second has to do with the manner in which the parties were informed of the decision. Mrs. Price found out about the decision when her husband called her about it from Greencastle Middle School, where he is the choir director. A co-worker had read the December 15, 2004 article in *The Banner Graphic* that day and informed him. According to the case docket, the decision was rendered on the previous day, with the nine page hard copy being mailed that same day. The mail does not leave the Greencastle post office until 9:00 am. In order to make it to *The Banner Graphic* in time to make the paper on the 15th, DePauw and the printer would have had to have received the decision late on the 14th or very early on the 15th. Even if the decision had been made at the very moment that the court convened on the 14th, it would have been difficult to get a hard copy to the newspaper office in enough time to compose and print an article about it. One reasonable conclusion that a person could reach was that DePauw was sent a fax or e-mail version of the decision on the 14th, while Mrs. Price had to wait for the U.S. Mail to deliver the blow. It is beyond reprehensible to give one party favoritism of this magnitude when rendering a legal decision.

Equally disturbing was what I found when I checked the DePauw University website on Sunday, December 26, 2004. I was curious to see what, if anything, was being said by the university about the Indiana Court of Appeals decision. The server directed me to a *DePauw Online* article about the appeal that looked very familiar. It was the same story that had been printed in *The Banner Graphic* on December 15. Most interestingly, the date of this issue of the online version of *The DePauw* was December 7, 2004, a full week before the decision was allegedly made.[391] Was this an honest error on the part of DePauw's webmaster, or did the university have knowledge of the ruling a full week before it was supposedly issued? This article did not appear in hard copy in *The DePauw* once classes began in February. As of April 1, 2005, the publication date on this story had not been changed. Perhaps they didn't think anyone would notice.

Another Appeal

It is quite obvious to the objective observer that Mrs. Price was severely wronged by DePauw University. Had she so chosen, she could have cited far more grievances than she did. Neither she nor John Price decided to take this travesty lying down.

> As you know, we have been reversed in the Court of Appeals of Indiana. I think their reasoning is circular and frankly, doesn't make a lot of sense, but at this point in time we have to consider what our next step is. The next legal step would be to petition the Indiana Supreme Court for review of the case.[392]

They decided to pursue the case, but one obstacle remained in the way. DePauw has bottomless pockets, allowing it to clog the legal system with nonsense for an indefinite period. Janis Price wasn't quite as fortunate. She had been surviving on three quarters of her salary, while her husband Geoff labored as a public school teacher. That amounts to a comfortable living under ordinary circumstances, but having to sue an employer for violating one's rights is no ordinary situation. They needed help, so John Price appealed to the Alliance Defense Fund for financial assistance.

> As you can see from the attached, the Indiana Court of Appeals has reversed the decision in our favor. There are two (2) troubling aspects of this decision. The first is that the Opinion ignores the difference between standard contract law and employment contract law. Under this holding, an employee who has been mistreated must terminate the relationship before seeking redress of grievances. Secondly, the Court of Appeals affirmed the trial court's ruling that DePauw University's religious discrimination policy, as found in the handbook, was meaningless. Because 36 other states apply handbooks in employment relationships, we think that there is a fair

chance that the Indiana Supreme Court could reverse the opinion.

My purpooc in writing, besides sharing the decision, is to make an expeditious request for financial assistance on the appeal. Under Indiana Trial Rules, we must prepare a Petition for Transfer to the Indian Supreme Court and file it on or before January 15, 2005. Though a petition to transfer under normal circumstances would be in the four to five thousand dollars ($4-5000.00) range, we are willing to prepare and file it for one thousand dollars ($1,000.00). If the ADF could assist us in this regard, it would be greatly appreciated. [393]

The Alliance Defense Fund wisely granted the request. It was the sworn duty of the Indiana Supreme Court to hear cases like this, but the court system in the state has shown itself to be motivated more by activist furor than by Constitutional duty.

Mrs. Price Goes to Law School

Janis Price was invited to speak as part of a panel at a March 29, 2005 conference on sexuality at the Indiana University School of Law in Indianapolis. It was a diverse group, with the head of the Indiana Civil Liberties Union, Ken Falk, U.S. Representative John Hostettler (R., 8th District, IN), Jesus Metropolitan Community Church minister Jeff Miner, and Face-to-Face Ministries director Brad Grammer participating as well.[394] Mrs. Price focused on her interaction with Dr. Eric Edberg.

Eric Edberg is well-known as a gay activist on DePauw's campus. After I filed the lawsuit, I saw Dr. Edberg on campus and as always, spoke to him. He told me that he hated what the university was trying to do to me and that if my case ever went to court that he would be willing to testify in my behalf.... It is of special note that Dr. Edberg was pressured by the DePauw lawyer to not testify and again was pressured to recant his testimony afterwards. He refused to be part of it.[395]

After the session ended, Jeff Miner, the pastor of the homosexual-supporting Jesus Metropolitan Community Church in Indianapolis, and Ken Falk of the ICLU told Mrs. Price that she had been terribly wronged by DePauw University. If one of the ACLU's surrogates realized that Janis Price had been persecuted for her faith, the university's actions must have been even more egregious than previously believed.

Supreme Injustice

On March 31, 2005, the Indiana State Supreme Court declared that it had chosen not to hear Janis Price's appeal.[396] With the stroke of a pen, yet another band of activist judges had denied the justice granted by a panel of six wise American citizens. Ken Owen was insufferably arrogant in his response to the ruling. "Indiana's highest court has effectively put her meritless claims to rest for good, which we applaud."[397] As has been shown in these pages, Mrs. Price's claims are just the tip of the iceberg at DePauw. It should come as no surprise that she was denied justice. Justice Theodore R. Boehm, appointed to the Indiana Supreme Court by Democratic governor Evan Bayh, had been employed by Baker and Daniels, which is the same firm retained by DePauw to handle this case.[398] It is very easy to get the verdict that you want if you have a former employee as the judge on one level, an alumnus and contemporary of your lead attorney on the next, and a former partner in the same firm as the afore mentioned lawyer at the top level. Janis Price herself summed up this turn of events masterfully. "I've learned through this process that justice and legality are not the same thing."[399]

The Irony is Delicious

DePauw University possesses many characteristics, the most intriguing of which would have to be a wonderfully infuriating sense of irony. On April 7, 2005, the Indiana Court of Appeals came to campus to hold a hearing. The intent was to educate the public as the workings of the judicial system. This was done at the behest of political science professor Bruce Stinebrickner. The three judge panel consisted of Justices Margaret G. Robb, and two judges with whom the DePauw community were familiar, Terry Crone and Patricia Riley.[400] What better way to reward a ruling in the university's favor than to invite two of the three justices to hold court on campus? This was either a very ironic twist of fate, or a calculated insult to Janis Price and her supporters. I for one found the brazenness of this to be quite offensive.

The Consequences of Judicial Activism

Janis Price's adventure through the Indiana legal system serves as painful evidence of the judicial oligarchy that has imposed itself upon the nation. Indiana is a state that prides itself on its conservative, Constitutional outlook. Despite that, our judiciary often resembles the 9th Circuit Court of Appeals or the Massachusetts Supreme Court. Hoosiers deserve better. Our juries come to the correct conclusions, thanks to old-fashioned common sense. This was quite evident in Mrs. Price's case. DePauw tried to distort the truth about the case in the media. Its lawyers twisted and bent the case until it became unrecognizable. A former employee served as the judge, gutting as much of the case as she safely could do. Despite this, a jury of six ordinary citizens ruled for Mrs. Price. Instead of conceding defeat, DePauw arrogantly appealed the case to places where no witnesses would take the stand. These courts issued rulings riddled with circular reasoning that would make a first year law student blush. Only under these circumstances could they get the ruling they desired. In the process, they trampled their own regulations, as well as the time honored principles of the United States Constitution. What price, victory? A legal landscape littered with human wreckage is far too great a price to pay to allow an arrogant institution to abuse its employees.

Chapter 13

Restoration

As of this writing, Janis Price had lost her final appeal within Indiana's legal system. The university's agents were gloating because it believed that this lawsuit could no longer harm them. On June 14, 2005, Janis Price was informed that the 2005-2006 school year would be her last at DePauw.

> In light of the reorganization of the Education Studies Department to serve new undergraduate and graduate programs and cirricula, this will be the last year of this position. While they may be positions open in the future for which you might apply, you should not expect your employment to continue beyond the 2005-2006 fiscal year.[401]

It seems rather suspicious to discontinue this position, given its importance to the Education Department's mission. DePauw University is using Janis Price as an example to other conservative Christians who refuse to worship at the altar of political correctness. The real question now is why should anyone, other than Mrs. Price and her immediate family, care what happened to her? Some might conclude that it was a sad case of Christophobia and abuse of power, but that the events of March 2001 really have no bearing on their lives.

The United States of America was founded by Christians on the principle that something greater than ourselves, the rule of law, governed society. In the Founding Fathers' eyes, no one was above the law. All Americans, from the humblest farmer to the president, had a code by which to live. The law was rooted in the Biblical principles passed down to us through the centuries. Disobeying the law was an act of defiance to God. Today, this concept has been nearly obliterated. Mrs. Price was punished by her employer for the simple act of refusing to check her Christian faith at the classroom door. If this travesty is permitted regarding Christians, rest assured that other groups will soon follow. In Nazi Germany, Christian churches were among the first institutions to be seized by the state. *The Holy Bible* and the Cross were replaced by *Mein Kampf* and the swastika.[402] If we continue to allow universities to persecute Christians, similar mischief will surely follow.

Christian people must take action now to turn the tide at the academy. It would certainly be cause for concern if Mrs. Price's case was unique to DePauw University. David Limbaugh documented the pervasive war being waged against Christians throughout American society in *Persecution.* Jim Nelson Black spent over three hundred pages in *Freefall of the American University* recounting numerous cases similar to Mrs. Price's at universities from coast to coast. These are just the tip of the iceberg. We will never know the true scope of the problem, as the majority of the victims of Christophobia have been unwilling to make their voices heard. The time has come to take back the academy!

Be Bold

Despite the best efforts of the mainstream media to say otherwise, Christians represent the mainstream of America. We have tremendous strength because of our vast numbers. This was made evident by the outcome of the 2004 election. We need to reassert ourselves in society in general and at the academy in particular. If a Christian student is harassed by peers, instructors, or administrators, we must speak out. The same is true if the victim is a professor or staff member. At many universities, Christians are afraid to mention their faith in the classroom. They fear the response by the politically correct elites. Homosexuals represent roughly 1.7% of the general population.[403] At a school the size of DePauw University, that amounts to less than fifty students. Even at a large state school of 40,000, this group would number less than seven hundred. By remaining silent, we have allowed a tiny, but vocal minority to control the agenda at the academy. Christians have the same right to speak their minds as atheists, Muslims, liberals, or any other group. We have abdicated our rightful place in society. Now is the time to reclaim that position. If our faith in Christ as the Redeemer of all mankind is at all real to us, we must not shrink from sharing it, be it at the library, in the classroom, or the dorm room. We owe it to our fellow citizens of this fallen world.

Close Those Checkbooks

The next step in reclaiming the academy lies in the hands of the alumni. Every contributor to his or her alma mater must make the effort to learn the true state of affairs at the university. Alumni publications only tell part of the story. Most members of DePauw's Class of 1935 would be shocked and appalled at the current condition of the university. The same would be true of their contemporaries at other colleges. A subscription to the campus newspaper would help these alumni make educated decisions about donating to their alma mater. Student writers often present the seamy side of the campus in their quest for "diversity" or "tolerance." In most cases, the university that alumni remember from decades past has been replaced by something that would have been too vile to imagine during their college days. It would be nice if the problem was localized to DePauw University, but almost every college and university in America has changed for the worse in the past half century. Alumni can make an impact by withholding donations from universities that promote programs that violate decent morals. Janis Price's treatment has already cost DePauw University several sizable donations. Some of these gentlemen were kind enough to explain their position when renouncing their gifts. We will never know how much this debacle has cost the university. Undoubtedly, the same scene has played out at other universities when their alumni got wind of the insanity running rampant on their campuses. It doesn't take much imagination to see what would happen if a few dozen big donors started withholding money from their schools. These universities would have no option but to listen to their alumni's concerns and correct their aberrant behavior.

Demand Change

The board of trustees is the most powerful organization at any college or university. They choose the president, who then chooses the rest of the administration. These administrators are responsible for hiring and managing the faculty. It is vital that a university president serve the best interests of his institution, not the whims of political correctness. Alumni who serve on these boards should do so out of love for their alma mater. If administrators engage in actions that undermine the well-being of the institution, the trustees are duty bound to correct these problems. They must listen carefully to the concerns raised by fellow alumni, even if they are demanding the removal of a corrupt administrator. The real power at the academy, as with the nation, lies with the people. A board of trustees that doesn't respond to the will of the people must be voted out of office immediately.

Better Professors Make Better Schools

Perhaps the biggest problem faced by the academy is the faculty's pronounced tilt to the Left. Finding a conservative on a college campus can be frustrating. Liberals, like DePauw's own political science professor Brent O'Bannon, often claim that conservatives simply aren't as intelligent as their liberal contemporaries. Such claims are demonstrably false. These are people who will tell you with a straight face that Karl Marx and Vladimir Lenin were economic geniuses while ignoring the chaos they caused in the former Soviet Union. Some of these people actually believe that humans evolved from primordial slime, without explaining how such complex beings arrived by chance. In late 2004 and early 2005, hate-inspired young leftists assaulted conservative speakers Ann Coulter, Bill Kristol, Pat Buchannan, and David Horowitz with pies during their lectures on college campuses.[404]   Most people outgrow such nonsense in preschool. Clearly, the Left doesn't have anything remotely resembling a monopoly on intelligence. The real reasons for the lack of conservative representation at the academy is far simpler.

> Liberals have maintained a lock on academia for one reason. They are human beings. As such, they like people who hold similar views. Consider the organizations to which you belong. The vast majority of the group typically agree on most items. When it comes time to hire a new faculty member, the natural inclination would be to hire another liberal.[405]

No matter how hard we try, human nature usually wins.

I would add one significant change to this statement. I wrote that prior to seriously starting work on my master's degree. I had forgotten how it felt to be the only conservative in the room. Well meaning, though very liberal, professors would say things that I knew not to be true. For the first time, I realized what it must be like to be the only conservative at a faculty meeting. Many of us are not willing to take the pressure of that kind of environment for the five to seven years that it takes to obtain a post graduate degree. Four years is more than enough for most conservatives, who then go on to lucrative careers outside academia. It is easy to see what would happen if more conservatives were willing to take eleven years of abuse. They would have a chance to tilt the scales back toward a balance at the university. The change would filter upward. With a larger pool of very qualified applicants vying for jobs, there would be a greater chance of getting conservatives as administrators. This change might take decades to complete, but I can see a day where students could have an equal opportunity to hear conservative and liberal views at the academy. The level of Christophobia would drop precipitously, as there would be conservative administrators to keep their liberal peers in check. All that is needed is a core of conservative intellectuals who are willing to tolerate years of abuse to obtain the Ph.D.s. Only then can we begin to undo the damage caused by decades of one party rule at the academy.

Legislative Remedies

In one of his many bombastic speeches, DePauw attorney John Neighbors claimed that the United States Constitution does not apply to the university.[406] On the surface, this claim is absurd. The Supremacy Clause is quite clear.

> This Constitution, and the laws of the United States which shall be made in pursuance thereof, and all treaties made, or which shall be made, under the authority of the United States, shall be the supreme law of the land: and the judges, in every State, shall be bound thereby, any thing in the Constitution or laws of any State to the contrary notwithstanding.[407]

Mr. Neighbors is correct in that private institutions in Indiana and other states have been allowed to act as if the United States Constitution doesn't apply. Following this line of reasoning, the Indiana Constitution would not apply either. Mrs. Price was forced to use the DePauw University Employee Handbook as her last line of defense. The Indiana Court of Appeals used the flawed logic of *Orr v. Westminster Village North (1995)* to rule that the handbook provided no protection. As a result, there is no rule of law at DePauw University or any other private school in Indiana. Employees are left to the mercy of the administration. Eight centuries of legal precedent must be ignored to arrive at this conclusion.

There is hope. Bad judicial rulings make terrible law. Indiana and other states with similar legal conditions must offer protection for employees. All employees at a university must be held to the same standard. If the institution is unwilling to acknowledge the supremacy of the Constitution, it should at least be required by law to follow its own handbook. This does not mean that the government should control the content of these manuals. That would eventually lead to greater mischief. It is in the best interest of the both the employer and the employee that they each understand expectations before employment begins. Making handbooks a legally binding part of a contract would protect both sides from abuse. Now is the time to demand that the state legislatures of Indiana and other afflicted states take action to undo the injustices of *Orr* and similar decisions.

Former radical David Horowitz has become a vocal champion of restoring balance to the academy. His "Academic Bill of Rights" deserves to be adopted by every college and university in the nation. In it, he lays out a handful of simple principles that would drastically improve the condition of our institutions of higher learning. Competence should be the determining factor with all faculty employment issues, not political or religious views. Students would be evaluated on similar criteria. Speakers of all political stripes would be given equal access to the academy. Civil exchange between groups with differing opinions must be promoted.[408] It seems like so little to ask from people who believe in tolerance and diversity. Administrators all across the nation vigorously oppose this common sense plan. It is our duty to promote it with even greater zeal.

Open Those Checkbooks

Janis Price would not have been able to press forward with her case against DePauw without financial assistance from hundreds of donors. The American Family Association was instrumental in directing its members' donations to Mrs. Price. Focus on the Family contributed to her legal fund corporately. The Alliance Defense Fund was very generous to Mrs. Price. These organizations do a lot of good in this country, and they are worthy of our financial support. Our donations will insure that these worthy organizations will be able to fight for the rights of other persecuted Christians.

Throw the Bums Out!

The final change that needs to occur to save the academy lies in the courts. From the Supreme Court on down, activist judges have sought to impose their distorted values upon the rest of us. Some in Congress, such as Senator Chuck Shumer (D. NY), have stated openly that Christians must be disqualified from serving as judges because of their "deeply held conservative religious views." It should come as no surprise that radicals oppose Christian judges.[409] Abortion, euthanasia, atheism in the classroom, and homosexual marriage are but a few of the issues that would never have seen the light of day within the democratic process. Every election day, citizens go to the polls to vote on issues dear to them. Usually, common sense prevails. Inevitably, a liberal judge has already declared this new law unconstitutional before the ink is dry. We are living in an oligarchy controlled by a tiny minority of activist jurists. Most people believe that judges are the final authority in matters of law and policy. The Founding Fathers had no intention of an un-elected cabal running the republic. The courts, with the exception of the Supreme Court, are a creation of the people's representatives.[410] All courts were created to serve the citizenry, not to enslave them. We have the final say in the scope of their power. "The judges, both of the Supreme and inferior courts, shall hold their offices during good behaviour..."[411] Elected judges that do not perform Constitutionally must be voted out of office at the earliest opportunity. Appointed judges are not invulnerable. The legislature can impeach and remove them if they fail to do their duty. Consider the case of Alabama Chief Justice Roy Moore. Judge Moore refused to obey an unconstitutional order handed down by an un-elected federal judge. He was removed from office by his peers in Alabama, despite being elected by the people of the state. It seems very reasonable that if an elected judge who followed the Constitution and the Bible can be removed from office, then liberal activists who trample the Constitution should meet a similar fate. This can only happen if the people demand that their representatives reign in an abusive and out of control judiciary. It is unlikely that every liberal activist would have to be removed. If a few of them lost their jobs for re-writing the Constitution, their peers might think twice before ruling against common sense and morality.

We are in Control!

It is easy to become discouraged. Mrs. Price won her case when tried in front of a jury, only to have it overturned by the ruling of a DePauw alumnus serving as judge. Neal Abraham, Esther Lee, Eva Weiss, and Angela Morris appear to have gotten away with their

Christophobic antics. Other Christians might take this as a sign to cower and remain silent, lest a similar fate befall them. That is exactly what I suspect that DePauw thinks will happen. However, "Pride goeth before destruction, and a haughty spirit before a fall."[412]

This case is not over by a long shot. Mrs. Price lost her appeal to the Indiana Supreme Court, but even now, we must take heart. DePauw's misdeeds have focused a national spotlight on the university. While the case has been ignored by the partisan media, the new media has taken the story and made sure that it received a fair hearing. There is no telling what the long term effects will be for the university. Alumni must make their displeasure known in the ways that they see fit. DePauw's Christian community should become emboldened. When the case was heard by a jury, DePauw lost, even with a former employee as the judge. We have seen that the unsubstantiated claims of a disgruntled student can do tremendous damage. Perhaps conservative students should make greater use of the grievance system when they are truly harmed by their professors. If administrators attempt something similar with other faculty in the future, perhaps Christians will rise to their defense more readily than they did in Janis Price's case. In Indiana, this situation should serve as an impetus to demand legislative reforms that would protect the rights of Christians and conservatives from overzealous administrators and Constitutionally-ignorant judges. On a national level, this case has focused attention on the university system. Perhaps ill-treated Christians at other colleges will not be cowed so easily and take the offenders to court. A lot of good can come from this situation. It can only happen if we, as Christians, patriots, and citizens demand change. It is my earnest hope that we take Janis Price's persecution and use it as an alarm to awaking the sleeping American giant.

"Operation Tidal Wave"

Some who read this will question why I spent two years of my life researching and writing an indictment of my alma mater. It is always a difficult task to critically examine one's heritage and then decide to take action to correct the problems found there. I saw many problems as an undergraduate, but I chose not to speak up. I was afraid of losing friends and ruining my grade point average. I let injustice happen without lifting a finger to stop it. I was a gutless coward. There comes a point in every man's life when he must decide to take a stand. In a previous generation, the place of that stand might have been in the skies over Ploesti, Romania, in August 1943. The refineries there had to be destroyed in order to deny the Third Reich its precious fuel supply. Five hundred forty airmen were lost during Operation Tidal Wave, but Germany staggered under the blow. For me, the first nudges toward action happened thanks to Esther Lee's pestering about my missing transcript. President Bottoms' August 2002 letter to the alumni sealed the deal. Like those brave bomber crews, I knew that failure was not an option. I'm not a lawyer, so I couldn't help correct the injustice in that arena. However, I am a writer. My first article in the local paper stirred a lot of interest. Many people praised my bravery in confronting DePauw, while a few questioned my intentions. I realized that one article couldn't correct the injustice meted out by DePauw. The press coverage to date has not fully explained the history behind DePauw's Christophobic behavior and showed how this affected their handling of a simple personnel matter. Only a carefully researched book could do that. I realized that it was not only my desire, but my duty to write an expose' on the Janis Price incident. This is my Ploesti.

I hope that real change occurs at DePauw and other universities because of my efforts. That change must begin in the hearts and minds of those misguided souls that persecute Christians like Mrs. Price on their campuses. Several years ago, I had the opportunity to speak with President Bottoms on a fairly regular basis. I found him to be a hard working and likable fellow who did what he thought was best for DePauw. I don't know Dr. Abraham, but I suspect that he too has a seed of decency that needs a chance to bloom. With that in mind, I have a great deal of hope that these people will come to see that their actions have not been in the best interest of my alma mater and make the necessary corrections.

As an undergraduate, I listened for hours as alumni told of DePauw's golden age in the 1930s. Even then at that young age, I knew that my university was a shadow of its former self. Most of those wonderful fellows have passed away now. In some ways, I'm glad that Gordy, Hank, and Harry didn't live to see their alma mater stoop to promoting anti-American rallies, condom distribution, co-ed dorm floors, and an annual "Drag Ball." Perhaps someday, those golden days of decades past will return. We can't sit idly by and hope that the university finds its way again. Alumni must raise their voices and demand restoration to DePauw founding principles. It is my prayer that this happens in my lifetime. Perhaps on some distant August afternoon, my son or daughter will be able to stroll across a campus where civilization's greatest triumphs are on display instead of society's basest elements. On that day, I will proudly don my tattered DePauw alumni cap and join them on a tour of my alma mater.

Appendix

Excerpts from the DePauw University Academic Handbook (2003 edition)

(no significant changes were made in these
sections from 2000 to 2003)
FACULTY PERSONNEL POLICIES PREFACE
1977
The material on faculty personnel policies consists of the following:

The "Standards and Guidelines for Decisions on Faculty Status",
passed by the Faculty November 18, 1974 (for the text, see the
minutes of October 14, 1974, pages 9 through 13).

The "Faculty Review Procedure," passed by the Faculty December
13, 1976. It was originally called a "Grievance Procedure," but the
name was changed to "Review Procedure" at the faculty meeting
May 16, 1977. This is now Section VII, pages 40 through 48.

Information on appointments and tenure in the DePauw "Handbook
for Faculty," 1971 edition, pages 25 to 27.

The documents were combined and revised by an ad hoc committee consisting of Professors William Cavanaugh, Underwood Dudley, John Morrill, Fred Silander, Howard Youse, Dean Robert Farber and President Richard Rosser. The Faculty passed the documents,. with minor amendments, on April 18, 1977, and the Board of Trustees accepted them as official policy on April 22. At the May 13, 1977 faculty meeting, some changes. suggested 'by the Board of Trustees were approved.

In a memorandum to the faculty on April
11, 1977, President Rosser said:

"In an attempt to develop policies which reflect a consensus between faculty and administration, we have made certain minor changes and clarifications of previous terminology. We should note that the grievance procedure assumes that the President and Dean are members of the Faculty Committee, and participate in all faculty personnel matters with the elected Faculty Committee on Faculty. In reference to the difficult problem of confidentiality of records, we have tried to strike a balance between the need for complete information and fairness to the individual."

Personnel Policies

I.   Appointment

A. Types of Appointment
1. Tenure positions carry academic rank and may be or are held without limit of time, subject to specified conditions. They may support either a full or partial load of teaching.
2. Term positions carry academic or nominal rank and are held for a specified period of time (e.g., two years). Ordinarily, they support a full load of teaching, advising, and committee responsibilities. They may be renewable. Some term appointments (directors of competence centers and librarians) support instructional and administrative responsibilities. These positions are made for fixed periods of time, renewable at the end of each period.
3. Part-time positions carry academic rank and are held for a particular semester. Ordinarily, they support one or two courses during that semester.
4. Administrative staff positions carry nominal rank and are held for a specified period of time. Ordinarily, they support administrative responsibilities but not a teaching load.

B. Recruitment
1. Tenure and term positions. Schools or departments, through their personnel and search committees, are the primary agencies in recruitment. They recommend job descriptions, recruit, and make the recommendations to hire, according to the goals of the University and their respective missions. The Vice President for Academic Affairs appoints search committees for term positions with administrative responsibilities.
2. A subcommittee of the Committee on Faculty shall participate in the interviews, make sure candidates receive clear and complete information regarding the policies and procedures (university, school or

department) under which they will work and by which they will be judged, and advise the Committee on Faculty and the Vice President for Academic Affairs regarding the school or department recommendation to hire.

C. Notice of Terms

Financial contracts are for one fiscal year only. In addition to this contract, a written statement of the precise terms of appointment shall be given to the appointee before the appointment is consummated.

D. Time Limits and Renewal
1. In the final year of the probationary period, the faculty member in a tenurable position must be either granted tenure or given a one-year terminal contract.
2. The conditions of possible renewal of term appointments shall be specified at the time of initial appointment. Faculty members with academic or nominal rank may serve in term appointments no more than six years, unless their administrative duties make them ineligible for tenure.

E. Qualifications for Rank and Promotion
Appointments shall carry rank appropriate to the degree and experience of the appointee.
Faculty members in tenure and term appointments shall be eligible for consideration for promotion according to the following schedule.
For promotion of persons with term appointments with administrative responsibilities and of administrative staff and part-time faculty, the time sequence may differ from this schedule owing to differences in continuity and extent of service and in patterns of career development. Consideration shall be conducted in a manner similar to that for faculty in tenure and term appointment, except that bodies or persons other than the committee on faculty shall evaluate the administrative performance of the faculty member.
1. Normally an _instructor_ must have the M. A., M. S., or equivalent degree. Promotion will follow immediately

upon completion of requirements of the doctorate or the appropriate terminal degree for the field or discipline.

2. Normally, an <u>assistant</u> <u>professor</u> must have the Ph.D. or equivalent degree. (Exceptions may be made for temporary appointments and when there are compensating factors.) He or she must have completed five years in rank at DePauw to be considered for promotion (ten years, if without the terminal degree). Exceptional performance may be considered for shortening the time in rank. In such cases, prior service elsewhere may also be considered as a factor in early promotion. If the assistant professor has completed five years in rank at DePauw at the time of the tenure decision (i.e., whose rank as Assistant Professor was established before December 31 of the first year of service), he or she shall be either granted tenure and promoted to the rank of associate professor or given a one-year terminal contract. In unusual circumstances, tenure may be granted without promotion, but the specific reasons for doing so must be made clear to all parties.

3. Normally, an <u>associate</u> <u>professor</u> must have the Ph.D. or equivalent degree. (Exceptions may be made when there are compensating factors.) When a faculty member is promoted to the rank of associate professor, he or she is entitled to tenure at that rank. He or she must have completed seven years in rank at DePauw to be considered for promotion to full professor (ten years if without the terminal degree). Exceptional performance may be considered for shortening the time in rank.

4. Normally, a <u>professor</u> must have the Ph.D. or equivalent degree. (Exceptions may be made when there are compensating factors.) There is no promotion beyond the rank of professor, but appointment at senior professor rank may follow upon retirement accompanied by continued teaching responsibilities.

F. Probationary Period and Tenure

Faculty appointed to tenurable positions shall serve a specified probationary period before being considered for tenure.

1. A faculty member in a tenurable position who is appointed for a seventh year is entitled to tenure, unless the contract specifies the appointment as terminal. However, the total probationary time for a person appointed initially as associate professor shall normally be no longer than three years. Initial appointment at the rank of professor may carry tenure, but normally it involves a probationary period of no longer than three years.

2. Prior service may be considered for shortening the probationary period (normally, six years). If so, the amount of credit shall be expressed in the initial statement of conditions.

3. If faculty members in term appointments are appointed to tenurable positions, the years spent in the term appointment shall count in the probationary period. At this time, a faculty member may negotiate for tenure and promotion credits based on previous service at other institutions.

G. Workload

The normal teaching workload of a full time member of the DePauw faculty shall be equivalent to twelve contact hours per week and the whole range of attendant duties involved in teaching (preparation, evaluation, and reflection) necessary to support these twelve hours. Departments are responsible for determining, with the approval of the Vice President for Academic Affairs, what counts as a normal teaching load under this general guideline.

II. Periodic Evaluation

A. Annual Consultation

For purposes of departmental self-study, the school dean or department chair shall confer annually with individual members of the school or department about their role in, and expectations for, the school's or department's mission in the University. With tenurable faculty members between interim review and tenure decision, this consultation provides opportunity to review progress toward tenure. (See statement on department chairs.)

B. Peer Observation

Peer observations of faculty members in tenurable positions

In the first year, peer observations are voluntary. If done, observations shall be initiated and arranged by the probationary faculty member. After visiting a class or classes, the observing faculty member should arrange a meeting with the first-year faculty member to provide feedback. Any written materials provided to the first-year faculty member based on these class observations shall be under the sole control of the first-year faculty member. Peer observations are required after the first year of the probationary period. Required course observations shall be conducted by tenured or tenurable faculty members who are appointed by the department chair in consultation with the DPC. Observers shall be from the probationary faculty member's department; in exceptional cases, as deemed appropriate by the chair, faculty members from outside the department may be chosen for this purpose. No single faculty member shall do a majority of the observations. At least half of the observations shall be done by tenured faculty. The timing of classroom observations shall be arranged by the department chair in consultation with the faculty member being observed. The courses observed should reflect the range and type of courses* normally taught by the observed faculty member . Each observation should cover an entire session of the class. Following the observation of each course, the observing faculty member shall provide both written and oral feedback in a timely fashion to the observed faculty member. The observer will also provide a copy of the written feedback to the chair and the Vice President for Academic Affairs to be placed in the observed faculty member's personnel file and in the decision file for interim and tenure reviews.

(a) In the second year, two courses shall be observed in each semester.

(b) In the third, fourth, and fifth years of the probationary period, a total of four courses (at least one course each year) taught by the probationary faculty member shall be observed.

(c) Probationary faculty can always request additional observations. Departments wishing to conduct more classroom observations than the required number shall do so only with the written consent of the probationary faculty member.

If the probationary period is three years or fewer, peer observations will be required in the first year and will follow the process outlined in 2(a).

* In the sciences, labs may count for one of the course observations

B. Evaluation of Faculty in Tenurable Positions
1. Following the end of each calendar year (except the interim and tenure review years) of the probationary period, the faculty member shall submit in writing to the Dean of the school or department chair a reasonably detailed evaluation of his or her performance of that year relative to the stated criteria for the award of tenure. A written response to the faculty member shall be made by the dean or chair following the consultation and written report.
2. At the end of each semester of the probationary period, faculty members shall arrange to have written student comments taken in each course, according to procedures approved by the committee on faculty and the administration. These evaluations will be kept with the personnel file used by the Committee on Faculty and the Vice President for Academic Affairs. Copies will be sent to the faculty member, the chair of the department, and the Vice President for Academic Affairs.
3. Requests for special leaves; released time for research, service, and innovative teaching programs; and grants for research projects, equipment, and continuing education are reviewed by designated faculty committees and approved by appropriate university officers if they lead toward professional development of the faculty member and further the goals of the University.

4. Interim evaluation. At the mid-point of the probationary period, an interim evaluation shall be made according to the following schedule.

   <u>Probationary Period</u> <u>Interim Review</u>

   6 years 3rd year

   5 years 3rd year

   4 years 2nd year

   3 years At the faculty member's option unless requested by the chair, the committee on faculty, or the Vice President for Academic Affairs

5. Tenure evaluation. In the final year of the probationary period, the tenure evaluation and decision are made, according to stated procedures and criteria.

C. Evaluation of Tenured Faculty

1. (In mandating merit awards, the Board of Trustees at its 1994 October meeting authorized the administration to change or supersede this paragraph. For current administration policy on evaluation see the special notice distributed by the Vice President for Academic Affairs.) Every third semester, student comments from each currently taught course of the tenured faculty member shall be taken according to procedures approved by the committee on faculty and the administration. These comments shall be returned to the faculty member for his or her own personal development and improvement.

2. Promotion evaluations (for associate professor and professor ranks) shall be carried out for candidates nominated for promotion to associate and full professor, using the stated guidelines, procedures, and criteria for promotion. (See below.)

3. Requests for sabbatical and special leaves; released time for research, service, and innovative teaching programs; and grants for research projects, equipment, and continuing education are reviewed by designated faculty committees and approved by appropriate university officers if they lead to toward professional development of the faculty member and further the goals of the University.

D. Evaluation of Faculty Members in Term Appointments

Such faculty shall be evaluated according to similar requirements for periodic evaluation as faculty members in tenurable positions. Those having completed two years of service and being considered for reappointment to another term shall be evaluated in a manner similar to the interim review of faculty members in tenurable positions. (See above II.A.4.)

Those term positions that combine both instructional and administrative responsibilities shall be evaluated as follows:

1. In their capacity as instructors or classroom teachers, these faculty shall be evaluated in a manner similar to the interim review of faculty members in tenurable positions.
2. In their administrative capacities, these faculty shall be evaluated by their superiors in accordance with their job descriptions.

E. Evaluation of Librarians Serving in Renewable Term Faculty Positions.

Beginning in the third year of service (and then in the seventh year, twelfth year, and every five years thereafter), the Vice President for Academic Affairs appoints a review committee consisting of the library director, all full-time professional librarians (excluding the candidate under review, and those in their first year of service), and two faculty from outside the library. The librarian develops a file for review in the same way as do other faculty members. The committee submits a report and recommendation to the President through the Committee on Faculty and the Vice President for Academic Affairs. The library director and assistant director are reviewed in this manner to evaluate their work as librarians; the Vice President for Academic Affairs separately reviews their administrative performance.

F. Evaluation of Faculty Members in Full-Time Temporary Appointments

Such faculty shall be evaluated according to requirements for periodic evaluation applicable to faculty members in tenurable positions. Those having been reappointed for a second year shall prepare for an interim evaluation, to take place in their third year.

III.   Guidelines for Decisions on Faculty Status
(Article written and approved by the faculty)

A. Decisions affecting faculty status, such as the granting of tenure and promotions in rank, shall both serve the programs and purposes of the University and the particular missions of the various departments within it.

B. Criteria and expectations for achievement, particularly in regard to tenure, shall be regarded as long-term standards, and changes may be made only after full discussion, agreement among all parties, and ample time for adjustments.

C. Candidates shall be promptly informed of the results of decisions and evaluations and, where appropriate, given clear specification of and adequate time for improvement in performance.

D. Personnel decisions shall avoid special interest (e.g., family) and participation at more than one level of decision making (e.g., both department and Committee on Faculty).

E. The reliability and credibility of those submitting information shall be tested or capable of being tested in a procedure which preserves the maximum possible openness of evidence consistent with the qualified privilege of confidentiality legally protecting those participating in personnel processes. Specifically, persons (employed by the University) giving and receiving information in personnel interviews shall be deemed to operate in the scope of their employment, thus enjoying the qualified privilege.
   1. All documents used in personnel decisions must be signed and placed in the decision file open to inspection by the candidate.
   2. Persons submitting information in committee interviews may have their names withheld from the record placed

in the decision file (but not from committee minutes) if they so request. The committee shall test such information and place what is credible and the results of corresponding investigations in the decision file.

3. After the final decision has been rendered, the candidate shall be informed of the results of any investigations not included in the decision file and permitted to place such results in the personnel file.

F. All decisions shall be based entirely and exclusively upon the material in the candidate's decision file with respect to the criteria stated in the <u>Academic Handbook</u> and only those additional criteria that have been clearly and publicly stated at the time of initial appointment or established later by mutual consent.

G. The candidate shall have opportunity to respond in person and in writing to all testimony and evidence <u>prior</u> to the recommendations or decisions of the respective committees or bodies considering the evidence.

IV. Procedures for Personnel Decisions

A. Personnel Committee
All personnel decisions shall be considered first by the personnel committee (membership of the committee is described in the By-Laws Art.IV.C.1.a) of the school or department. However, any tenured faculty member may nominate a colleague for promotion. Such nomination should be sent to the relevant personnel committee and the Committee on Faculty. Receiving such nomination and the consent of the nominee, the personnel committee shall prepare and send a recommendation to the Committee on Faculty.

B. Preliminary Steps
(1) The chair of the Committee on Faculty and the Vice President for Academic Affairs shall meet with candidates preparing for personnel decisions in order to explain the processes and answer questions. (2) The chair of the Committee on Faculty shall make known

the names of persons being considered for interim review, tenure, and promotion and request relevant information.

C. Personnel Committee Procedure

The committee shall follow a standard procedure approved by the Committee on Faculty, the administration, and the faculty. It shall include the following steps.

1. The candidate shall submit material to the personnel committee of the school or department. This may include evaluation of the candidate's merits by persons in and outside the University who are qualified to judge them.

2. Faculty members who feel that they have information which would be helpful in the tenure decision of any candidate should (a) submit this information in writing and signed to the chair of the personnel committee or Committee on Faculty or b) request interviews with the personnel committee or the Committee on Faculty.

3. The committee may solicit other relevant information from the following:

   a. a representative sample of students who have had course work under the candidate regarding the candidate's teaching effectiveness.

   b. colleagues in the University who are qualified to judge regarding the candidate's teaching effectiveness, professional competence, and service.

   c. persons outside the University who are qualified to judge an appropriate aspect of the decision file. The committee must notify the candidate that it intends to seek letters from persons outside the University. The committee must limit its solicitation to external evaluators agreeable to both the candidate and the committee.

4. All materials received or generated by the committee shall be placed in the candidate's decision file.

5. The personnel committee shall provide an opportunity for the candidate to inspect the decision file, make written response, and respond in person.

6. Report. The personnel committee shall (a) in the case of interim review, make an assessment of the evidenced

strengths and weaknesses of the candidate according to the criteria for tenure, clearly stating areas of desirable or necessary improvement or (h) in the cases of tenure and promotion, make a recommendation, stating clearly the evidence and the reasons for the recommendation. The preparation of a consensus report is strongly encouraged. However, if after prolonged discussion the personnel committee is unable to attain consensus among all of its members then the majority shall write and sign its report. The minority member or members shall together or separately write, sign and append their report(s) or statement(s) of their reasons for not agreeing. All members of the Personnel Committee shall have access to the entire document (i.e., both the majority and the minority reports). The entire report and any documentary evidence shall be sent to the COF and the Vice President for Academic Affairs. The entire report shall be sent to the candidate. If members of the personnel committee do not agree with the report, they shall write separate reports or a statement of their reasons for not agreeing. The committee conclusions, documentary evidence, and any separate reports shall be sent to the Committee on Faculty and the Vice President for Academic Affairs. In addition, the conclusions shall be sent to the candidate.

D. Committee on Faculty Procedure
  1. Evidentiary sessions. The committee is required to (a) receive the documents and recommendations of the personnel committee; (b) receive any related information or concerns from the President and/or Vice President for Academic Affairs; (c) receive further written evidence that might be offered from members of the University community; (d) read the decision file; (e) interview any faculty member who has indicated in writing that this is the manner in which he or she wishes to communicate relevant information. In order to gain additional relevant evidence the committee may (f) interview anyone from whom the committee wishes to solicit information; (g) collect statistical information. After collecting all required and additional information

188

the committee shall (h) provide opportunity for the candidate to inspect the decision file and to respond in writing and/or in person to the committee.

2. Deliberation and decision sessions
    a. The committee, using the criteria stated in Section V. and any additional criteria of the school or department, shall consider the (1) adequacy of the procedures, (2) the propriety of the evidence, (3) the warrants for the conclusion of the personnel committee, and (4) the relevance and value of the additional evidence.
    b. The committee and the Vice President for Academic Affairs present their tentative conclusions to each other and discuss their respective reasons with openness to any opposing points of view. The following options are possible.
        1. If the report of the personnel committee is judged inadequate, that committee may be asked to reconsider and resubmit its report, at which time deliberation and decision recommence.
        2. The Committee on Faculty may investigate further and then return to deliberation and decision.
        3. If the personnel committee's conclusions are judged valid and the additional evidence at least not in conflict with that conclusion, the committee and the Vice President for Academic Affairs, together or separately, shall either concur or conclude on their own, then submit such to the President.
        4. Either party (the Committee on Faculty or the Vice President for Academic Affairs) not concurring with the personnel committee's conclusions shall make its own conclusion and submit it to the President.
    c. The chair of the Committee on Faculty shall communicate the action of the committee to the President, who may meet with the committee for further clarification.
3. If the President is considering a decision against the recommendation of the Committee on Faculty, he or she

shall communicate this and the reasons to the committee. The committee shall respond to the President regarding the decision and the reasons.

4. The President shall inform the candidate of the decision in writing. Reasons for the President's decision will be presented to the candidate orally, and, at the candidate's request, in writing.

5. After the President has informed the candidate and if the candidate requests, the Committee on Faculty shall release its initial recommendation and/or final assessment.

V. Criteria for Decisions on Faculty Status

(Article mutually agreed to by administration and faculty) Decisions should express judgments about candidates' merit and service using the principle of equity, which considers each individual faculty member in terms of his or her unique talents, abilities, and accomplishments in relation to the criteria for personnel decisions, and quality. A large amount of activity per se does not necessarily contribute to a superior academic environment. Criteria for possible dismissal (VI.A. below) are also applicable to decisions on faculty status.

Interim review. Required: effective teaching during the probationary period, satisfactory growth in the professional competence category, and contribution to school, department, or university programs.

Tenure decision. Required: effective teaching, including teaching in the school or department in which tenure will be granted, demonstrable achievement or unquestioned promise of accomplishment in the professional competence category; and contribution to school, department, or university programs.

Promotion to associate or full professor. Required: continued effectiveness of teaching; significant achievement or contribution in either professional competence or service to the school, department, or the University since the initial appointment to the preceding rank; and at least adequate performance in the other category.

A. Teaching effectiveness shall be considered paramount in all personnel decisions.

Candidates are required to provide broad-based and representative evidence of teaching effectiveness. Tenured faculty under consideration for promotion can satisfy this requirement most easily by providing complete sets of student evaluation for three or four semesters. "Complete sets" means all forms that have been filled out by students, the original jackets supplied by the Office of Institutional Research (which includes data on the number of students enrolled in the course and the number of students present and completing the forms and the statistical reports of the OIR.) If such evaluations are not provided, other evidence of teaching effectiveness (including broadly-based student input) must be submitted. Such "other evidence" might include the following procedures conducted by the DPC or by appropriate evaluator(s) external to the department or the University: systematic peer observation and evaluation of classroom, laboratory, and studio teaching; thorough and representative sampling of the judgments of former students; in-depth interviews of students; and detailed evaluation of syllabi. Candidates are required to show evidence in <u>all</u> <u>of</u> <u>the</u> <u>following</u>:

1. content and rigor (evidence to be drawn from course goals, syllabi, examinations and assignments, texts, other course materials, distribution of grades, etc.; evidence should demonstrate that courses meet scholarly standards and are offered at an appropriate level of difficulty);

2. teaching methods (evidence to be drawn from teaching philosophy, course goals, syllabi, examinations and assignments, other course materials, etc.; evidence should demonstrate that teaching methods are appropriate, given the contexts of discipline and topic and the specific characteristics of a given class); effectiveness (evidence to be drawn from student evaluations, peer observations, self reports, etc.; evidence should demonstrate that the candidate has been successful in implementing her

or his teaching methods, has treated students with professional fairness and integrity, and has established relations with students that arc conducive to the learning process).

B. Professional growth shall be given full consideration in personnel decisions. Candidates are required to show evidence in the following; however, for (2) and (3), more in one category may compensate for less in the other.
   1. Continued development of professional competence in the field(s) or discipline(s);
   2. Professional contributions or scholarly outreach beyond the university community;
   3. Intellectual liveliness within the university community.

C. Service to the school, department, and the University shall be considered in personnel decisions. Candidates are not required to show evidence in all or any one category unless there are special departmental requirements or responsibilities stated in the job description.
   1. effective participation in school, department or university governance, including committee assignments;
   2. effective participation in program development and resource acquisition within the school, department, or the University;
   3. effective participation in curricular development for school, department, competence, special, or general education programs;
   4. effective counseling and advising of individual students and student organizations related to academic life.

D. Librarians serving as renewable term faculty are evaluated in the areas of teaching, professional development, and service, with the following difference: in the evaluation of teaching, the evaluation has a primary focus on library effectiveness. Librarians may also show evidence related to teaching effectiveness, but they must show evidence in at least two of the following areas of library effectiveness:
   1. reference services for the university community;
   2. development of library collections and information resources;

3. provision of bibliographic organization and control over library collections;
4. instruction in the use of information resources and services including workshops, bibliographic instruction sessions, and research consultations;
5. creation of instructional materials and tools on the use of information resources and services including catalogs, bibliographies, and indexes.

VI. Standards for Release, Dismissal and Non-appointment
(Article mutually agreed to by administration and faculty)

A. Release and dismissal.

Faculty members in all categories of appointment may be released for stated reasons or dismissed for adequate cause. This action may be taken by the President after consultation with the school dean or department chair, the Committee on Faculty, and the Vice President for Academic Affairs, and it must follow a stated procedure.

Release must be based on one of the following reasons: (a) bona fide financial exigency; or (b) discontinuance of program, school or department.

Dismissal must be based on adequate cause: (a) dishonesty in teaching or research; (b) substantial and clear neglect of duty; (c) personal conduct which substantially impairs the individual's fulfillment of his institutional responsibilities; (d) moral conduct unfitting the position; or (e) performance which falls distinctly below the standards which the University may justly expect in terms of the criteria for personnel decisions.

B. Non-reappointment (before the end of the term or probationary period)
1. Conditions. Term and probationary appointments may be terminated (and tenure denied, if applicable) before the end of the term or probationary period only if the following conditions are met: (a) the decision does not violate the faculty member's academic freedom or punish him or her for exercising academic freedom in the performance of duties inside the University

or responsible civil activities; (b) the decision is not arbitrary or capricious; (c) the decision represents the deliberate exercise of professional judgments in the particular institutional circumstances.

2. Reasons. Term and probationary appointments may be terminated before the end of the term or probationary period if the decision is based upon one or more of the following reasons: (a) failure to meet the institution's stated conditions for reappointment, such as receipt of terminal degree by a specified date; (b) undistinguished performance, according to the institution's stated criteria for personnel decisions (See V. above.); (c) substantial change in the institution's academic program requiring a change in the job description under which the faculty member was hired; (d) violation of standards of integrity (not serious enough to warrant immediate dismissal); (e) bona fide budgetary constraints necessitate elimination of the faculty member's position; (f) discontinuance of an academic program or department.

3. Notice. Notice of non-reappointment shall be given: (a) in the first academic year of service, not later than March 1 if the appointment expires at the end of that year; or at least three months in advance of its termination if a one-year appointment terminates during an academic year; (b) in the second year of academic service, not later that December 15 if the appointment expires at the end of that year; or at least six months in advance of the termination if an initial two-year appointment terminates during an academic year; (c) after two or more years in the institution, at least twelve months before the expiration of an appointment.

VII. Reconsideration and Review in Release, Dismissal, and Non-Reappointment Cases
(Article mutually agreed to by administration and faculty)

Even with the best standards and procedures, faculty who have been released, dismissed, or not reappointed may believe that they have been improperly judged or unfairly treated and may wish a reconsideration or review of the case. Such faculty shall have such an opportunity, and the reconsideration or review shall be in accordance with the faculty review procedure.

VIII. Part-time Faculty
(Article written by the administration)

Part-time faculty are recognized as members of the faculty and are accorded some of the rights and privileges pertaining to faculty status. However, part-time faculty may not be granted tenure as long as they are part-time; they may attend faculty meetings and participate in debate, but not vote; and they may not serve on the faculty's coordinating or executive committees, though they may accept appointments to other regular and <u>ad hoc</u> committees and subcommittees. In principle, part-time appointments should meet emergency needs and certain on-going needs of the schools and departments which may require special expertise or routine assistance where tenure or term appointments may be unwarranted.

Part-time teachers should be current and pursue professional development in their fields, and they should be afforded all due professional courtesies and supports.

A. Initial Appointment.
Appointments shall be made by the President or the Vice President for Academic Affairs after consultation with the dean of the school or department chair who requests such appointments. Each appointment should carry with it a designation of rank and should be for a specific semester or academic year. No announcement of courses to be staffed by part-time faculty should be made without prior approval of the Vice President for Academic Affairs. Contracts stating conditions should be executed in all cases, and these should make provision for possible cancellation based upon registration. The contract should include a provision for compensation for preparation time for courses that have been cancelled by the University. Appointments or contingency plans should be made in time to allow adequate course preparation, and contracts should be executed as soon as possible after agreement has been reached. A person may receive reappointment at a higher rank consistent

with degree status, teaching effectiveness, professional development, and quality of service.

B. Compensation.
The basis for compensation of part-time faculty should reflect both prevailing market conditions and the levels of compensation paid to faculty in tenure or term positions holding the same rank and having comparable experience. This basis for compensation as defined by the President of the University should be consistently applied; however, in cases of special need for tutorial courses, compensation may be below the defined standard. Standards for enrollment minimums should be alike for tenure, term and part-time teachers. Part-time teachers who must commute more than 50 miles (one way to the campus) should receive a travel allowance according to a policy defined by the President of the University.

C. Continuation of Employment.
The University, by employing a part-time faculty member once or repeatedly, is not undertaking a commitment to provide future employment. Nevertheless, when part-time teachers have satisfactorily performed their contractual obligations, they should receive special consideration when a school, department or program selects part-time faculty in their discipline and should be informed as early as possible about the probability of their continued or repeated employment.

D. Evaluation.
The dean of school or program or the department chair should be responsible for continuing evaluation of part-time faculty members, as described in the <u>Academic Handbook</u>. Course evaluations shall be administered every semester for the first six semesters of teaching and at least every third semester of teaching thereafter. All required evaluations will be sent to the faculty member, and copies will be sent to the department chair to be placed in the departmental personnel file. Peer evaluation, professional activities, service to the University and participation in faculty development should also figure in the evaluation. In determining the impact of

the evaluation, the Vice President for Academic Affairs will consult with the chair or dean concerned, but, in view of the limited term of part-time teachers and of the fact that they are ineligible for tenure, the decision of the Vice President for Academic Affairs about compensation and continued employment should be final.

E. Rights and Privileges.
With regard to faculty governance, the faculty will define rights and privileges of part-time faculty. Part-time teachers may apply for funds for professional development, including faculty development and travel funds according to guidelines determined by the faculty development committee and the administration. They are also entitled to participate in other faculty development programs and activities. They should be given the same initial instruction and continuing information concerning academic and community affairs as is given to faculty in tenure and term positions. Each should have access to the university's instructional services, including office space, telephone, secretarial aid and library and audio visual support.

IX.   Faculty Review Procedure
(Article written and approved by the faculty)

A. Review Committee--Scope
The faculty shall have a Review Committee which, on the request of any member of the faculty, shall review personnel decisions affecting the tenure, terminal reappointment, nonreappointment of that faculty member. The committee also may review a personnel decision affecting the salary or promotion of a faculty member. Any grievance which a faculty member may have must be brought before the Committee on Faculty before it may be reviewed under this procedure.

B. Review Committee--Membership Elections, Alternates
The Review Committee shall consist of eight tenured members of the full-time faculty two from each division who are not members of the Committee on Faculty. No person shall be a member of the Review Committee unless

the terms of his or her appointment are subject in whole or in part to action by the Committee on Faculty. Persons granted leaves of absence for all or part of the review Committee's term of office <u>are</u> eligible for election to the committee. Voting for members of the Review Committee shall be restricted to members of the faculty whose terms of appointment are subject in whole or in part to action by the Committee on Faculty, and to the President and the Vice President for Academic Affairs. Eight alternate members of the Review Committee shall also be elected; they may be called upon to serve when regular committee members disqualify themselves as too directly involved in a grievance to render an objective decision.

1. The election of the Review Committee shall be conducted at the time of the spring elections for faculty committees. Review Committee members shall serve for one year; they are eligible for re-election.

2. Members of the Review Committee shall take office at the beginning of the second semester of the academic year following their election.

3. In the nomination phase of the balloting, each division will submit <u>four</u> names.

4. In the final balloting, the two candidates from each division receiving the highest number of votes shall take office. The nominees ranking third and fourth in their division shall be alternates, and shall all be considered equally available. If additional alternates or replacements are needed, they shall be chosen by the Division Nominating Committees.

5. If a new Review Committee takes office while a petition is pending, the preceding Review Committee may decide whether to complete the review or to hand it over to the new committee.

C. Petitioner's Request for Review
    No request for review may be made unless the faculty member (hereafter called "the petitioner") has, within 14 days after having been informed in writing of the Committee on Faculty's decision, requested in writing that the committee review the personnel decision. It is expected that the petitioner will consult with his or her department

chairman and with the Vice President for Academic Affairs regarding the questioned decision before requesting such review.

1. The Committee on Faculty shall honor any request from a faculty member for review regarding his or her tenure, reappointment, salary, and/or promotion, provided it has been made in writing within the 14-day period specified above. Within 10 days of receiving the petitioner's request, the committee shall respond in writing. If the original decision goes unchanged, this response shall include a written statement of the reasons for the original decision and a written statement detailing the procedure followed and listing the persons consulted in reaching the original decision. If the petitioner finds this response unsatisfactory, he or she may, within three days after being informed in writing of the action, submit a request for review by the Review Committee to the Chair of the Faculty, who shall convene the Review Committee, including the alternates, within four days.

2. The request for review shall be in writing and shall include a detailed statement of the petitioner's reasons for requesting review, and an explicit waiver by the petitioner of any right to non-disclosure of the grounds for the decision. It is intended that the disclosure of grounds be restricted to persons authorized under this grievance procedure. The petitioner shall provide the Chair of the Faculty with three copies of the request for review.

3. All references to specified periods of time in this section and hereafter shall be computed--unless the context specifically indicates otherwise--on the basis of "in-session" time. In-session days are those from the first day of registration through the last day of classes (excluding Saturdays and Sundays) of the fall and spring semesters, plus the week days of the Winter Term. Vacation days (fall and spring recesses, Thanksgiving, Christmas, and summer recesses, any other recess days, etc.), Saturdays and Sundays are not counted as in-session days. A mediation panel or an appeals panel may recess at any time; that is, it may delay proceedings without counting any days as part of the stated time limits, because of

absence or illness of the panel members or one of the parties, because of self-disqualification of a Review Committee member, or for other reasons.

D. Review Committee--Selection of Mediation Panel and Review Panel

For each petition there shall be two panels: a three-member mediation panel whose function shall be to seek resolution, not necessarily by compromise, of the case and a five-member appeals panel whose function shall be to conduct a formal hearing, if required. On being convened by the Chair of the Faculty, the Review Committee shall, for each case, select the two panels, observing the following regulations:

1. Each panel shall select its own chairperson at the time the Review Committee is convened by the Chair of the Faculty.

2. After the panel chairpersons are selected, the members of the appeals panel shall withdraw and shall have no further involvement in the case unless a formal hearing is requested as prescribed below.

3. After the members of the appeals panel have withdrawn, the Chair of the Faculty shall transmit to the mediation panel the petitioner's statement requesting review.

4. A member of the mediation panel shall remove himself of herself from participation in any case with respect to which he or she feels disqualified because of bias or interest. All vacancies shall be filled as described in Section B, (4). A replacement for a panel member shall serve for that one case only (unless specifically called upon to serve in other cases as they arise).

5. Under normal circumstances, the Review Committee and any of its panels shall meet and conduct business only when all members are present. An appeals panel may meet with one member absent. If any member resigns from a panel for any reason while the procedure is continuing, a replacement shall be chosen from the alternates in the manner described in IX B (4) and IX D (6). The chairperson of the appeals panel shall vote only in the event of a tie.

6. At the first meeting of the Review Committee and alternates, the members shall determine, by lot, the

order in which the alternates will be called on to serve. The order will be determined with no reference to Division membership or to the number of votes received in the committee election.

7. No member or alternate shall serve on more than one appeals panel at any one time, and no member or alternate shall serve on more than two panels at any one time.

E. Procedure for Tenure Decisions and for Promotion or Salary Decisions
   1. In cases involving tenure, terminal reappointment, or non-reappointment, review shall proceed upon request as prescribed below.
   2. In cases involving promotion or salary, the mediation panel shall, within three days after receipt of the request for review, meet with the petitioner on the basis of this meeting and the petitioner's written statement, the panel shall decide whether the review shall proceed. Normally, review shall not be deemed merited unless there has been a prolonged denial of promotion or the petitioner has received salary increases below the median over three successive regular periodic salary considerations. When a promotion or salary case is accepted for review, the review shall proceed as prescribed below.

F. Advisers
   Each party may have an adviser of his or her choice, drawn from the faculty, who may represent or advise him or her at any stage of the proceedings. A representative of the Committee on Faculty shall speak for the committee in all proceedings before the mediation and appeals panels. By "a member of the Committee on Faculty" is meant a member at the time the petition is being considered; preferably the member shall have been a member of the committee when it made its original decision. The representative of the

committee shall have a clear mandate to discuss the original decision and to explain Committee on Faculty procedures.

G. Mediation Panel--Procedures

Within three days of the meeting described in IX E (2), or if there is no such meeting (as in cases involving tenure, terminal reappointment, or non-reappointment), within three days of the receipt of the request for review, the chairperson of the mediation panel shall invite the petitioner to meet with the mediation panel for the purpose of facilitating the panel's understanding of the nature of the grievance as defined in the petitioner's written statement.

1. At the same meeting the petitioner shall provide the chairperson of the mediation panel with three copies of all the documents which the petitioner wishes to submit in support of his or her written statement defining the nature of the grievance.

2. The chairperson of the mediation panel shall promptly submit the petitioner's statement to the Committee on Faculty which shall, within three days after its next meeting, provide the panel with:

    a. a written response to the petitioner's definition of the grievance (this will usually be approximately the same reply which the Committee on Faculty sent directly to the petitioner, C1);

    b. a copy of the written statement of reasons for the original decision (already sent to the petitioner, C1);

    c. a written statement detailing the procedure followed and listing the persons consulted in reaching the original decision, and

    d. copies of all documents (The faculty committee shall provide, in place of those documents which it judges to be highly confidential, copies of the documents with all identifying material blocked out. The sources may remain confidential.) in deliberations leading to the original decision. With the approval of the panel, the Committee on Faculty may provide access to these documents for panel members and shall then provide copies of only those documents specifically requested.

e. At this point, the mediation panel shall not disclose these statements to anyone who is not a member of the panel.

H. Mediation Panel--Attempt at Resolution

After consideration of all written materials provided under Section G, the mediation panel shall seek informally to bring about a resolution in the case, not necessarily by compromise. The mediation panel is not an advocate for any party to the dispute. The role of the mediation panel is to assist both the petitioner and the Committee on Faculty to discuss the case and reach some agreement.

1. In seeking a resolution, the mediation panel may meet with the petitioner and/or with the Committee on Faculty (or its designated representative) and/or both together. Individual members of the panel shall not meet with individual members of the committee, unless they have been designated by their respective bodies for such a discussion. The panel shall not disclose confidential documents.

2. If the mediation panel decides early in its proceedings that mediation will not be effective, it will report its decisions and the reasons for it to the petitioner, to the chair of the Committee on Faculty, and to the chair of the appeals panel.

3. The mediation period shall normally not exceed 14 days from the time the mediation panel receives from the Committee on Faculty the documents described in G2 above. The mediation period shall be extended by at most seven days by mutual agreement of the two parties. The mediation panel's success or failure at bringing about a resolution of the case shall be communicated in writing by its chair to the petitioner, to the chair of the Committee on Faculty, and to the chair of the appeals panel.

I. Mediation Panel--Conclusion

Whether resolution has been achieved or not, the mediation panel shall return all materials to the persons from whom they were received. If resolution has not been achieved, the mediation panel shall submit to the appeals panel (with a copy to the petitioner) a statement which defines the nature of the grievance which has been subject to mediation efforts.

1. On receipt of notification of failure of mediation, the petitioner may, within four days, submit to the chairperson of the appeals panel: (1) a written request to institute a formal review and (2) a copy of the detailed statement of reasons for requesting the review, as previously submitted to the Chair of the Faculty (C.2). Within an additional three days, the petitioner shall give to the chairperson of the appeals panel: (3) his or her statement detailing the precise nature of the grievance, or else an explicit endorsement of the mediation panel's statement with whatever exceptions or qualifications the petitioner may desire to make, and (4) copies of all documents which the petitioner wishes to submit in support of his or her statement.

J. Appeals Panel--Procedures

Within three days after receiving the request for a formal hearing, the chair of the appeals panel shall meet with the other members of the panel. (Members may disqualify themselves at this meeting, as provided in J (1) below.) The chair shall then invite the petitioner to meet with the appeals panel for the purpose of assuring the panel's understanding of the nature of the grievance as defined by the petitioner (or endorsed) in writing. No arguments or evidence will be presented at this time.

1. A member of the appeals panel shall remove himself or herself from participation in any case with respect to which he or she feels disqualified because of bias or interest. All vacancies shall be filled as described in Section B (4) and D (6). A replacement for a panel member shall serve for that one case only (unless specifically called upon to serve in other cases as they arise).

2. Within two days of the receipt of the petitioner's request for a formal hearing, the chair of the appeals panel will notify the Committee on Faculty of that request. The Committee on Faculty shall, within three days of its next meeting, send to the chair the same documents which it

had earlier sent to the chair of the mediation panel, as listed in VII G (2).

3. Within three days after its first meeting with the petitioner, the appeals panel shall meet to discuss the procedures for the hearing. The petitioner and a representative of the Committee on Faculty may attend this meeting, and each may have an adviser. The appeals panel will state its understanding of the grievance, and the parties may respond. No oral arguments or evidence will be presented at this time. The appeals panel will describe the procedures for the formal hearing and will set the date for the start of the hearing.

4. The appeals panel shall promptly schedule a hearing for the purpose of oral argument and for the presentation of additional information. Copies of all documents submitted by the petitioner and the Committee on Faculty shall be made available to both parties at least four days prior to the hearing, unless an earlier hearing date is agreed to by both parties. (Either party may have a three-day recess for the purpose of preparing a response to any document presented at the hearing which had not been previously disclosed.) None of these written materials shall be released or disclosed in whole or in part by anyone other than the immediate parties and their advisers.

K. Appeals Panel--Hearings
The following procedures shall apply in all hearings:

1. The burden of proof shall rest initially with the petitioner unless the case involves the dismissal of a tenured faculty member. By "burden of proof" is meant the responsibility for affirmatively proving, by a preponderance of evidence, disputed facts bearing on the issues described in section L below.

2. The hearing shall be closed and its proceedings confidential. Each party may have in attendance an observer of his or her choice drawn from the general faculty (in addition to an adviser).

3. A written or taped record shall be kept of the proceedings, to which both parties shall have reasonable access. Two copies of this record shall be kept in control of the

chairperson of the appeals panel until final disposition of the case. After the appeal panel's recommendation to the President (M, below), both copies of the record of the proceedings and one copy of all official documents shall be deposited in the University Archives for confidential storage, in accord with usual archival procedures. The documents will be available to the President during his consideration of the appeals panel's recommendation.

4. Both parties shall be afforded an opportunity to present oral testimony (bearing on the case as defined) directly or through witnesses and to question any person presenting testimony. However, no person testifying before the panel shall be required to disclose confidential sources. No member of the mediation panel shall testify as a member of that body, and no member of Committee on Faculty except the chair or another designated representative shall speak for the entire Committee on Faculty.

5. The appeals panel shall not be bound by strict rules of legal evidence, but the findings shall be based solely on the hearing and the documents considered by the appeals panel.

L. Appeals Panel--Scope of Inquiry
During the formal hearings, the appeals panel shall restrict its inquiry to the following questions:

1. Was all material evidence considered? If not, would consideration of all such evidence have justified a different decision?

2. Was any improper evidence considered? If such evidence had not been considered, would a different decision have been made?

3. Was the decision in any other way so inappropriate that a new decision should be recommended?

M. Conclusion and Recommendation
The formal hearing shall be completed within 21 days. Within 3 days after the appeals panel shall report its findings in writing to the petitioner, to the Committee on Faculty, to the Vice President for Academic Affairs, and to the President. The panel's report shall be accompanied by a full statement

of the reasons for the recommendation, including responses to all the points raised by the petitioner.

1. If the appeals panel finds that the Committee on Faculty made a correctable procedural error, it shall direct the committee to correct the error and reconsider the original decision. (A "reconsideration" does not necessarily mean a modification or reversal of the original decision.)

    a. The Committee on Faculty shall report its decision, with a statement of reason, within 10 days, to all the parties. Within 3 days after the receipt of the committee's report, the appeals panel shall state its opinion of that report in writing to all the parties.

2. If the appeals panel finds that an error other than a correctable procedural error has been made, it shall report its findings to all parties, with a recommendation to the President for retaining, modifying, or reversing the original decision. The findings of the appeals panel might include the following:

    a) bias or prejudice;
    b) unavailability of pertinent documents or testimony;
    c) a decision inappropriate in light of the evidence;
    d) a violation of academic freedom.

        NOTE: Cases involving academic freedom will be reviewed in accordance with the principles of the American Association of University Professors, as found in the "Statement on Proceedings," "1968 Recommended Institutional Regulations on Academic Freedom and Tenure," and other documents.

N. Interpretation of the Review Procedure

All matters of interpretation of this faculty review procedure shall be resolved by the Review Committee or its panels.

By-Laws and Standing Rules of the Faculty

I. **The Faculty**
The faculty consists of the President and those persons appointed to tenure, term, or part-time positions with <u>academic</u> rank in a discipline or to term or administrative staff positions with <u>nominal</u> rank ("with rank of . . . ").

II. **Faculty Meetings**

A. Regular and Called
There shall be one regular meeting of the faculty each month of the academic year. Additional meetings when desired may be called by the Chair of the Faculty.

B. All faculty members may attend faculty meetings and participate freely in discussions.

C. Voting
1. Faculty members holding tenure and term positions may vote. (Those faculty members who hold other positions at the time this revision is approved and who have been eligible to vote shall continue to enjoy this privilege.)
2. A quorum shall consist of 40% of the faculty eligible to vote and not on approved leave (rounded to the nearest whole number). This number shall be determined for each semester by the Vice President for Academic Affairs, using the faculty roster as of the Friday immediately preceding the first faculty meeting of each semester. Immediately after the call to order at the first faculty meeting of each semester, the Vice President for Academic Affairs shall announce the quorum requirement for that semester. The next order of business after the call to order at each faculty meeting shall be the verification of a quorum by the Chair of the Faculty (for the first meeting of the semester, the quorum verification shall occur after the Vice President for Academic Affairs has announced the requirement).

3. Senior Professors are eligible to vote during any semester in which they are teaching at least one course.
4. Faculty members who are on sabbatical leave or special leave are eligible to vote. The Chair of the Faculty shall send ballots only to the university addresses of the voting faculty.
5. All voting in meetings, unless otherwise stipulated, shall be by show of hands. However, at the' request of any faculty member the vote shall be by secret ballot.

D. Order of Business
At all regular faculty meetings the following shall be the order of business:
1. Call to order
2. Correction and approval of minutes
3. Reports from Coordinating Committees
4. Reports from other Committees
5. Remarks from the Vice President for Academic Affairs
6. Remarks from the President
7. Old Business
8. New Business
9. Announcements
10. Adjournment

III. The Officers

A. The Presiding Officer
The Chair of the Faculty shall preside at all meetings of the faculty. In the event of absence due to illness, a substitute designated by the Chair of the Faculty shall preside.

B. The Chair of the Faculty
1. The Chair of the Faculty shall be a tenured faculty member elected by the faculty for a term of three years under the election rules provided in Article V, Section E.
2. The Chair of the Faculty shall appoint an assistant to help in preparing the first draft of the minutes of the faculty meeting, with faculty elections, with maintenance of the Academic Handbook, and any other record keeping functions. The Chair, aided by the assistant, shall have

responsibility for the tabulation of ballots in any faculty election, and shall be responsible for the Academic Handbook. The Chair shall provide each new member of the faculty with a copy of the Academic Handbook. He or she shall provide every faculty member with copies (or access to electronic editions) of all revisions, amendments and new editions of the Academic Handbook. Financial and resource support for the assistant and the functions of the Chair shall be given by the chief academic officer of the university.

C. The Parliamentarian
The Parliamentarian shall be a tenured faculty member elected by the faculty for a term of three years under the election rules provided in Article V, Section E. The Parliamentarian shall advise the Chair on rules of procedure in the faculty meeting and shall have final authority to resolve disputes regarding those rules. In case of vacancy in the office of Parliamentarian, the Chair shall appoint an Interim Parliamentarian and conduct an election for a new Parliamentarian to serve a full term as soon as possible.

IV.   Schools and Departments

A. Academic Positions
Faculty members with academic rank shall be appointed to positions in schools or departments.

B. Responsibilities
Schools and departments shall have immediate supervision over:
1. their respective fields and disciplines and the courses of instruction;
2. the definition of teaching positions in those fields and disciplines;
3. recruitment, appointment, evaluation, tenure, and promotion of their faculty members;
4. the definition of major and minor concentrations of studies in their respective fields and disciplines;
5. their schedules of courses and laboratories;

6. their organizational structure, except where specified by faculty action;

7. and the support personnel and budget needed to carry out their respective missions.

C. Committees

1. Personnel Committee

   (procedures described under Procedures for Personnel Decisions in the Personnel Policies section of the Handbook)

   a. Membership.

   A personnel committee shall consist of all continuing tenure and term faculty members of the department except the person being reviewed, those on non-academic leave, and those in their first year of service. Faculty members on academic leave and nontenured members of the department may withdraw from any case. If there are fewer than three eligible department members or if the tenured members do not constitute a majority, the committee shall select additional tenured members from related departments, according to a procedure established by the Committee on Faculty and the administration. It is expected that all members of a personnel committee shall fully participate in the activities of the committee. When conducting a search or considering a recommendation from a search committee, a personnel committee shall include two members from other departments, approved by the Vice President for Academic Affairs. (See below IV.C.2.a.) A personnel committee may delegate responsibilities to subcommittees.

   b. Function.

   1. The personnel committee makes requests for faculty positions to the appropriate faculty committee(s) and administrative officer(s),

   2. writes the job description to meet publicly defined criteria and stated policies of equal opportunity and affirmative action, and

   3. prepares the advertisement for appropriate journals.

4. It may act as the search committee or receive the report of the search committee; and it makes the recommendation to hire.
5. It insures that job candidates are fully apprized of the primacy of teaching, the nature of student-faculty relationships, and the kinds of professional and service activities required by the University and any departmental expectations for tenure and promotion.*
6. The committee investigates, considers evidence, and makes recommendations regarding all other personnel decisions affecting members of the department.

   *The job description and the school or department expectations shall be given to the committee on faculty prior to campus interviews of candidates.

   c. Chair. The department chair serves as committee chair and communicates in writing the recommendations of the committee to the candidate for promotion or tenure, the Committee on Faculty, and the Vice President for Academic Affairs, including any separate reports by members of the committee.

2. Search Committee
   a. Membership

   A search committee may be constituted by the department with three or more members drawn from its continuing tenure and term faculty members and two additional members from each of two other departments, chosen after consultation with the Vice President for Academic Affairs. Additional members from other departments are not required in searches for positions lasting one year or less. In special circumstances, members may be appointed from other faculty of the department, such as those who are leaving the department or the University at the end of the year. If there are fewer than three eligible department members, with approval of the Vice President for Academic Affairs the personnel committee shall select additional search committee members from related departments.

   b. Function

The committee:

1. screens applicants, arranges off- and on-campus interviews, including those with the Vice President for Academic Affairs and President, if appropriate;
2. arranges on campus presentations and performances;
3. confers with all regular members of the department and others, such as emeriti and part-time teachers, regarding assessment of the candidates interviewed; and
4. formulates a recommendation and brings it to the personnel committee.

   c. Organization and Chair. The chair of the department shall be responsible for the organization of the committee and may be its chair.

D. Dean of the School; Chair of the Department

1. The Dean of the School of Music and department chairs are appointed by the President on the recommendation of members of the department and the Committee on Faculty, and in consultation with the Vice President for Academic Affairs. The term of appointment is three years, with evaluation in the third year of the term and the possibility of renewal. Ordinarily, for <u>chairs</u>, no more than two terms will be served. A dean or chair [may] receive a stipend or carry a reduced teaching load according to a published schedule. If there are co-dean or co-chairs or associate deans or associate chairs, similar arrangements shall be followed.

2. Deans and chairs are expected to be leaders within the University at large through consultation with the administration and committees. They meet from time to time as a body to discuss mutual concerns and share expertise. They may select officers, organize committees, conduct workshops, etc., to expedite their work.

3. Deans or chairs lead curriculum planning within the school or department, chair the personnel committee,

and prepare and administer the school or department budget. In all of these areas, they should lead, but also consult, others in the school or department and involve them in the decision-making process. They are responsible for maintaining good morale within the school or department and for encouraging excellence in teaching and other professional activities.

4. Deans or chairs link department and other university constituencies, serving as a spokesperson for departmental interests, but also interpreting for the department the larger needs and goals of the University.

5. Deans or chairs serve as mentors to the members of the school or department, particularly the newer members, informing them of development opportunities, facilitating peer teacher observations, communicating university and departmental expectations, and helping faculty to meet those expectations. For purposes of school or department self-study, the deans or chairs confer annually with individual members about their role in, and expectations for, the school's or department's mission in the University.

6. Deans or chairs assist school or department members in preparing materials for personnel reviews and assure that the school or department has thoroughly investigated and submitted all relevant information.

7. Deans or chairs participate in disciplinary procedures of the school or department.

V.   The Divisions

A. Definition and Function
Faculty members appointed to teaching and library staffs shall be grouped (by departments) into divisions for the purpose of coordinating the work in related fields and for equitable distribution of committee memberships. Divisions may submit matters of concern to an appropriate faculty coordinating or executive committee. Each division shall present nominations for divisional and at-large membership

on coordinating and executive committees and for the Chair of the Faculty.

B. Department Grouping
    Division I - Art; School of Music; Kinesiology; Communication Arts and Sciences; Librarians with faculty rank.
    Division II - Classical Studies; English; Modern Languages; Religious Studies.
    Division III - Biology; Chemistry; Computer Science; Geology and Geography; Mathematics; Physics and Astronomy; Psychology.
    Division IV - Economics and Management; Education; History; Philosophy; Political Science; Sociology and Anthropology.

C. Divisional Officers
    The chair and the secretary of each division shall be elected annually and the names reported to the Chair of the Faculty. No chairperson of a division shall be eligible to succeed himself or herself in office.

D. Divisional Nominating Committees
    There shall be a divisional nominating committee made up of the chair, the secretary, and one other elected annually by the division, no two from the same department.

E. Nominations
    The Divisional Nominating Committee shall present a slate of candidates at the divisional meeting. Nominations may be made from the floor also. No persons shall be nominated without their consent.

F. Interim Appointments
    In the event of a vacancy in a position of a representative of a division to a faculty committee, the divisional nominating committee shall appoint a replacement who will serve until the position can be filled through the regular faculty election process.
    1. In the event of a vacancy in a position of a member elected at-large to a faculty committee, the nominating

committee of that member's division shall appoint a replacement who will serve until the position can be filled by the faculty at the next election.

2. In the event of a vacancy in an elected faculty office other than on faculty committees, the nominating committee of that member's division shall appoint a replacement who will serve until the position can be filled by the faculty at the next election.

3. No persons shall be appointed to any vacancy without their consent.

4. All interim and temporary appointments shall be reported to the Chair of the Faculty by the secretary of the division making the appointment.

G. Meetings of Divisions

The chairperson of each division shall choose a time and place for division meetings which seem likely to make possible the largest attendance at each meeting. Before each meeting of a division the secretary of the division shall send a notice to every member of the division including a designation of the time and place of the meeting and a list of nominations to faculty committees to be made and/or agenda for other business to be transacted. Such a notice must be received in the offices of the division members no later than four calendar days before the meeting.

H. Reporting Divisional Elections

1. Following the meeting of a division at which nominations to faculty committees have been made, the secretary of the division shall deliver at once to the Chair of the Faculty a complete listing of all candidates for all vacant positions. The Chair of the Faculty will supervise a secret ballot canvas of all divisional members to determine the divisional representatives and at-large nominees from that division.

2. The Chair of the Faculty shall announce the divisional nominations to the faculty meeting, and they shall be confirmed by a vote of the faculty.

VI.   Faculty Committees

A.   Coordinating Committees
The faculty shall elect committees to supervise and integrate, singly or in conjunction, the formulation and execution of policy in four areas: academic policy and planning, operations, scholastic life and academic atmosphere, and faculty. They shall recommend all policies to the faculty for adoption. They shall be responsible for the interpretation of policy in their respective areas.

They shall consider the policy recommendations submitted to them by executive committees. They may request and receive reports of particular actions of executive committees.

They shall report to the faculty at each faculty meeting.

B.   Executive Committees
The faculty shall elect committees to carry out specific policies and programs in the areas of their respective assignments. They shall submit their policy recommendations to the relevant coordinating committees for consideration, and they may report such recommendations directly to the faculty. Upon request of the appropriate coordinating committee they shall present a report of their particular actions.

These committees may be assisted in the execution of their duties by an administrative director appointed by the President.

C.   Delegation of Powers
Faculty committees may delegate matters of specialized study, program direction, and administration to ad hoc or permanent sub-committees. (The members of such sub-committees need not be members of the committee making the delegation.)

D.   Eligibility, Restrictions, Terms
1.   Faculty members appointed to tenure and term positions are eligible for elected positions on most faculty committees. (The committee on faculty [see VII.

B.2]and the review committee [see VIII.E.2] have other restrictions.)

2. All faculty members are eligible for appointed positions on faculty committees, where such positions exist and subject to restrictions that may be imposed on each committee.

3. All terms of service on faculty committees filled by elections shall be three years, unless otherwise specified. Members may be re-elected.

4. No faculty member may serve in an elected position on more than three committees nor on more than one coordinating committee.

E. Method of Election

1. No later than one month before the end of the second (spring) semester each year the Chair of the Faculty shall deliver to the chairperson of each faculty division all the materials pertinent to the annual faculty election, and he/she shall list the results of the divisional nominations to committees, the election of faculty members at large to committees, and the election of faculty members to faculty offices, at least in the minutes of the last faculty meeting of the year and, if at all possible, in the minutes of the next-to-the-last meeting. If an election to fill vacancies in committees is held at the beginning of the school year in the fall, the Chair to the Faculty shall deliver the materials pertinent to that election to the divisional chairperson as soon as possible after the beginning of classes, but in no case later than one month after classes begin; and he or she shall report all the results of this election in the next minutes of the faculty which he or she distributes.

2. If at the beginning of the school year in the fall there are vacancies in one or more of the coordinating committees or in faculty offices essential to the conduct of faculty business, there shall be a general election according to the procedure outlined above or as may be determined by means of a motion suspending the By-Laws.

3. A fall election may be held at the discretion of the Chair of the Faculty to fill committee vacancies. Other special

elections may be held at the discretion of the Chair of the Faculty or at the direction of the faculty.

4. All offices for the same committee which have the same term shall be considered as one group in the election of at-large faculty representatives to faculty committees. Each division shall select one nominee for each vacant office. Nominees receiving the highest numbers of votes in the general election shall be elected. Voting shall be conducted by an electronic ballot available to all voting members of the faculty for at least three week days. The names of the individuals nominated by the divisions shall be arranged in random order on the official ballot. The Chair of the Faculty, with the assistance of two tellers appointed by him or her, shall conduct all elections.

5. The election of divisional representatives to faculty committees shall take place at a divisional meeting in accordance with procedures outlined in Article IV.

6. Student members of faculty committees will be chosen by the Student Congress in accord with the following principles:

   a. Any student in good standing shall be eligible (definition of good standing shall be in accord with the University Bulletin).

   b. There shall be petitions for committee membership. (1)There shall be established closing dates for the petition. (2) There shall be established election dates (if possible, the replacement for the retiring committee member shall be held in the spring following the academic year)

   c. Positions shall be filled by appointment by the Student Congress. (1) Appointment shall be made from among those students petitioning.

VII. Coordinating Committees

A. Committee on Academic Policy and Planning
   1. Function. This committee shall be responsible for general and long-range academic policy and planning, and it shall recommend to the faculty policies and programs relating to academic interest of the University.

This committee shall supervise programs and recommend policies relating to: admissions requirements, Aerospace Studies, Army ROTC, Experimental Division, University Studies, Winter Term, graduation requirements, pre-professional programs, public occasions, and other programs of similar relevance to academic policy. All new majors and minors, whether departmental or interdisciplinary in nature, shall be considered by CAPP and subsequently voted on by the faculty.

This committee shall coordinate the Executive Committees of the Athletic Board, International Education and Off-Campus Programs, and Teacher Education.

2. Membership. Voting members: The President of the University; the Vice President for Academic Affairs (or his or her appointed representative); six elected faculty members (one elected from each division and two elected at large), of which no more than two may be from one division and no more than one from each department, and two students. Ex-officio members (without vote): the Dean of the School of Music.

3. The Resource Allocation Committee is a subcommittee of the Committee on Academic Policy and Planning. The Resource Allocation Committee considers those departmental requests for new faculty forwarded to the Resource Allocation Committee by the Vice President for Academic Affairs, and sends to the Committee on Academic Policy and Planning their recommendations concerning granting or not granting requests. RAS shall be appointed by the Committee on Academic Policy and Planning as needed.

4. The Winter Term Committee is a subcommittee of the Committee on Academic Policy and Planning. It is composed of four full-time faculty (appointed by CAPP, one from each division, for three year staggered terms), two students (appointed yearly by Student Congress), the Vice President for Academic Affairs (or his or her representative), and the WT Coordinator as an ex-officio member. The committee should report to CAPP in the spring of every year. The responsibilities of the WT Committee are the following: 1) review policies,

procedures, and standards pertaining to all Winter Term programs 2) oversee and make final recommendations about the staffing of WT programs 3) review and approve all proposed WT projects and courses - both on-campus and off-campus 4) evaluate Winter Term on an annual basis, and make recommendations to CAPP regarding policy changes.

5. *The First Year Seminar Committee is a subcommittee of the Committee on Academic Policy and Planning. It is composed of four full-time faculty members (appointed for three year staggered terms by CAPP in consultation with the FYS Committee and the Vice-President for Academic Affairs with consideration given for representation of the academic divisions of the University and diverse faculty rank), and three representatives of Academic Affairs. Non-voting members may include people invited to participate on the committee in an advisory capacity by the Vice-President for Academic Affairs. The responsibility of the First Year Seminar Committee is the oversight of the FYS program including such duties as: developing and articulating the goals of the program, soliciting and approving seminar proposals, training faculty to teach FY Seminars, coordination of FY Seminars with academically-related social activities, evaluation of the seminar program, and reporting on developments in the program to CAPP and the faculty.*

B. Committee on Faculty
   1. Function. The committee shall represent the faculty by (a) recommending policy and procedures for personnel decisions to the faculty; (b) communicating procedures for personnel decisions to faculty members; (c) ensuring that candidates interviewing for initial appointment are informed of the procedures and criteria by which they will be evaluated; (d) considering evidence and testimony and consulting with and making recommendations to the President of the University in the following areas: appointment of new faculty members when requested by the Vice President for Academic Affairs; retention, advancement to tenure, promotion and dismissal of

faculty members; and appointment, reappointment, and evaluation of school deans and department chairs; (e) considering the legal propriety and risks of all faculty personnel procedures, including those at the school and department level; and informing all faculty participants in personnel procedures of possible legal concerns. The committee should be informed by a lawyer knowledgeable in the application of law to institutions of higher education.

2. Membership. Nine tenured faculty members each with at least four years of service at DePauw. Five shall be elected at large and one representative by each division. No more than two members may be from one department and no more than four may be from the same division. Each divisional representative must be nominated and elected by that particular division, but the representative's actual membership in that division is not mandatory. The committee will usually meet with the Vice President for Academic Affairs, though the Vice President for Academic Affairs does not vote. The Vice President for Academic Affairs shall have the other privileges granted to members of the committee, including receipt of minutes (which shall include all committee discussions of the merits of personnel cases) and opportunity to hear all testimony. The Vice President for Academic Affairs and the committee shall meet together upon the request of either, and the President and the committee shall meet together upon the request of either.

3. Organization and orientation
   a. Members of the committee shall be elected by the faculty during the spring election (described in VI. E.).
   b. The committee of the coming year shall elect as its chair a member with experience on the committee.
   c. A quorum shall consist of the chair and five other committee members.
   d. At an early meeting in the academic year, there shall be an orientation to the work of the committee in which both faculty members of the committee and administrators will discuss their respective

roles; the personnel decision calendar; types of admissible evidence; hypothetical difficult cases and the procedures for dealing with such; and legal guidelines and risks.

4. Subcommittees. The Committee on Faculty may form subcommittees (e.g., those to consider interims, reviews, candidate interviews, review of school deans or department chairs), but the committee shall act on all recommendations.

5. Responsibilities and privileges of the chair
   a. The chair with the Vice President for Academic Affairs shall arrange the agenda of the committee, setting the calendar for its orientation, the evidentiary and deliberative sessions, and shall arrange the keeping of personnel documents.
   b. The chair shall preside at the sessions of the committee and report to the faculty and the university community regarding the progress of the committee.
   c. The chair assisted by designated members of the committee shall provide notice and guidance to those participating in personnel matters (school or department personnel committees, nominations for promotions, candidates for personnel action, etc.) regarding the time and form of recommendations, procedures for gathering and evaluating evidence, and statement of reasons for the recommendations.

6. Secretary of the Committee.
   a. The secretary shall be a staff person provided by the office of the Vice President for Academic Affairs.
   b. The secretary shall attend and keep the minutes of the organization.
   c. The secretary shall assist the chair, the Vice President for Academic Affairs, and the chairs of subcommittees in preparing and maintaining documents, including model documents that might be helpful to the school or department personnel committees, to recommenders, and to candidates for personnel actions, and in communicating with others participating in personnel matters.

C. Committee on Management of Academic Operations

    1. Function. This committee shall be responsible for policies and actions of the Faculty relating to the daily operation of academic programs, and it shall have the responsibility for making recommendations to the faculty concerning the institution and implementation of these policies and details.

    This committee shall supervise the Area Major, scheduling, registration, classrooms, course changes, calendar, the grading system, comprehensives, academic counseling, learning resources, the libraries, and the Computer Center. MAO shall consider all changes to existing majors or minors and subsequently bring those changes to a vote before the faculty. If MAO determines that a proposed change to a major or minor represents a significant change in policy, MAO will also refer the proposal to CAPP for consideration before bringing the changes to a vote before the faculty.

    This committee shall coordinate the activities of the executive committees on Petitions and Academic Standing.

    2. Membership. Voting members: The President of the University; the Vice President for Academic Affairs (or his or her appointed representative); six elected faculty members (one elected from each division and two elected at-large), of which no more than two may be from one division and no more than one from each department; and two students. Ex-officio members (without vote): the Registrar, and the Dean of the School of Music.

D. Committee on Student Life and Academic Atmosphere

    1. Function. This committee shall be responsible for the policies and actions of the faculty relating to student life and general academic atmosphere of the university.

    This committee, with faculty approval, shall deal with policies, guidelines, and information on all factors affecting student life and campus-wide academic atmosphere; these factors include policies stated in the Student Handbook (e.g., academic dishonesty, the student judicial process, or sexual harassment), policies on campus-wide academic atmosphere (e.g., collecting data on university-wide GPAs or studying the effects of social activities on classroom work), and policies which encourage faculty-student interactions which foster the intellectual life of the university.

This committee shall coordinate the faculty representation on those committees, councils, and boards which supervise student life and campus-wide academic atmosphere issues participated in jointly by faculty members and students including the University Review Committee (which deals with grade grievances and cases of academic integrity) and the Community Conduct Council.

2. Membership. Voting members: The President of the University; The Vice President for Academic Affairs (or his or her appointed representative); The Vice President for Student Services (or his or her appointed representative); six elected faculty members (one elected from each division and two elected at-large), of which no more than two may be from one division and no more than one from each department; and two students.

Ex-officio members (without vote): the Dean of Students, the Dean of the School of Music, the Director of the Office of Institutional Research, the President of the Student Body, and one other student to be designated by the Student Congress by virtue of the office which she or he holds.

VIII. Executive Committees

A. Athletic Board
1. Function. This committee shall determine policies related to intercollegiate athletics including schedules and athletic awards, though basic policies are subject to ratification by the faculty.
2. Membership. Voting members: The Vice President for Academic Affairs; six elected faculty members (one elected from each division and two elected at large), of which no more than two may be from one division and no more than one from each department; and two students, one of whom shall have participated in intercollegiate athletics. Ex-officio members (without

vote): the Director of Athletics, the Director of Alumni Services, one alumnus/alumna elected by the Board of Directors of the Alumni Association for a term of three years, a coach of a men's intercollegiate athletic team, and a coach of a women's intercollegiate athletic team.

B. Faculty Development
    1. Function. This committee shall plan and execute faculty development programs within the University and coordinate institutional programs with faculty development programs of outside agencies. The committee will cooperate with the Committee on Faculty in establishing policies for faculty development.
        This committee shall make recommendations to the President of the University concerning the granting of institutional research and development funds, leaves of absence, and selection of institutional nominees for grants or awards given by outside agencies. Policies and procedures of faculty development programs are outlined in detail in the Faculty Development Handbook which is available from the Academic Affairs Office.
    2. Membership. Six elected faculty members (one elected from each division and two elected at-large) of which no more than two may be from one division and no more than one from each department. Ex-officio members (without vote): the Vice President for Academic Affairs (or his or her appointed representative); the Coordinator for Faculty Development. The chair for this committee shall be chosen from among the elected faculty members.

C. International Education and Off-Campus Programs
    1. Function. This committee shall be responsible for overseeing International and Off-Campus Programs in which DePauw students participate and for international students studying on the campus. This committee shall consider all academic aspects of International and Off-Campus Programs including the following:
        a. the general development of International Education, both on- campus and off-campus;

b. the selection of DePauw and non-DePauw students for DePauw programs;

c. the approval of non-DePauw programs for DePauw students;

d. the recruitment and supervision of international students attending DePauw (in cooperation with the Offices of Admissions and Financial Aid);

e. the offering of courses on and off-campus as related to International Education;

f. the amount of credit a student shall earn during an off-campus experience (in cooperation with appropriate academic departments).

2. Membership

Voting Members: The President of the University, the Vice President for Academic Affairs (or his or her appointed representative); the Director of International Education and Off-Campus Programs; the Registrar (when he or she has a vote at faculty meetings); eight elected faculty members (two elected from each division); of which no more than two may be from one department; and three students, including one international student and another who has studied abroad.

Ex-officio member (without vote: the Registrar (when he or she does not have a vote at faculty meeting), the Vice President of Admission and Financial Aid, and the International Student Advisor.

D. Petitions

1. Function. This committee shall consider and decide upon student petitions concerning academic matters as detailed in the University Bulletin.

2. Membership. The Vice President for Academic Affairs (or his or her appointed representative), the Dean of Academic Support Services, the Dean of Students, the Registrar, and the four elected faculty members of the Committee on Academic Standing.

E. Review

1. Function. This committee shall, on the request of any member of the faculty, review decisions affecting the tenure, terminal reappointment, or non-reappointment

of that faculty member. The committee may also review decisions affecting the salary or promotion of a faculty member.

2. Membership. Eight elected tenured faculty members, two from each division; members of the Committee on Faculty are not eligible.

F. Academic Standing
   1. Function. This committee shall consider all matters affecting academic classification and standing of students, including level of scholarship, probation, dismissal from and readmission to the University.
   2. Membership. Voting members: A representative appointed by the Vice President for Academic Affairs, the Dean of Academic Support Services, the Dean of Students, the Dean of the School of Music (for music students only), the Registrar, and four elected faculty members, one from each division.

G. Teacher Education
   1. Function. This committee shall advise the Vice President for Academic Affairs and the certification officer on all matters relating to the preparation of teachers and the certification requirements which should be met by students desiring certification. This advising shall include approving students applying to the teacher education program and making recommendations for departmental certification patterns and making recommendations to the faculty concerning the teacher education program.
   2. Membership. The Vice President for Academic Affairs (or his/her appointed representative); two members of the Education Department, one from elementary and one from secondary education, one of whom is the Chair of the Education Department; six elected faculty members (one elected from each division and two elected at large), of which no more than two from one division and no more than one from each department. The chair shall be the Chair of the Education Department.

H. Public Occasions
   1. Function. This committee solicits suggestions for campus convocation speakers and events with either small-group or campus-wide appeal. It then approves and funds programs which, with the President, it determines to be beneficial to the University community.
   2. Membership. Six faculty members (one from each division and two at large) for four-year terms, of which no more than two from one division and no more than one from each department; the Coordinator of Convocations; the Vice President for Academic Affairs (or his/her representative); and the Director of Public Relations (non-voting ex-officio).

I. Library Advisory Committee
   1. Function. This committee advises the library staff and administration on matters of library policy and assists in formulating plans, goals, and priorities, and in determining the overall role of the library in support of the academic program.
   2. Membership. Voting members: four elected members of the faculty, one from each academic division; the Director of Libraries; one additional librarian elected by the faculty; the Vice President for Academic Affairs (or his or her designated representative); and two students, one designated by Student Congress and the other appointed by the library advisory committee in consultation with the library staff.

IX. **Committees of the Administration**
Faculty members may be elected to serve on the following committees authorized by the administration or by the Board of Trustees of the University: Administration Committee; Board of Control of Student Publications; Joint Committee on Honorary Degrees; and Hartman Center Steering Committee. Descriptions of these committees are included in the Appendix to the By-Laws.

X.   Election of Officers of Faculty Committees

The chair and secretary of a faculty committee shall be chosen from the elected faculty members at the last meeting of the academic year except where otherwise specified. They shall begin their duties at the beginning of the next semester. Officers shall serve only one year. No person shall serve two years in succession. Officers of committees shall have voting rights.

XI.   Special Committees

Members of all special committees shall be elected by the faculty, except in cases where the faculty, by a two-thirds vote of those present and voting, shall authorize some other procedure.

XII.   Communications and Reports

Minutes and agenda of coordinating committees shall be distributed to all academic departments of the University. Each coordinating committee shall report regularly to the faculty meeting.

XIII. Parliamentary Procedure

A. The following shall be circulated at least three days before each faculty meeting: copies of the minutes of the last meeting; an agenda including the specific committee motions to be voted on at the next meeting. All committee motions on which there is to be a vote at a faculty meeting must have been announced in the agenda circulated before that meeting.

B. All business shall be conducted according to proper parliamentary procedure as set forth in *Robert's Rules of Order.*

XIV.   Amendments

Amendments proposed for these By-Laws must lie on the table one month and may be passed at any regular faculty meeting by a majority vote of those present and voting.

Standing rules may be amended at any regular meeting by a two-thirds vote of those present and voting.

XV.   Suspension

By-laws relating to the transaction of business (such as order of business and method of election) may be suspended by two-thirds vote of those present and voting at any regular faculty meeting. Any motion to suspend the By-Laws at a faculty meeting must be announced in the written agenda circulated at least three days prior to the meeting.

XVI. Standing Rules

A. The regular meeting of the faculty shall be held once a month during the academic year. The time and place of these regular meetings shall be determined and announced, by the chair of the faculty, to all faculty members by May 1 of the previous academic year.

B. The following persons may attend faculty meetings:
    1. faculty members (Article I. Section B.),
    2. any other persons appointed to the teaching staff (Article I. Section A. Number 1, Item a.) during the semester in which they hold such appointments,
    3. student members of coordinating committees,
    4. the President of the Student Body,
    5. the Director of Public Relations and News Bureau,
    6. and others to whom permission is granted by majority faculty vote at the beginning of the meeting.

C. The following persons may attend faculty meetings and, when recognized by the Presiding Officer, make presentations, respond to questions, participate in discussions, but not vote:
    1. non-faculty persons with teaching responsibilities during the period in which they teach,
    2. Vice Presidents
    3. Deans: Academic Affairs, Academic Services, Admissions, Students;
    4. Registrar.

D. The following persons may attend faculty meetings as observers, and, by prior agreement with the Presiding Officer, make presentations and respond to questions, but not vote:
1. Executive Director of Development;
2. Director of Public Relations;
3. Director of Fifth Year and Travel Grant Programs and Winter Term Coordinator;
4. student members (2) of three coordinating committees;
5. President of the Student Body;
6. representatives (2 from each) of The DePauw, WGRE, and the Student TV Board; additional representatives may be permitted at the discretion of the Presiding Officer before the meeting starts;
7. and others to whom permission is granted by majority faculty vote at the beginning of the meeting.

Appendix

XVII. Descriptions of Administration Committees

A. Committee on Administration
1. Function. This committee shall advise the President on matters of administration. When the Academic Affairs Committee of the Board of Trustees want faculty representation, the three at large members elected by the faculty will serve in this capacity.
2. Membership. Membership of this committee shall be appointees of the President and seven faculty members elected by the faculty, of which no more than two may be from one division and no more than one from each department. Each division shall elect one member from their division to serve a two-year term (two divisional members will be replaced each year.) Additionally, three faculty members shall be elected at large to serve three-year terms (one at large member being replaced each year.)

B. Board of Control of Student Publications
1. Function. This committee shall exert final authority over The DePauw and the Mirage. The board functions much

as would the owner of a private publishing operation except that it does not dictate editorial policy.

    2. Membership. The Vice President for Academic Affairs (or his/her appointed representative), a permanent treasurer appointed from the faculty by the President, the instructor of the journalism courses, four faculty members elected by the faculty to serve two-year terms (two members being replaced each year), and six students chosen by Student Congress in the manner prescribed.

C. Committee on Honorary Degrees

    1. Function. This committee shall survey candidates for honorary degrees and present a slate of candidates to the faculty for recommendation to the Board of Trustees. Members of the faculty and of the board may offer names of possible candidates. The Trustees and faculty delegate the approval of an honorary degree for the commencement speaker to a joint subcommittee of the Nominations and Trusteeship of the Board of Trustees, composed of three Trustees, including the Chairman of the Board and the three faculty members elected to the Committee on Honorary Degrees. An affirmative vote shall require approval of four of the six members.

    2. Membership. Three members of the faculty are elected by the faculty to serve three-year terms (one member being replaced each year) and to sit with members of the subcommittee of the Nominations and Trusteeship of the Board of Trustees.

D. Hartman Center Steering Committee

    1. Function. The role of the Hartman Center Steering Committee is to evaluate and develop Hartman Center programs. Additionally, this committee will develop long-range plans for the center.

    2. Membership. Director of the Hartman Center, a representative from CAPP, an administrator, the Chair of the Volunteer Student Council of the DCS, the Chair of the Volunteer Student Council of the WTIS, the Indiana Campus Compact and Recorder, three faculty members elected at-large, and three student members.

E. Diversity and Equity Committee

In matters regarding diversity, inclusiveness, and equity, the Diversity and Equity Committee: advises the Administration and the faculty on policy; presents educational sessions for all employees; identifies issues regarding diversity and equity in campus life and refers them to the appropriate university office and/or committee(s) for action; annually reviews and assesses aspects of the University's efforts to attract and retain a diverse campus community.

Membership

Faculty:

4 full-time, appointed by COF (3-year terms)

1 part-time, appointed by COF

Administration:

2 administrators appointed by the president (3-year terms)

Director of Human Resources (or representatives)

Director of Multicultural Affairs

Hourly Staff:

2 appointed by the Hourly Support Staff Committee (2 year terms)

Students:

2 appointed by the Student Congress (1 year terms, renewable)

XVIII. Election of Faculty Members to Administration Committees

Except where otherwise indicated in the committee descriptions above, each faculty member of an administration committee shall be elected and shall serve in accord with the procedures of Article V, Sections D and E of the faculty By-Laws. Terms of service are subject to amendment at the discretion of the administration committee, the President, or the Board of Trustees.

XIX. The Constitution and Authority of the Faculty

(from Charter and By-Laws of DePauw University, 1986)

Section 1. <u>Members</u>. The Faculty shall consist of the President, all professors, associate professors, assistant professors, instructors, and lecturers on full-time appointment, and others officially admitted to faculty membership by action of the Trustees, all of whom may participate freely in discussions, provided, however, that on matters of academic policy and practice only those persons who have been on the faculty or admitted to faculty status for such period as determined by the faculty may vote.

Section 2. <u>Appointment</u>. Professors, associate professors, assistant professors, instructors, lecturers and other assistants required by the educational program of the University shall be appointed by the President subject to review by the Board. After an appropriate period of service, faculty members in the rank of professor, associate professor, and assistant professor may enjoy the privilege of tenure as this privilege arising from academic custom and usage among American colleges and universities is specifically defined by faculty personnel policies approved by the Board of Trustees.

Section 3. <u>Duties</u>. Subject to the final authority of the Board, the faculty shall have charge of and responsibility for the institution and implementation of policies and programs relating to the academic interests of the University, including the fixing of academic requirements for admission, class advancement and graduation, the institution, development and supervision of courses of instruction, the procedures for the conduct of studies, the promulgation of rules for the conduct of students in the classrooms and the granting of degrees to be conferred by the University. The faculty shall adopt its own rules relating to the academic interests of the University, including the fixing of academic requirements for admission, class advancement and graduation, the institution, development and supervision of courses of instruction, the procedures for the conduct of studies, the promulgation of rules for the conduct of students in the classrooms and the granting of degrees to be conferred by the University. The faculty shall adopt its own rules of order and procedure, keep minutes of its meetings, and make reports to the Board of Trustees.

Section 4. Relations with Board of Trustees. All actions of the faculty materially affecting any segment of the University shall be reported to the Academic Affairs Committee which shall be responsible for determining the matters to be referred to, reviewed and approved as necessary by the Board of Trustees. Reasonable opportunity shall be provided for faculty representatives to attend meetings of the Academic Affairs Committee and to present to the Trustees their recommendations concerning the University.

Endnotes

1   Clifton J. Phillips and John Baughman, *DePauw: A Pictorial History* (Greencastle, Indiana: DePauw University, 1987), 7.

2   Ibid., 5.

3   William Warren Sweet, *Indiana Asbury-DePauw University 1837-1937: A Hundred Years of Higher Education in the Middle West* (New York: The Abingdon Press, 1937), 25-27.

4   Phillips and Baughman, 5.

5   Sweet, 28-30.

6   Ibid., 31.

7   Ibid., 31-32.

8   Ibid., 39.

9   Ibid., 45-47.

10 Phillips and Baughman, 18.

11 Sweet, 51.

[12] Ibid., 48.

[13] Ibid., 52.

[14] Phillips and Baughman, 23.

[15] Ibid., 22-23.

[16] Sweet, 63.

[17] Ibid., 66.

[18] Ibid., 66-67.

[19] Ibid., 89.

[20] Ibid., 120.

[21] Phillips and Baughman, 49.

[22] Sweet, 126-156.

[23] Phillips and Baughman, 52.

[24] Ibid., 60.

[25] Ibid., 48.

[26] Ibid., 41.

[27] Sweet, 114.

[28] Phillips and Baughman, 38.

[29] Ibid., 51-52.

[30] Ibid., 62.

[31] Ibid., 61.

[32] Ibid., 71.

33   Ibid., 74.

34   Ibid., 74.

35   Ibid., 107.

36   Ibid., 121.

37   Ibid., 111.

38   Ibid., 123-124.

39   Ibid., 99.

40   Ibid., 129-130.

41   Ibid., 144-146.

42   Ibid., 148-149.

43   Ibid., 171-172.

44   Ibid., 182-186.

45   Ibid., 205.

46   Ibid., 186.

47   Ibid., 207.

48   Janis Price, interviewed by author, 21 June, 2004, Greencastle, IN.

49   Leonard DiLillo, provost, DePauw University, to Janis K. Price, administrator and instructor, DePauw University, 25 August, 1992.

50   Janis Price Interview.

51   J.K. Wall, "More professors make for smaller classes," *The DePauw*, 27 August, 1999.

52   DePauw University, IRS Form 990, Schedule A, 2000.

53   Eva Weisz, professor, DePauw University, to Jeff Shively, student, DePauw University, 29 November, 2000. Email.

Eva Weisz, professor, DePauw University, to Jeff Shively, student, DePauw University, 4 December, 2000. Email.

Matthew Huber, teacher, Greencastle Middle School, to Jeff Shively, student, DePauw University, and Eva Weisz, professor, DePauw University, 6 December, 2000. Email.

Matthew Huber, teacher, Greencastle Middle School, to Jeff Shively, student, DePauw University, and Eva Weisz, professor, DePauw University, 2 January, 2001. Email.

54   Price interview.

55   Wall, "More professors make for smaller classes."

56   Price interview.

57   Brooke Hefner, student, DePauw University, to Dr. Marcelle McVorran, Education Department chair, DePauw University, 13 May, 2002.

58   Ibid..

59   Ibid..

60   Janis Price, "Course Syllabus for Education 375," Spring 2001.

61   Angela Morris, "Morris responds to Janis Price Lawsuit," *The DePauw*, 20 September, 2002.

62   Brooke Hefner, interviewed by author, tape recording, Terre Haute, Indiana, 3 June, 2004.

63   Neal Abraham, deposition regarding Janis K. Price, Plaintiff, vs. Neal B. Abraham, Individually and as Vice-President for Academic Affairs of DePauw University; and DePauw University, Indianapolis, Indiana, 3 June, 2003, 37.

64   Hefner interview.

[65] Brooke Hefner, "Price did nothing wrong," *The DePauw*, 15 October, 2002.

[66] Ibid..

[67] Ibid..

[68] Ibid..

[69] Ibid..

[70] Ibid..

[71] J. Budziszewski, "But what do I say?" *Teachers in Focus*, October 2000, 4-9.

[72] Heather Koerner, "Love Won Out," *Teachers in Focus*, October 2000, 10-12.

[73] Dr. Joseph Nicolosi, "Is This Really Good for Kids?" *Teachers in Focus*, October 2000, 14-18.

[74] "Pen Master," "Notes From the Underground," *Teachers in Focus*, October 2000, 20-21.

[75] John Bunyan, "To Those Far Off," *Teachers in Focus*, October 2000, 22-23.

[76] Abraham deposition, 48.

[77] Hefner interview.

[78] Abraham deposition, 42.

[79] Abraham deposition, 43.

[80] "Statement of Janis Price," Exhibit #3, Trial Notebook, Cause # 11C01-0301-P-30, *Janis K. Price v. DePauw University*, 30 April 2001.

[81] Abraham deposition, 43.

[82] Abby Lovett, "In Support of Both Teams," *The DePauw*, 28 August, 1998.

83   Janis Price, administrator and instructor, DePauw University, to Tona Dobson, teacher, South Putnam Junior-Senior High School, 2 February, 2001.

84   Tona Dobson, teacher, South Putnam Junior-Senior High School, to Janis Price, administrator and instructor, DePauw University, 15 May, 2001.

85   Ibid..

86   Janis Price, administrator and instructor, DePauw University, to Angela Morris, student, DePauw University, 13 July, 2001, e-mail.

87   Tona Dobson, "Evaluation of Angela M. Morris," Spring 2001.

88   Esther Lee, Education Department chair, DePauw University, to Janis Price, administrator and instructor, DePauw University, Eva Weisz, professor, DePauw University, and Jamie Stockton, professor, DePauw University, 4 September, 2001. e-mail.

89   Price interview.

90   Marnie McInnes to Janis Price, 8 October 2001, e-mail.

91   Price interview.

92   Marnie McInnes to Janis Price, 2 October, 2001, e-mail.

93   Price interview.

94   Neal Abraham, vice president of academic affairs, DePauw University, to Angela Morris, student, DePauw University, 11 October, 2001.

95   Dobson, "Evaluation of Angela Morris."

96   Janis Price, "Class Enrollment for Education 275-276/375," In exhibit 11, Trial Handbook, *Price v. DePauw*.

97   Price interview.

98   Gilbert Herdt, *The Sambia: Ritual and Gender in New Guinea* (Chicago: The University of Chicago, 1987), 79.

99   Janis Price, "Meeting Notes", 7 May, 2001. In exhibit 3, Trial Notebook, *Price v. DePauw.*

100   Neal Abraham, vice president of academic affairs, DePauw University to Janis Price, administrator and instructor, DePauw University, 17 July, 2001.

101   Janis Price, "Enrollment for Education 275, 276, 375, and 351." In exhibit 11, Trial Handbook, Price v. DePauw.

102   Janis Price, "Record of Semester Totals for Field Experience Placements." In exhibit 12, Trial Handbook, Price v. DePauw.

103   Neal Abraham, vice president of academic affairs, DePauw University, to Janis Price, administrator and instructor, DePauw University, 17 July, 2001. Letter #1.

104   Ibid..

105   Ibid..

106   Ibid..

107   Abraham deposition, 142-143.

108   Mitch Merback, professor of art history, DePauw University, faculty, DePauw University, 19 February, 2004.

109   Letter #1 from Neal Abraham to Janis Price, 17 July, 2001.

110   Janis Price, "Harassment of Janis Price- Avenues and Methods of Harassment"

111   Letter #1 from Neal Abraham to Janis Price, 17 July, 2001.

112   Ibid..

113   Neal Abraham, vice president of academic affairs, DePauw University, to Janis Price, administrator and instructor, DePauw University, 17 July, 2001. Letter #2.

114   Abraham deposition, 110-111.

115 Janis Price, "Quarterly Report and Annual Report Dates."

116 Ibid..

117 Janis Price, "Quarterly Report," 14 January, 2002.

118 Judy Miller, director of assessment, Indiana Professional Standards Board, to unit heads, 20 September, 2001, e-mail.

Marie Theobald, executive director, Indiana Professional Standards Board, to licensing advisors, 21 March, 2002, e-mail.

119 Price interview.

120 Ibid..

121 Dr. Wilson Warren, history professor, Indiana State University, to Jeffrey Shively, student, DePauw University and Indiana State University, 2 January, 2001. e-mail.

122 Esther Lee, Education Department chair, DePauw University, to Janis Price, administrator and instructor, 1 November, 2001, e-mail.

123 Esther Lee, Education Department chair, DePauw University, to Janis Price, administrator and instructor, 20 November, 2001, e-mail.

124 Esther Lee, Education Department chair, DePauw University, to Janis Price, administrator and instructor, 20 February, 2002, e-mail.

Registrar, Indiana State University, to Jeffrey Shively, "Receipt for Transcript," 22 January, 2002.

125 Shawn Sriver, director of licensing, Indiana Professional Standards Board, to Esther Lee, Education Department chair, 5 December, 2001, e-mail.

126 Esther Lee, Education Department chair, DePauw University, to Janis Price, administrator and instructor, DePauw University, 7 December, 2001, e-mail.

127 Janis Price, "Response by Janis Price to Fourth Quarterly Performance Assessment of Janis Price," June 2002.

[128] Janis Price, administrator and instructor, DePauw University, to Esther Lee, Education Department chair, DePauw University, 20 November, 2001.

[129] Esther Lee, "Fourth Quarterly Performance Assessment of Janis Price," 29 May, 2002.

[130] Neal Abraham, Executive Vice President, Vice President of Academic Affairs and Dean of the Faculty, to faculty and staff, DePauw University, 9 June, 2005, e-mail.

[131] Jeff McQuary, "Eley describes gay life at DePauw", *The DePauw*, 13 May, 1986.

[132] Jeff McQuary, "Gay students suffer loneliness, alienation," *The DePauw*, 13 May, 1986.

[133] Leanne Longstreth, "Support Group Formed," *The DePauw*, 18 February, 1988.

[134] Hung-Yang Chen, Carol Eukon, "Action conquers silence," The *DePauw*, 12 April, 1988.

[135] "Blue Jean Day supports gays," *The DePauw*. 12 April, 1988.

[136] Joe Walusel, "Homosexuality is a mental disorder," *The DePauw*, 18 April, 1988.

[137] Resse Watt, "Biblical stance on homosexuality examined," *The DePauw*, 6 May, 1988.

[138] Hung-Yang Chen, "Homosexuality fits in religion, science, morality, society?" *The DePauw*, 22 April, 1988.

[139] Lucinda DeWitt. Dick Kelly, Bob Garrett, Felix Goodson, Steve Raines, Don Ryujin, Kevin Moore, "Psychology professors clarify poor definition," *The DePauw*, 22 April, 1988.

[140] Jay Hosler, "Bible cites other sins," *The DePauw*, 26 April, 1988.

Amie Klempnauer, "Morals point refuted," *The DePauw*, 22 April, 1988.

[141] Catherine Bauer and Karen Klingaman, "Conformity reigns here," *The DePauw*, 26 April, 1988.

[142] Nancy Adams, "Parent commends Gardner," *The DePauw*, 10 May, 1988.

Dr. Ray L. Swihart, assistant professor of Education, "God provides escape from judgment of sins," *The DePauw*, 30 November, 1989.

Eric J. Vale '81, "Scripture challenges homosexuals to change their ways, *The DePauw*, 6 May, 1994.

[143] Jamie Prime, "ROTC homophobia questioned," *The DePauw*, 16 November, 1989.

Jamie Prime, "ROTC policy condemned, controversial program stays," *The DePauw*, 12 February, 1990.

Rod Clifford, "Administration, faculty lock gays in 'the closet," *The DePauw*, 12 February, 1990.

Constance Ford '88, "Faculty ROTC decision shocking," *The DePauw*, 13 March, 1990.

Milo Hanke, "Pressure on ROTC policy increasing," *The DePauw*, 11 May, 1990.

[144] Ed Clare, "Fate of ROTC rests in the hands of trustees," *The DePauw*, 20 April, 1993.

[145] John Ohle, "Remove ROTC from curriculum," *The DePauw*, 13 March, 2001.

Andrew Tangel, "Should ROTC kindly hit the road," *The DePauw*, 10 April, 2001.

[146] R. Brandon Sokol, "Freshman in critical condition after car accident," *The DePauw*, 6 February, 2004.

[147] Kate Holloway, "Students fill Kresge for services," *The DePauw*, 10 February, 2004.

[148] Laura Rich, "Trustee incident prompts new policy," *The DePauw*, 28 April, 1992.

[149] Jessica Rupp, "DePauw students plan to break the bubble to march for gay civil rights," *The DePauw*, 20 April, 1993.

[150] Chillemi, Carol, "Parent credits DePauw marchers," *The DePauw*, 4 May, 1993.

[151] Ellen Morrison, "Denim Day to recognize gay rights at DePauw," *The DePauw*, 4 May, 1993.

[152] Ellen Morrison, "Denim Day deemed a success," *The DePauw*, 7 May, 1993.

[153] Jason Anders, "New Group attempts to 'unite' DePauw gays," The DePauw, 18 March, 1994.

Tedra Williams, "Support United DePauw," *The DePauw*, 15 March, 1994.

[154] Keith Borden, "Support groups embrace gays,"," *The DePauw*, 15 March, 1994.

[155] Rob Riemersma, "Greek fraternities homophobia outweighs campus as a whole," *The DePauw*, 12 April, 1994.

[156] Rod Clifford, "Gay prejudice still at DePauw," *The DePauw*, 12 April, 1994.

Jon Jenkins, "Attitudes toward gays have a long way to go," *The DePauw*, 18 April, 1994.

Jon Jenkins, "Homosexual students at DePauw challenged, diverse," *The DePauw*, 3 May, 1994.

[157] "Nick L." interviewed by author, Greencastle, Indiana, 6 November, 2004.

[158] Lewis Grizzard, *I Haven't Understood Anything since 1962*, (New York: Villard Books, 1992), 124.

[159] "Nick L." interview.

160 Kristen Ingwell, "Baseball Caps Mar Denim Day," *The DePauw*, 6 May, 1994.

161 Claire Goldstein, "Profs offer support to gays, bisexuals," *The DePauw*, 2 May, 1995.

162 Richard Buino, "Gay rights supported with denim Thursday," *The DePauw*, 29 April, 1997.

163 Tedra Williams, "Support United DePauw," *The DePauw*, 15 March, 1994.

164 Keith Borden, "Campus dialogue about homosexuality has fallen silent," *The DePauw*, 21 April, 1995.

165 Emily Plemons, "Queer Center will be inclusive," *The DePauw*, 16 March, 1999.

166 Jessica Schaab, "Queer Center gets new look," *The DePauw*, 22 September, 2000.

167 Brian Thompson, "United DePauw plans to spend money wisely," *The DePauw*, 5 September, 2001.

168 Rorry Kinnally, "Students in search for J.C.," *The DePauw*, 9 November, 1998.

169 Rorry Kinnally, "Rite of Passage: Coming out at DePauw," *The DePauw*, 15 October, 1999.

170 Brian Thompson, "United DePauw plans to spend money wisely," *The DePauw*, 5 September, 2001.

171 Ryan Pugliano, interviewed by author, Greencastle, Indiana, May 2004.

172 "DePauw celebrating Gay History month," *The DePauw*, 14 October, 1997.

173 Kim Bousquet, "United DePauw plans to start GLBT panel," *The DePauw*, 8 September, 1998.

174 John Ohle and Anisah Miley, "Observe and support Coming Out Day," *The DePauw*, 9 October, 1998.

175 Ryan Slabough, "Students protest silence," *The DePauw*, 30 October, 1998.

176 Belles of...," *The DePauw*, 14 October, 2003.

"Doing the Drag at DePauw," *The DePauw*, 4 February, 2003.

"Drag Ball at the Walden," *The DePauw*, 30 November, 2001.

"Drag queens and kings show DePauw how its done," *The DePauw*, 4 February, 2003.

"Dragging at DePauw," *The DePauw*, 5 December, 2000.

Amber Foreman, "Doing drag; What it feels like for a girl," *The DePauw*, 7 December, 2001.

Anisah Miley, "Drag Ball not hypocritical," *The DePauw*, 8 December, 2000.

Amanda Sidebottom, "Image to icon: explaining Drag Ball theme," *The DePauw*, 30 November, 2001.

Doug Waters, Jeff Wright, Merideth Douglas, James McQuiston, Lindsey Parsons, " United DePauw Apologizes," *The DePauw*, 11 February, 2003.

177 Matt Claus, "Eyeliner, feathers and boas, oh my!" *The DePauw*, 4 December, 2001.

178 Abby Tonsing," Speakers Bureau makes house calls with information," *The DePauw*, 16 March, 1999.

179 Robert Maril, "UD Festival draws small crowd," *The DePauw*, 10 November, 1998.

180 Rachel Kovac, "Bornstein speaks during Women's Week," *The DePauw*, 9 March, 2001.

[181] Abby Lovett, "Students coming out for United DePauw," *The DePauw*, 6 October, 2000.

[182] Don Kelley, " Activist group screams to protest silence,' *The DePauw*, 11 April, 2003.

[183] Amber Foreman, "Just call me Queer," *The DePauw*, 28 August, 2001.

Lindsay Hay, "Don't forget queer community," *The DePauw*, 26 October, 1999.

Matt Kappel, "New dialogue urgently needed for the Q-Word," *The DePauw*, 28 August, 2001.

Rorry Kinnally, "Junior breaks the mold of DePauw students" *The DePauw*, 15 October, 1999.

Paula Kirlin, "Unconditional love important," *The DePauw*, 25 September, 1999.

Paula Kirlin, "Make DPU a better place for all students," *The DePauw*, 5 October, 1999.

Paula Kirlin, "Sharing her coming out story," *The DePauw*, 15 October, 1999.

Paula Kirlin, "Understanding 'queer' terms," *The DePauw*, 7 December, 1999.

[184] Emily Plemons, "Christians still hypocritical about homosexuality," *The DePauw*, 23 October, 1998.

[185] Luke 21:16-17, *Holy Bible*, King James Version.

[186] Dr. Howard Brooks, "Faculty Resolves to support Denim Day," *The DePauw*, 5 May, 1995.

[187] "Today's faculty lesson- lifestyle tolerance," *The DePauw*, 2 May, 1995.

[188] Martha Rainbolt, English professor, DePauw University, faculty, DePauw University, "Teaching Roundtable on Monday, April 21," 14 April, 2003, e-mail.

[189] Abraham Deposition, 246-247.

[190] Abraham Deposition, 243.

[191] Lane Rogers, "Campus gay rights group reaches one year mark," *The DePauw*, 2 May, 1995.

[192] "Counseling Services congratulates all those celebrating Coming Out Day!" *The DePauw* October, 1998.

[193] "A flippin' good time," *The DePauw*, 5 September, 2003.

[194] Eric Assjen, "Hate crimes may be added to the handbook," *The DePauw*, 13 October, 1998.

[195] Jamie Aussieker, "University proposes stricter hate crime guidelines," *The DePauw*, 17 March, 2000.

[196] Rajai Bimbo, Takiyah Brooks, Larissa Train, Eboni Walker, "Hate crime happens," *The DePauw*, 22 February, 2002.

Rachel Kovac, "Armstrong pleads guilty to battery charge," *The DePauw*, 30 August, 2002.

Rachel Kovac, "Student charged in battery," *The DePauw*, 7 May, 2002.

Rachel Kovac, "University investigates bias-motivated incident," *The DePauw*, 23 April, 2002.

[197] "Obituary of Charles Bruner Thomas," *The Banner Graphic*, 10 June, 1985.

[198] Kenneth Jennison, "Graduation Trauma," *The DePauw*, 14 May, 1985.

[199] *The Mirage* (Greencastle, Indiana: DePauw University, 1912), 129.

[200] Council of Delta Kappa Epsilon, *General Catalog of Delta Kappa Epsilon Fraternity* (New York: Council of Delta Kappa Epsilon, 1913), 934.

[201] Jennison.

[202] "Obituary of Charles Bruner Thomas."

[203] *The Mirage* (Greencastle, Indiana: DePauw University, 1913), 106.

[204] Jennison.

[205] Mary Tesmer, Charles Bruner Thomas' guardian, interviewed by author, Greencastle, Indiana, 29 October, 2004.

[206] Ibid..

[207] Phillips and Baughman, 123.

[208] Ibid..

[209] Ibid..

[210] Ibid., 131.

[211] "Dean arrested for drinking and driving," *The DePauw*, 6 May, 1997.

[212] J.K. Well, "Professors support Rabbi Bogage," *The DePauw*, 26 September, 2000.

[213] Dr. Glen Kuecker, "Florida vote was racially biased," *The DePauw*, 4 May, 2001.

[214] Dr. Glen Kuecker, "What if students were drafted?' *The DePauw*, 21 February, 2003.

[215] Craig Greiwe, "School of Americas ignites sharp debate," *The DePauw*, 6 October, 2000.

Rachel Kovac, "DePauw students risk arrest to protest SOA," *The DePauw*, 1 December, 2000.

[216] Craig Greiwe, "Students to protest SOA with Peace Camp," *The DePauw*, 20 October, 2000.

[217] Rebecca Martinez and Dan Kelley," Students react to professor's arrest," *The DePauw*, 23 August, 2003.

[218] Ibid..

[219] Melanie Tacoma and J.K. Wells," The Buzz on 'Buz," *The DePauw*, 3 October, 2000.

[220] J.K. Well and Jessica Schaab, "Bogage suspended," *The DePauw*, 22 September, 2000.

[221] J.K. Well, "Professors support Rabbi Bogage," *The DePauw*, 26 September, 2000.

[222] Mitch Merback, "Bogage story indefensible," *The DePauw*, 26 September, 2000.

[223] Micah Ling, "Bogage too important to lose," *The DePauw*, 26 September, 2000.

[224] "Don't fire Rabbi Bogage," *The DePauw*, 29 September, 2000.

[225] Melanie Tacoma, "Bogage investigation complete," *The DePauw*, 29 September, 2000.

[226] Melanie Tacoma, "Bogage stays," *The DePauw*, 3 October, 2000.

[227] Andrew Tangel, "Greiwe's complaint against University dropped," *The DePauw*, 17 September, 2002.

[228] Craig Greiwe, "Questions surround quest for faculty diversity," *The DePauw*, 4 December, 2001.

[229] Ibid..

[230] Ibid..

[231] Ibid..

[232] Ibid..

233   DePauw University, IRS Form 990, Schedule A, 2000.

234   Andrew Tangel, "Greiwe's complaint against University dropped," *The DePauw*, 17 September, 2002.

      Andrew Tangel, "University Investigates Abraham," *The DePauw*, 3 May, 2002.

235   Craig Greiwe, "Former student questions integrity of University leaders," *The DePauw*, 17 September, 2002.

      Tangel, "Greiwe's complaint against University dropped."

236   Ibid..

237   Ibid..

238   Miranda Ast, "Retaliation: The Taylor Case and the 9 Day Policy," *The Voice*, May 2003, 18.

239   Ibid..

240   Ibid..

241   Ibid., 18-19.

242   Ibid..

243   "DPU class examines religion in America," *The Banner Graphic*, 5 February, 2005.

244   Adam Cohen, "There's more than one way to get to heaven," *The DePauw*, 25 September, 2001.

245   John 14:6, *Holy Bible*, King James Version.

246   Jen Nielsen, "Faculty approves Jewish Studies minor in monthly meeting," *The DePauw*, 4 December, 2001.

247   Sarah Craft, " Students prepare for High Holy Days," *The DePauw*, 26 September, 2003.

248 Kristen Earhart and Becky Marfoe, "Students get Muslim Tips," *The DePauw*, 4 March, 1994.

249 Cassie Trueblood, "Muslims meet misunderstanding at DePauw," *The DePauw*, 13 April, 1999.

250 Gene Rhea, "Religious group fasts from dawn to dark," *The DePauw*, 30 November, 2001.

251 Jesse Rochrich, "Buddhism reaches some DePauw students," *The DePauw*, 2 April, 1999.

252 Bobbi Kay Ruehter, "Christmas isn't universal," *The DePauw*, 8 December, 1998.

253 "Monks bring different kind of chanting to campus," *The DePauw*, 6 September, 2002.

254 "DePauw celebrates the arts," *The DePauw*, 5 November, 2002.

"Mandala colors Arts Festival," *The DePauw*, 8 November, 2002.

255 Anne Hunter, "Crystals: New Age healing or fashion statement," *The DePauw*, 5 October, 1990.

256 "Pentagram mystery solved," *The DePauw*, 26 April, 1991.

"Roller Rink Obstacle," *The DePauw*, 23 April, 1991.

257 Katherine Wright," The truth about Rede," *The DePauw*, 27 April, 2004.

258 Colin Mathers, "Bible instructs for slavery and sexism, not life," *The DePauw*, 25 February, 1992.

259 Marthe Chandler, Philosophy Professor, "Letter to the Editor, "*The DePauw*, 28 February, 1992.

Paul Linge, "Why should anyone believe anything?' *The DePauw*, 21 February, 1992.

260 Kay Weaver, "Do not criticize Linge for his beliefs," *The DePauw*, 3 March, 1992.

[261] Damon Xanthopoulos, "Give more this year," cartoon, *The DePauw*, 5 December, 2003.

[262] Christine Cercone, " Church and State should be separate," *The DePauw*, 4 April, 1989.

[263] Joe Mason, "God and Government," *The DePauw*, 23 October, 1989.

[264] Lindsay Hey, "Other's stories provide insight," *The DePauw*, 1 October, 1999.

[265] Scott Liepis, "Christian ideals not for everybody," *The DePauw*, 3 November,1998.

[266] Matt Claus, "The frighteningly amusing side of Catholicism," *The DePauw*, 11 February, 2000.

[267] "Interfaith Commencement Worship Service," *The DePauw*, 7 May, 2002.

[268] "Can I get an amen? with a side of anti-Islamic propaganda," *The DePauw*, 7 December, 2001.

[269] Matt Santoro, "Religious extremism can not be ignored," *The DePauw*, 23 September, 2003.

[270] J. Kyle Sturgeon, "Wrong to violate document that allows religious freedom," *The DePauw*, 12 September, 2003.

[271] Rorry Kinnally, "Students in search for J.C.," *The DePauw*, 9 November, 1998.

[272] Brian Thompson, "United DePauw plans to spend money wisely," *The DePauw*, 5 September, 2001.

[273] Nick Partlow, "Student Congress Allocations Announced," cartoon, *The DePauw*, 4 May, 2001.

[274] Ad For Religious Life Groups and Activities, *The DePauw*, 18 August, 2001.

[275] Pam Munch, "Student funds allocated based on breadth of activity," *The DePauw*, 30 August, 2002.

[276] Nicolas Raleigh, "J.C. article shows lack of partiality," *The DePauw*, 3 November, 1998.

[277] Josh Harrison, "What would Josh do?" *The DePauw*, 6 November, 1998.

[278] J.K. Wall, "Students find faith at J.C.," *The DePauw*, 27 October, 1998.

[279] James Pate, "Christian ideas should not be restrained," *The DePauw*, 6 November, 1998.

[280] Alexander W. Scott, "Christianity based on including others," *The DePauw*, 6 November, 1998.

[281] Clarinda Crawford, "Christian does not mean homophobic," *The DePauw*, 13 October, 1998.

[282] James Pate, "Tolerance not the same as acceptance," *The DePauw*, 27 October, 1998.

[283] "Agape 2003," *The DePauw*, 18 April, 2003.

"Get your praise on," *The DePauw*, 30 April, 2004.

Nathan Richardson, "Christian music, testimonies revive campus," *The DePauw*, 18 April, 2000.

[284] "Should the University be allowed to regulate religion in the classroom?" *The DePauw*, 30 August, 2002.

[285] "Sex Week schedule set," *The DePauw*, 20 September, 1991.

Special Sex related insert in *The DePauw*, 26 March, 1991.

[286] Jamie Prime, "Dorms to receive condom machines," *The DePauw*, 22 February, 1991.

[287] Nancy Adams, "Mother says; Condoms bad, abstinence good," *The DePauw*, 11 September, 1990.

[288] Jennifer Hartpence, "Preventing AIDS at DePauw: Are we doing enough?" *The DePauw*, 28 September, 1989.

Mary Reilly, "Abstinence, denial not valid solutions," *The DePauw*, 14 September, 1990.

Kristen Sites, "Condom-nation," *The DePauw*, 14 September, 1990.

[289] Dale Hrebik, "Say Yes! to condom machines and help prevent itchy diseases," *The DePauw*, 2 October, 1990.

[290] Claire Goldstein, "Students collect 2000 free condoms," *The DePauw*, 8 March, 1994.

[291] Rush Limbaugh, *The Way Things Ought To Be* (New York: Pocket Books, 1992), 132.

[292] "Planned Parenthood moves clinic closer to campus," *The DePauw*, 4 November, 1988.

Jeremy Rogalski and Sarah Sargent, "Planned Parenthood increasing hours to better serve community," *The DePauw*, 30 October, 1990.

[293] Sara White, "Planned Parenthood President to speak," *The DePauw*, 2 March, 1990.

[294] Sara White, "Pro-life committee hosts open meeting," *The DePauw*, 2 March, 1980.

[295] Colleen Harding, "A voice from the bubble takes its case to Washington," *The DePauw*, 14 April, 1992.

"Pro-choice Hoosiers mobilize in November," *The DePauw*, 6 November, 1989.

Kristen Sandstrom, "D.C. rally insists 'Bush has no womb to talk," *The DePauw*, 16 November, 1989.

[296] Ronda Merryman, "College Democrats plan to support pro-choice candidates," *The DePauw*, 9 March, 1990.

[297] Seanna Murphy, "Student angered with letter's pro-life view," *The DePauw*, 16 March, 1989.

[298] Joe Mason, "Pro-life: lack of choice," *The DePauw*, 4 December, 1989.

[299] Human Life Alliance, "What you don't know can hurt you," *The DePauw*, 16 November, 1998, supplement.

Susan Watt, art gallery director, "Ad insert shouldn't have been run in paper," *The DePauw*, 3 December, 1999.

[300] Dale Hrebik, "Women's Week begins on Sunday," *The DePauw*, 3 March, 1989.

[301] "Mendenhall lecturer Trible to give feminist viewpoint on the Bible," *The DePauw*, 29 October, 1991.

[302] Jacqueline Nats, "Plaskow speaks on religion and sexual ethics," *The DePauw*, 12 March, 2002.

[303] Lauren Bustard, "Is DePauw still Methodist?" *The DePauw*, 4 November, 2003.

[304] Emily Lewinski, "Coming Out Week concludes today," *The DePauw*, 11 October, 2002.

[305] Janis Price, administrator, DePauw University, to Max Bryant, assistant director of human resources, DePauw University, 30 July, 2002.

[306] Abraham deposition, 190-199.

[307] Program, "The One Hundred and Thirty-Second Annual Commencement ", DePauw University, 23 May, 1971.

[308] *Janis K. Price vs. Neal Abraham and DePauw University*, 17 April, 2002, 8-9.

[309] Ibid., 9.

[310] Ibid., 10.

[311] Ibid., 11.

[312] Ibid., 12-13.

[313] "Courthouse reception for Judge LaViolette Thursday afternoon," *The Banner Graphic*, 27 December, 2004.

314   Janis Price, "Reasons why Judge Diana LaViolette should recuse herself."

315   "Combining law, teaching a difficult task," *The DePauw*, 14 October, 1986.

316   Appeal from the Clay Circuit Court, *DePauw vs. Janis K. Price*.

317   Ibid..

318   Ibid..

319   Jim Poor, "Reflections and Comment on Clay County Trial, *Price vs. DPU*."

320   Ibid..

321   Ibid..

322   Janis Price, interviewed by the author, Greencastle, IN, 5 April, 2005.

323   Poor.

324   Ibid..

325   Price.

326   Poor.

327   Price.

328   Janis Price, interviewed by author, Greencastle, IN, 14 April, 2005.

329   Poor.

330   Ibid..

331   Poor.

332   Ibid..

333 Price.

334 Poor.

335 Ibid..

336 Ibid..

337 Rachel Kovac, "Price wins lawsuit, awarded $10, 401," *The DePauw*, 4 November, 2003.

338 Judge Diana LaViolette, *Janis K. Price vs. DePauw University*, Order Granting Costs.

339 Sarah Preuschl, "Price explains faith, faces student opposition," *The DePauw*, 5 December, 2003.

340 Ibid..

341 Ibid..

342 Meredith Douglas, "Price's victory breeds fear," *The DePauw*, 18 November, 2003.

343 Board of United DePauw, "Silence broken in Price case" *The DePauw*, 18 November, 2003.

344 "Free Speech?" Andrea Garrett, *The 700 Club*, aired 10 July, 2002.

345 Ibid..

346 Ibid..

347 Ibid..

348 Ibid..

349 Ibid..

350 Ibid..

351 "Interview with David Limbaugh," *The 700 Club*, aired 29 October, 2003.

352 "Price Victory," Andrea Garrett, *The 700 Club*, aired 3 November, 2003.

353 Robert G. Bottoms, president, DePauw University, to alumni, DePauw University, 29 July, 2002.

354 Dr. Robert Bottoms, "Address to 2002-2003 Faculty Institute," Meherry Hall, DePauw University, 16 August, 2002.

355 Ibid..

356 Ibid..

357 Jeffrey Shively, "DePauw Letter Inaccurate," *The Banner Graphic*, 16 August, 2002.

358 "Letter Winner," *The Banner Graphic*, 19 August, 2002.

"Not the High Road," *The Banner Graphic*, 21 August, 2002.

359 "Two sides to every story," *The Banner Graphic*, 21 August, 2002.

360 Janelle van Buiten," Christians not anti-gay," *The DePauw*, 4 October, 2002.

361 Jim Poor, "Alumnus Ashamed of DPU," *The Banner Graphic* , 21 August, 2002.

362 Jim Poor, "Aid a Christian Struggle," *The Banner Graphic,* 2 October, 2002.

363 Jeffrey D. Shively, "Take Heart, America, *The Banner Graphic*, 14 November, 2003.

364 Jeffrey D. Shively, "Rule of Man or Rule of Law?" *Hoosier Topics*, 30 December, 2003

365 Marcella Fleming, "Prof's lawsuit roils DePauw," *The Indianapolis Star*, 22 August, 2002.

Ruth Holladay, "DePauw dispute highlights diversity- of aggrieved parties," *The Indianapolis Star*, 22 August, 2002.

"Lawsuit against DePauw sent back to state court," *The Indianapolis Star*, 18 October, 2002.

"Judge: College didn't curb teacher's rights," *The Indianapolis Star*, 13 March 2003.

Ruth Holladay, "Conversation could have kept teacher out of court," *The Indianapolis Star*, 23 November, 2003.

366 Patty Quchenbush, "Price should have used other sources in class," *The DePauw*, 27 August, 2002.

367 Damon Xanthopoulos, "DePauw is intolerant of my intolerance!" cartoon, *The DePauw*, 30 August, 2002.

368 Damon Xanthopoulos, "We won, Janis!" *The DePauw*, 11 November, 2003.

369 Ryan Pugliano, "Rambling thoughts from a random man," *The DePauw*, 7 May, 2002.

Ryan Pugliano, "Price acted within her rights," *The DePauw*, 30 August 2002.

Ryan Pugliano, "Baraka promotes same intolerance as Price," *The DePauw*, 13 September 2002.

Ryan Pugliano, 'Building a hypocritical community," *The DePauw*, 14 October, 2003.

Ryan Pugliano, "Holding nothing back," *The DePauw*, 11 May, 2004.

370 Drew Humphrey, "Coming Out Week contradicts Price punishment," *The DePauw*, 14 October, 2003.

Seth Kinnett, "Academic freedom for everyone," *The DePauw*, 3 September, 2002.

371 Jason Column, "University faces lawsuit for religious discrimination," *AFA Journal*, October 2002; available from http://www.afa.net/journal/October/2002/anti_christian_bias.asp; Internet; accessed 20 December, 2004.

372   "Instructor wins motion in DePauw case," AFA Journal, March, 2003; available from http://www.afa.net/journal/March/2003/noi.asp; Internet; accessed 20 December, 2004.

373   David Limbaugh, *Persecution* (Washington D.C., Regnery Press, 2003), 118-119.

374   David Limbaugh, forward in Norman Geisler and Frank Turek's, *I don't have enough faith to be an atheist* (Wheaton, Illinois: Crossway Books, 2004), 9.

375   Jim Nelson Black, *Freefall of the American University*, (Nashville, TN: WND Books, 2004), 263.

376   Andrew Tangle, "Price lawsuit affects alumni donations," *The DePauw*, 19 November, 2002.

377   Eloise G. Davis, to Robert G. Bottoms, President, DePauw University, 12 August, 2002.

378   P. William Davis, Ph.D., alumnus, DePauw University, Robert G. Bottoms, president, DePauw University, 14 October, 2002.

379   W. Eugene Danneberg, "DPU bequests renounced," *The Banner Graphic*, 18 December, 2002.

380   Appeal from the Clay Circuit Court, *DePauw vs. Janis K. Price*.

381   *DePauw University vs. Janis K. Price,* Indiana Court of Appeals.

382   "Ruling vs. DePauw overturned," *The Banner Graphic*, 15 December 2004.

383   Terry A. Crone biography, Indiana Court of Appeals website; available from http://www.in.gov/judiciary/appeals/bios/crone.html; Internet; accessed 26 December, 2004.

384   Program, " The One Hundred and Fifth-fifth Annual Commencement Program," DePauw University, 18 May,1974.

385   *The Mirage*, (Greencastle, Indiana: DePauw University, 1971), 178-179.

386 Patricia A. Riley biography, Indiana Court of Appeals website; available from http://www.in.gov/judiciary/appeals/bios/riley.html; Internet; accessed 26 December, 2004.

Nancy H. Vaidik biography, Indiana Court of Appeals Website; available from http://www.in.gov/judiciary/appeals/bios/vaidik. html; Internet; accessed 26 December, 2004.

387 Appeal, 5.

388 Appeal, 6-7.

389 *Orr v. Westminster Village North (1995)*, 651N.E. 2nd 795 June 8, 1995

390 Ibid..

391 "Court of Appeals Overturns Janis Price Case," The DePauw.com, 7 December, 2004 [newspaper online]; available from http://www. thedepauw.com/dynamic/news.php?date=2004-12-07&id=780; Internet; accessed 26 December, 2004.

392 John Price, attorney at law, Janis Price, Administrator, DePauw University, 16 December, 2004.

393 John Price, attorney at law, Brett B. Harvey, director, Grants and Funding, Alliance Defense Fund, 20 December, 2004.

394 Program for "Sexual Orientation and Familial Status," Indiana University Law School, Indianapolis, IN, 29 March, 2005.

395 Janis K. Price, "My Perspective on Sexual Orientation and Familial Status," Indiana University Law School, Indianapolis, IN, 29 March, 2005.

396 Randall T. Shepard, Chief Justice, Indiana Supreme Court, "Denial of Appellee's Petition to Transfer Jurisdiction, *DePauw University v. Price, Janis K.*"

397 "Court Rules for DePauw in Janis Price Case," *The Banner Graphic*, 5 April, 2005, 1.

398 "Biography of Justice Thomas R. Boehm," Indiana Supreme Court website; available from http://www.in.gov/judiciary/supreme/bios/html; Internet; accessed 26 December, 2004.

399 Jason Moon, "Price disappointed by court decision," *The Banner Graphic*, 6 April, 2005.

400 "Court of Appeals bringing session to DPU April 7," *The Banner Graphic*, 29 March, 2005.

401 Neal Abraham, Executive Vice President, Vice President of Academic Affairs and Dean of the Faculty, to Janis K. Price, Administrator, DePauw University, 14 June, 2004.

402 Special Services Division, The War Department, "Prelude to War," motion picture, 1943.

403 Jennifer Roback Morse, "Sex Fiction," *The American Enterprise*, April-May 2005, 11.

404 Ann Coulter, "It's only funny until someone loses a pie," Townhall. com website; available from http://www.townhall.com/columnists/anncoulter/ac20050414shtml; Internet; accessed 14 April, 2005.

405 Jeffrey Shively, "The Intellectual Soundness of Conservativism," *The Banner Graphic*, 29 August, 2003.

406 Paul Stolarczuk, "A Chill Descends Over DePauw," *The Wabash Commentary*, October 2003, 9.

407 U.S. Constitution, art. 6.

408 David Horowitz, "The Academic Bill of Rights," in *Freefall of the American University* by Jim Nelson Black, 320-323.

409 Don Wildman, founder and chairman, American Family Association, Jeffrey Shively, 13 April, 2005. e-mail.

410 U.S. Constitution, art 3, sec 1.

411 Ibid..

412 Proverbs 16:18, *Holy Bible*, King James Version.

About the Author

Jeffrey D. Shively is a passionate historian, finding greatest interest in the Second World War, automotive history and political history. He earned a Bachelor of Arts degree in History from DePauw University in December 1994. Five years later, he returned to school to add an Indiana teaching license to his credentials. Currently, Mr. Shively is completing a Masters of Arts degree in History at Indiana State University while teaching at a local community college.

Mr. Shively has many interests outside of writing and history. He is a fan of all genres of jazz, but Glenn Miller is his favorite bandleader. The efforts of Stan Getz and Chet Baker have struck his fancy lately. He has played the trumpet for twenty years. A fan of traditional patriotic band music, Mr. Shively has spent the past nineteen summers playing in community bands. A lover of fine things, he collects antique Cadillacs. Currently, his stable includes models from 1941, 1960, 1965, and 1992. He has served as director of the Indiana Region of the Cadillac-LaSalle Club since 1999 and is active in the Auburn-Cord- Duesenberg Club and Classic Car Club of America. Whenever possible, Mr. Shively cruises the forgotten roads of yesteryear, be it the National Road, the Lincoln Highway, or Route 66.

As a lifelong Hoosier, Jeffrey Shively has had traditional American values instilled in him since birth. Mr. Shively believes that strong, moral, Christian men are the bedrock of American society, so he has been involved with Promise Keepers for six years. He currently resides in Greencastle, Indiana.

Printed in the United States
35795LVS00008B/1-15

9 781420 859638